LEVERAGE

THE CEO'S GUIDE TO CORPORATE CULTURE

JOHN R. CHILDRESS

Published by The Principia Group 2013
Copyright © John Childress 2013

The right of John Childress to be identified as the Author of the Work has been asserted by him in accordance with the Copyright, Designs and Patens Act 1988

All rights reserved. No part of this publication may be reproduced, stored in a retrieval system, or transmitted, in any form or by any means without the prior written permission of the publisher nor be otherwise circulated in any form of binding or cover other than that in which it is published and without a similar condition being imposed on the subsequent purchaser.

The Principia Group
27 Brook Green
London W6 7BL
ISBN: 9780957517974

Printed by Lightning Source Lightning Source UK Ltd.

For speaking engagements, consulting, or other business matters, contact:
John R Childress, Managing Partner, The Principia Group
john.childress@theprincipiagroup.com
www.theprincipiagroup.com

Few concepts in business contain so many powerful truths, and at the same time so much crap as corporate culture.
~ John R. Childress

Table of Contents

Overview   3

What's all the fuss?   7

Section One: The Rise, and Rise, and Rise of Corporate Culture   17
    Chapter 1: Just What is Corporate Culture?   21
    Chapter 2: The Hijacking of Corporate Culture   35
    Chapter 3: 'Seeing' and Understanding Corporate Culture   47
    Chapter 4: The Missing Link: The Impact of Culture on Performance   63

Section Two: It's Complicated . . .   75
    Chapter 5: In the Beginning . . . Where Culture Comes From   77
    Chapter 6: The Culture Continuum   103
    Chapter 7: Culture by Design or Default?   115

Section Three: Leadership and Corporate Culture   129
    Chapter 8: Shadow of the Leader   131
    Chapter 9: You Get The Culture You Allow   145

Section Four: Strategy and Corporate Culture   159
    Chapter 10: Culture and Strategy: Paper, Rock, Scissors   161
    Chapter 11: Good Culture, Bad Culture   169

Section Five: Measuring Corporate Culture   183
    Chapter 12: Culture Surveys and Assessments   185

Section Six: Culture Change   215
    Chapter 13: The Inside and Out of Culture Change   219
    Chapter 14: The Human Brain and Culture Change   233
    Chapter 15: Instant, Sheep-dip or Viral?   241

John R. Childress

Chapter 16: Rethinking Culture Change — 255

Section Seven: Culture Clash — 265
Chapter 17: Corporate Culture and M&A — 269

Section Eight: Corporate Culture Myths — 277

Section Nine: The Culture of Banking is Broken — 287
Chapter 18: Why Banks Should Focus on Culture, Now More Than Ever — 289
Chapter 19: Banking Leadership? — 303

Section Ten: Q&A about Corporate Culture — 309

Section Eleven: The Future of Corporate Culture — 317
Chapter 20: Corporate Culture Ain't What it — 319

So, Just What the Heck is Corporate Culture? — 329

Acknowledgements — 333

About The Author — 337

About The Principia Group — 339

Citations — 341

References — 346

Overview

Few concepts in business contain so many powerful truths, and at the same time so much crap, as Corporate Culture.

It is nearly impossible to pick up any business article, no matter what the industry, and not see the words **corporate culture**. And headlines abound: *The Culture of Banking Is Broken; The Profit Power of Corporate Culture; How Innovative Is Your Company's Culture?; Corporate Culture: The Only Truly Sustainable Competitive Advantage; Demystifying Corporate Culture.*

Books about corporate culture populate the business best-seller lists: *Corporate Culture and Performance; Leading Culture Change in Global Organizations; Toyota Culture: The Heart and Soul of the Toyota Way; The Corporate Culture Survival Guide,* to name just a few. Even the giant Internet shoe retailer, Zappos.com, has produced a book about its famous corporate culture!

A recent Google search for the phrase "corporate culture" turned up 621 million hits in 0.21 seconds. (a search for "leadership" turned up just 456 million, while "productivity" only 264 million hits). And it's not just newspapers and Human Resource journals that publish articles on corporate culture, but academic and professional journals such as the Harvard Business Review, MIT Sloan Management Review, The Economist, Forbes and Fortune magazine. The list of books and articles are endless, as are the definitions of corporate culture.

Leverage

> *Give me lever long enough and a fulcrum on which to place it, and I can move the earth. ~Archimedes*

Archimedes was a Greek mathematician, physicist, engineer, inventor and astronomer who lived between approximately 287 BC – 212 BC in the city of Syracuse. He is perhaps best known for his explanation of the Principle of Leverage, using a lever and fulcrum to lift objects that would otherwise have been too heavy to move.

The job of the CEO and business leader calls for heavy lifting and the movement of some pretty stubborn and immovable objects. Not only does the CEO have to divine a winning strategy, but has to align and launch the human energies of hundreds to thousands of individuals, each with multiple agendas, towards a common objective in a cost effective efficient manner and in the fasted time possible to stay ahead of the competition.

For that task some real leverage is needed. Leadership is the lever and corporate culture is the fulcrum.

A weak culture will not sustain the force required for change. An unaligned culture will cause the lever of leadership to lose balance and be inefficient. But a strong culture, aligned with the strategy, and supported by beliefs and behaviors that match the task at hand, can create a powerful force in the business world.

This Guidebook . . .

The problem with experts is they know too much and understand too little.

It is my job in this short guidebook to clear up some of the mystery and misconceptions of what corporate culture is, why it matters, its impact on performance, where culture comes from, how to understand the strengths and weaknesses of your own culture, and ultimately, how to develop and shape a corporate culture that supports and propels your organization towards its business and strategic objectives.

Big goals for such a little book! But I have had the help of some of the most talented and respected CEOs, senior executives and business leaders from around the world, who have built, led and worked in large global organizations as well as small to medium enterprises. Together we have talked about, explored, dissected, inspected, studied, mapped, and shifted corporate cultures, all with the goal of improving the lives of customers, employees, the environment, shareholders and other stakeholders. The experiences and insights gained from my 35-year career working with many CEOs and senior executive teams on corporate culture and culture change form the basis for this guidebook.

LEVERAGE:

WHAT'S ALL THE FUSS?

There is no problem so big it cannot be run away from.
~ Charles M. Schulz

The weather in the Gulf of Mexico was calm on the evening of April 20th, 2010 when a gas blowout and subsequent explosion occurred on the Deepwater Horizon oil rig, ultimately causing what many have described as the worst oil spill in history. Eleven people died in the explosion and fire, which damaged the rig to the point where it sank the next day. Fortunately 115 people were safely rescued, but over the next 87 days an estimated 4.9 million barrels (210 million US gallons) of oil spilled into the Gulf of Mexico before the well hole, 5,100 feet below the surface, was finally capped.

A loss of life product disaster is every senior executive's worst nightmare and the Deepwater Horizon catastrophe ultimately cost Tony Haywood, CEO of British Petroleum (BP), his job. So far BP has spent an estimated $41 billion in recovery costs, set asides and settlements, and the litigation continues.

What is instructive about this unfortunate disaster to those interested in the concept of corporate culture is the way BP leadership responded in the early days of the accident. Initially BP downplayed the incident. Its CEO Tony Hayward called the amount of oil and dispersant *"relatively tiny in comparison with the very big ocean"* [1]. Either he was purposefully playing down the extent of the disaster, or the lines of communication within BP were so poor that he really didn't know what was going on, or perhaps nobody was willing to tell the boss the truth! Later, he drew an outpouring of criticism when he commented that the spill was a disruption to Gulf Coast residents and to himself, adding during a rather heated press grilling, *"You know, I'd like to have my life back"* [2].

British Petroleum, founded in 1909 as the Anglo-Persian Oil Company and now the fifth largest corporation in the world, is by all financial measures a successful company. Prior to the Deepwater Horizon accident its share price had been steadily increasing, outperforming the FTSE 100 index. Fundamentally, BP is a company with an intense focus on the bottom line and with cost control being paramount to improving share price performance. It is also a company highly invested in the global politics of oil and gas and spends massive amounts of executive time and money engaged in global lobbying and political influencing of key figures in the industry. Here is where we begin to see the real corporate culture of BP.

In 2011, a White House commission blamed the disaster on BP and its partners for a series of cost-cutting decisions and an insufficient safety system [3]. At the time of the accident, the Deepwater rig was over budget and behind on its production schedule, more pressure to move faster and return a profit.

As a result of how it handled the accident, BP has been vilified in the press and blogs the world over. The BP share price has yet to recover to its pre-accident level, and litigation is expected to go on for another 10 years. On April 19th, 2010 (the day before the accident) the Market Capitalization of BP was $188 billion. Just 2 weeks later it had plummeted to $91 billion, and today hovers around $133 billion. An expensive accident, but this one accident offered the world a rare insight into how BP is managed, the quality of its leadership and its corporate culture.

Chicago, 1982

Here's another unfortunate corporate disaster with loss of life.

In Chicago in 1982 someone put deadly cyanide into bottles of Tylenol Extra-Strength pain reliever. Seven people died from poisoning. The media exposure around the Tylenol poisonings was the largest since the 1963 assassination of President John F Kennedy. Tylenol, the best selling pain reliever in the US, had a 38% market share prior to this disaster.

The business press quickly took up the story, with the Wall Street Journal predicting the demise of Johnson & Johnson, the parent company. But Johnson & Johnson reacted quickly as well. A brand manager, not the CEO, made a quick decision to pull all Tylenol products off of all shelves, nationwide, a $100 million impact. Then the company moved all its various resources into action to protect the public, make certain an accident like this could never happen again, and recover the reputation of the brand and the company.

Quickly TV ads were placed by Johnson & Johnson telling people not to use any Tylenol product and to return current bottles for free replacement. The company then began to work with doctors and nurses to explain that the situation was a one-time tampering by an unknown individual, not a company manufacturing issue. They then embarked on an R&D effort that resulted in the introduction of a new product safety standard for the pharmaceutical industry, the tamper-proof bottle with safety cap.

Even though J&J's market share dropped from 38% to 8% immediately after the event, six months later, thanks to numerous speeches, appearances in advertisements and on TV by company executives and the then CEO, James Burke, Tylenol's market share had risen to 27% and within a year regained and maintained its dominant market share.

CEO James Burke, in his speeches and articles, credited J&J's quick response to protect the public, no matter what the cost and to make certain such events as this could never happen again, to the *Johnson & Johnson Credo*, set down by the company's founder, Robert Wood Johnson in 1943, and still very much a part of the J&J way of doing business. Basically the credo puts the company's responsibilities in the following order: doctors, nurses and patients first, employees second, communities third and shareholders fourth (last).[4]

Then, only a few years later, another Tylenol tampering scandal broke out in 1986 when a New York woman died after ingesting capsules again laced with cyanide. Again J & J stopped production of capsules, opting for pills and caplets. The recalls cost the company more than $200 million. But because of the CEO's openness and J&J's introduction of tamper-resistant packaging, the market share of Tylenol bounced back to its dominant position.

The way that Johnson & Johnson and British Petroleum responded to these two very different disasters, each with loss of life and intense media and public scrutiny, clearly shows corporate culture at work. One culture, very cost focused and financially driven with all eyes on share price and productivity, with visible behaviors of blame and executive arrogance (Edersheim, 2010). The other, guided by a fundamental set of shared beliefs and leadership behaviors putting the welfare of the users of their products first, and profit last.

From these two events it is easy to see that culture matters, big time!

Compromising on culture is mortgaging the future.
~ HubSpot Culture Code

Not Another Culture Book?

Corporate culture is one of the most written about (and talked about) subjects in business today, and one of the least understood!

When I first began to give presentations and have meetings with CEOs about corporate culture back in 1978, most would look at me with blank stares. And employees on the shop floor were even more direct. I recall one burly shop steward, after I explained that I was a consultant conducting a culture survey, who replied: *"What the hell do I care about yogurt cultures, we make military vehicles here."*

The situation is very different today. Everybody is talking, writing and pontificating about corporate culture. And consultants dealing with culture, culture change, culture assessments and cultural integration abound. One of our CEO clients was so fed up with the avalanche of calls and solicitations from culture consultants that she coined the term *'Culture Vultures.'*

And for a concept that has so much written in the press and academic journals, not to mention the several hundred books on corporate culture, even the experts can't agree on a clear and encompassing definition. So if we can't really define corporate culture, then what makes us think we can understand it, yet alone manage or improve it?

When there is genuine interest in a subject that is shrouded with confusion, complexity and misunderstanding, there is fertile ground for an explosion of consulting advice. After all, if everyone is talking about culture and senior executives don't really understand it fully, then the experts (consultants) must be the ones in the know! And they are knocking (banging) on your door.

This book is designed to assist you, the CEO, senior executive, business and government leader in developing your own understanding of corporate culture, it's role in your quest for improved performance, and how you can best shape, guide and lead your corporate culture. And if and when you do interact with culture consultants, I trust you will be able to ask the important and hard questions to test their level of competence and capabilities.

Why Focus on the CEO?

> *There is nothing more difficult to take in hand, more perilous to conduct, or more uncertain in its success, than to take the lead in the introduction of a new order of things. ~ Niccolo Machiavelli*

Because it's the CEO who gets fired if the company doesn't perform. And corporate culture does impact performance, either positively or negatively. CEO's who don't understand or who ignore corporate culture often do so at their peril.

Ron Johnson took over as CEO of underperforming retailer J. C. Penney in 2011 to accolades from all corners of the business world as the savior of a once venerable brand [5]. The man credited with the success of the Apple stores and the reinvigoration of the American retailer, Target Stores, he seemed to be the perfect choice. Seventeen months later, Johnson was fired for a litany of mistakes, all seemingly revolving around his lack of understanding of the strength of the J. C. Penney culture and the brand expectations of its core customers.

Carly Fiona, the celebrity CEO of Hewlett-Packard was fired for trying to turn a culture of *'technical excellence'* into a *'sales culture.'* It was a change too far and the HP culture was too strong.

> *"HP's culture, since the days of William Hewlett and David Packard, was engineering-driven and very*

paternalistic. Its fundamental focus was employee autonomy and creativity. Former CEO Carly Fiorina tried to impose a sales culture, first by fiat, then indirectly by merging with Compaq, which was decidedly sales-focused." [6]

Michael Woodford, the British senior executive elevated to CEO in a bid to revive the Japanese technology firm, Olympus, was fired just a few months later, the Japanese Chairman citing that Woodford did not understand or respect the *'culture'* of decision making in Olympus [7].

The role of the CEO is a 24/7 nonstop tsunami of issues that could potentially harm your business, destroy brand value, demoralize employees and alienate customers and shareholders. We now live in an era of explosive global competition, a large portion of which are not yet on the radar screen, and these emerging competitors are hungry to take away your customers. New regulations are creating more and more barriers to business efficiency and cost effectiveness. Climate change is impacting all businesses, from large to small. And the global economy is becoming a more and more a volatile, complex and risky place to do business. All these forces are forcing organizations to change, adapt and respond. A CEO who understands the strengths and weaknesses of their company culture will be better able to respond appropriately.

CEOs can talk and blab all day about culture, but the employees know who the jerks are.
~ Jack Welch

Why Me?

My fascination with corporate culture took firm root in 1978 when I met my soon-to-be business partner, Dr. Larry E. Senn. Up to that point, I had been a Vice-President for a large US-based personal development and leadership training company. From my work with large groups of 200-plus participants in 4-day personal development seminars, to facilitating small groups of men and women intent on becoming better leaders in business and the community, it was becoming increasingly obvious to me that personal change and self-improvement are heavily impacted by the work environment people find themselves in.

For example, many participants would report back on dramatic change in their outlook, self-esteem, energy levels, family relationships and work productivity for several months following their initial seminar experience. But then, increasingly, more and more would confide that even though they had changed, their workplace hadn't, and it was beginning to take its toll on them. The new tools and ways of thinking learned in the seminars weren't being reinforced at work. In fact, just the opposite. People at work felt threatened by their new levels optimism and self-confidence. And the policies and procedures at work were just as onerous as before. As we all know, it takes a habit to replace a habit and without daily reinforcement, old habits come roaring back.

At the time we met, Larry was running a small, retail focused, operations improvement-consulting firm based in Long Beach, California. However, his 1970 doctoral dissertation at UCLA had been on *Organizational Character as a Tool in the Analysis of Business Organizations*, showing that organizations, like people, have a definable personality, which in many ways determines how they react and behave. When we met, Larry had recently attended a personal development seminar and was enthralled with the *'soft'* training technology used to help people change and improve and was beginning to use a few of these techniques in his retail consulting assignments, to great success.

We both asked the same question: *Why couldn't we do the same for businesses?* He had the consulting experience and I had the personal development *'soft'* technology for change, so a partnership, a business and an industry, culture change, was born.

LEVERAGE:

In 1978 Larry and I co-founded a consulting firm specializing in reshaping corporate culture and aligning senior executive teams, *The Senn-Delaney Leadership Consulting Group*. Since the term corporate culture hadn't been popularized yet, we talked about the *'personality of the organization'* and its impact on performance.

Then in 1982 Tom Peters and Bill Waterman published their hugely popular book, *In Search of Excellence*, and suddenly everyone was talking about corporate culture. Well, our firm had first mover advantage and for the next 20 years we grew the firm significantly with offices in Long Beach, New York and London, and had the opportunity to work with many major US and global businesses. Again, working with the senior team to help them understand that "*organizations are shadows of their leaders*" (that's the good news and the bad news) and that senior team alignment and culture change could, in many cases, be a key to improved business performance.

After over 20 years as President and CEO of the Senn-Delaney Leadership Consulting Group and several million frequent flyer miles, I retired in 2000 and took my family to live in the South of France for a couple of years. It was there that I had the time and the luxury to review the past several decades of consulting assignments and to figure out just exactly what I had learned. And more importantly, just what the heck is corporate culture?

This book is a result of those assessments and reflections, as well as additional work between 2003 and the present, with CEOs and senior teams across the US, UK, Europe, Asia, Africa and the Middle East, on culture change, senior team alignment, strategy execution and leadership mentoring.

True Lies . . .

Half the lies they tell about me aren't true. ~Yogi Berra

As you will see in this book, if you haven't already in your day to day business life, everyone is talking about corporate culture, touting culture change, providing culture assessments, and using culture as an explanation for spectacular business successes, and dramatic business failures.

Let's be realistic. Culture is only one dimension of organizational success and failure. However, to sell books and consulting services, consultants and academics often put culture front and center as the major culprit. It makes a good story, but to say that corporate culture was *'the cause'* of the demise of a company or the failure of a merger is about as factual as saying the cause of the fall of the Roman Empire was only due to a decline in morals. This was just one of the many contributing factors, along with rapid geographic over-expansion, conflict between the Emperor and the Senate, unemployment of the working classes, political corruption, the rise of the powerful and corrupt Praetorian Guard, Barbarian knowledge of Roman military tactics and numerous other social and environmental factors. Corporate culture is just one of the factors in organization success and failure.

Yet make no mistake. Culture matters and in many ways corporate culture impacts the performance of your business. That is why I hope, in this book, to separate the useful from the exaggerated, the fundamental principles from the pontifications, and the BS from the fertilizer, in order to provide you with not only an informed and mature understanding as to what corporate culture is all about, but also some tools to manage and leverage your corporate culture to the advantage of your customers, employees, communities and shareholders.

Caveat Emptor ("Buyer Beware")

Section One: The Rise, and Rise, and Rise of Corporate Culture

Every company has its own language, its own version of its own history (its myths), and its own heroes and villains (its legends), both historical and contemporary.
~ Michael Hammer

The term corporate culture burst onto the business world in spectacular fashion in 1982 with the publication of a book by two former McKinsey & Company consultants, Tom Peters and Robert Waterman. The book, *In Search of Excellence*, shot to number one not only for business books, but also became a New York Times best seller and sold 3 million copies in its first four years. It launched Tom Peters, the more outspoken of the two, into stardom as a management guru, public speaker, and sought after culture consultant. Since the publication of *In Search of Excellence*, Peters has authored 12 more business books, all with corporate culture as a fundamental platform for business success.

Had you purchased shares in each of the 46 excellent companies profiled in the book in 1982 and held them for 20 years, your total return would have been 1,300% compared to around 800% for the Dow and 600% for the S&P 500.[8]

Corporate culture soon moved from a popular concept into academic credibility and greater rigor when Edgar Schein, a professor at the MIT Sloan School of Management, published *Organizational Culture and Leadership* in 1985. Schein's work was the first to really attempt to rigorously define corporate culture (he uses the term 'organizational culture' and for all practical purposes, both terms are referring to the same basic phenomenon of organizational life).

John P. Kotter and James L. Haskett, both Harvard professors, really kicked the term corporate culture into the stratosphere and onto the desks of almost every CEO with the 1992 publication of *Corporate Culture and Performance*, for the first time making a solid connection between culture and business performance, both good and bad.

In addition to these three seminal publications, numerous professors and consultants have added to the growing pile of books and articles on corporate culture. One of the more comprehensive recent works, *Corporate Culture: The Ultimate Strategic Asset* by Eric Flamholtz and Yvonne Randle is based on extensive discussions and examples from organizations large and small, from the US to Europe and China. And on the other side, one of the less scholarly but more engaging is *The Advantage: Why Organization Health Trumps Everything Else in Business*, by best selling business fable author and culture guru Patrick Lencioni.

And to show how deep corporate culture has been engrained in the modern business experience and lifestyle, there are even Apps available to help you understand and change culture!

The 'Culture Sage' from Omaha

Warren Buffett, one of the more savvy investors of the past three decades, made a bold and profound statement in a recent annual letter to the Berkshire Hathaway shareholders:

> *"Culture, more than rule books, determines how an organization behaves."*

As for the management at Berkshire Hathaway, Buffett insists that a culture of *'personal ownership'* prevails there as well.

> *Our compensation programs, our annual meeting and even our annual reports are all designed with an eye to reinforcing the Berkshire culture, and making it one that will repel and expel managers of a different bent.* [9]

Chapter 1: Just What is Corporate Culture?

What's in a name? That which we call a rose
By any other name would smell as sweet.
~ William Shakespeare, Romeo and Juliet

The concept of *'corporate culture'* is not only talked and written about almost daily, but also is described using several different terms, such a the recently popular phrase 'organizational health', and the classical academic term *'organization culture.'*

Another business concept that many tend to equate with corporate culture is *'organizational engagement'*, often simply called *'employee engagement'*. While not as comprehensive as the broad concept of corporate culture, engagement is definitely one of the many elements of culture and many authors use the two interchangeably.

Throughout this book I will use the term **corporate culture**, or just plain **culture**. While the academics may take issue to my lumping of these various terms under the umbrella of culture, this is not an academic review but a practical guide book for the CEO, senior executives and other business leaders to help them better understand and shape their corporate culture. As one pragmatic CEO told me: *"Spare me the academic mumbo jumbo and consultant gobbledygook and give me something I can use to improve my business and the lives of my employees!"*

A Short History of Corporate Culture

There are generally two types of literature on corporate culture: the Mythic and the Academic. The Mythic consists of confident assertions and descriptions. These are long on narrative and expert interpretations and short on data and metrics. The Academic literature is either theoretical (Mythic disguised in academic language) or research-based. Unfortunately for the CEO and business leaders tasked with moving their organizations forward and creating competitive advantage, much of this written material is mixed up and not easily accessible.

If you want to make sense of the world today, read history.

As far as I can tell, the first real mention of corporate culture in a business context comes from the pioneering work of Elliott Jaques (1917–2003) a Canadian psychoanalyst and organizational psychologist who studied the human dynamics within a manufacturing factory, with a particular emphasis on layers of management and how people behaved in carrying out duties and work orders from above. This first mention of culture appeared in his book *The Changing Culture of a Factory: A Study of Authority and Participation in an Industrial Setting* (Jaques, 1951)

> *The culture of the factory is its customary and traditional way of thinking and of doing things, which is shared to a greater or lesser extent by all its members, and which new members must learn, and at least partially accept, in order to be accepted*

into service in the firm. [It] consists of the means or techniques which lie at the disposal of the individual for handling his relationships, and upon which he depends for making his way among, and with, other members and groups.

In 1972 Roger Harrison published an article in the Harvard Business Review that put forth a model to describe four different types of corporate cultures, based on two perpendicular axes (High to Low Formality, and Degree of Centralization). This model was later expanded upon by Charles Handy in his book, *Gods of Management.* (Handy, 2009)

Handy gave highly descriptive names to these four types of corporate culture:

Role Culture: highly specialized, with many procedures for communication and for the resolution of disputes. This culture is typical of a bureaucracy.

Power Culture: based on a central source of power - a key individual or individuals. There are few procedures or regulations. Control is exercised personally by the center and through the selection of key individuals.

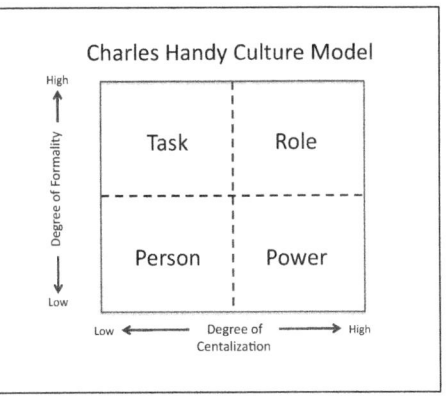

Task Culture: achievement-orientated, values teamwork, adaptability and co-operation in pursuit of project goals.

Person Culture: mainly values the people within the organization, and is not aimed at producing goods and services for customers. This type of culture may be found in social clubs and societies.

A few other researchers made side references to the culture of organizations between the 50's and 70's, without much fanfare, probably because at that time the business world was dominated by accountants and operations executives taking advantage of the explosive growth opportunities of post WWII expansion.

However, in the early 1980's the US economy was stagnating and all eyes were on the economic miracle of Japan and its use of *Total Quality Management* (supported by the speeches and writing of Edwards Deming). TQM's main focus was on improving productivity through people.

In an attempt to revitalize US companies and regain global competitiveness, four major books hit the US market that put corporate culture at the center of the debate on improving productivity and business performance.

William Ouichi, a professor at the UCLA Andersen School of Business, spent several years studying Japanese management methods and searching for an understanding of why the Japanese were outcompeting the US. In 1981 he published the controversial, *Theory Z: How American Management Can Meet the Japanese Challenge.*

Basically Ouichi was preaching that to be competitive, North American management would have to put a greater focus on the well-being and development of employees and not just a single-minded focus on productivity and costs. He described the Japanese management culture as responsible for getting high levels of employee productivity and loyalty.

The book was accepted by some managers in the West as a new way forward, but rejected by many others as being too different from Western management training and practices. *"That will never work here"* was the overriding sentiment.

Terrance Deal, an educator, and Allan Kennedy, a management consultant, really fired the interest in culture when they published *Corporate Cultures: The Rites and Rituals of Corporate Life*, in 1982. By studying the behavioral *'rites and rituals'* that go on inside of companies, they were able to categorize organizational culture along two dimensions: Level of Risk and Speed of Marketplace Feedback. This allowed them to build a 2X2 matrix resulting in four basic types of cultures:

Tough-Guy, Macho: This culture contains a world of individualists who enjoy risk and who get quick feedback on their decisions. This is an all-or-nothing culture where successful employees are the ones who enjoy excitement and work hard to be stars. The entertainment industry, investment banking and advertising are great examples of this cultural type.

Work – Hard / Play – Hard:
This culture is the world of sales (among others). Employees themselves take few risks; however, the feedback on how well they are performing is almost immediate. Employees in this culture have to maintain high levels of energy and stay upbeat. Heroes in such cultures are high volume salespeople.

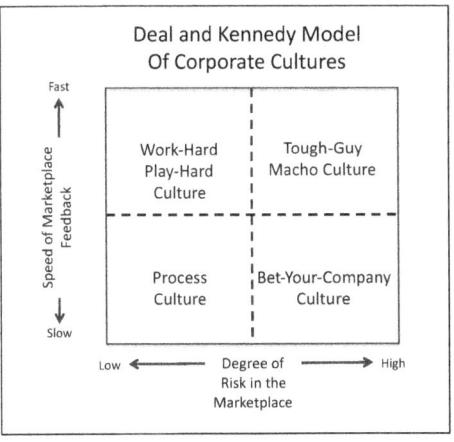

Bet-Your-Company: Here, the culture is one in which decisions are high risk but employees may wait years before they know whether their actions actually paid off. Pharmaceutical companies are an obvious example, as are oil and gas exploration companies. Because the need to make the right decision is so great, the cultural is long-term focused and there is a collective belief in the need to plan, prepare and perform due diligence at all stages of decision making.

Process Culture: In this culture, feedback is slow, and the risks are low. Large retailers, insurance companies and government organizations are typically in this group. No single transaction has much impact on the organization's success and it takes years to find out whether a decision was good or bad. Because of the lack of immediate feedback, employees find it very difficult to measure what they do so they focus instead on how they do things. Technical excellence is often valued here.

The Classic Culture Study: *In Search of Excellence*

Tom Peters and Roger Waterman were former McKinsey & Company consultants who looked at the common characteristics of what they called *"excellent companies"* in order to distill what separated high performing organizations from the mediocre. The result was the hugely popular book, *In Search of Excellence*, described by Forbes as one of the top 10 business books of all time.

Excellent companies (and therefore excellent cultures) shared many of the following eight characteristics:

- **A bias for action**: active decision making - *'getting on with it'*. Quick decision making and problem solving tends to avoid bureaucratic control.
- **Close to the customer**: listening to and learning from the people served by the business.
- **Autonomy and entrepreneurship**: fostering innovation and nurturing 'champions'.

- **Productivity through people**: treating rank and file employees as the source of quality.
- **Hands-on, value-driven management**: a philosophy that guides everyday practice - management showing its commitment.
- **Stick to the knitting**: stay with the business that you know.
- **Simple form, lean staff**: some of the best companies have minimal HQ staff.
- **Simultaneous loose-tight properties**: autonomy in shop-floor activities plus centralized values.

Great Place to Work®

While almost purposefully avoiding the word culture, Robert Levering and Milton Moskowitz, two business journalists, were asked by a New York editor to write a book called *The 100 Best Companies to Work for in America*, which was published in 1984. It quickly became a New York Times bestseller. This initial foray into great places to work so intrigued Levering that he set up the Great Places to Work® Institute to conduct further research and gain insights into what makes some companies great workplaces and others not.

His research revealed that a great workplace culture is one where employees trust the people they work for, take pride in what they do, and enjoy the people they work with. And further research has shown that companies who score high on these three factors tend to outperform their peer group in stock returns, growth and reduced turnover. In 1997, Fortune Magazine commissioned the annual Great Place to Work® survey, which has been conducted every year since and lists the top 100 companies with Great Workplaces.

Of the four business books about corporate culture published between 1981-1984, the more theatrical style of Tom Peters, along with his alleged *'research based'* assessments of strong and weak cultures, made *In Search of Excellence* a New York Times best seller for several years and was instrumental in spawning the industry of culture consulting.

Corporate Culture and the Academics

While Tom Peters tells engaging stories about corporate culture using examples of customer service and other actions from his growing list of companies with *'excellent'* cultures, MIT Professor Edgar Schein (often referred to as the father of corporate culture) put culture on a more solid academic footing when he published *Organizational Culture and Leadership* in 1985.

Schein breaks corporate culture into three parts: artifacts, espoused values and assumptions. The figure below illustrates the various layers of culture, with artifacts being at the surface and the most obvious to see in daily business life, and assumptions at the core and the least visible.

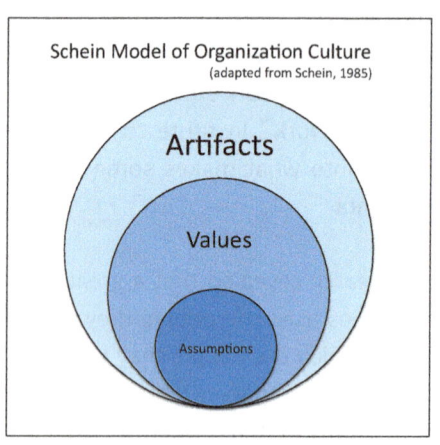

Artifacts are the visible elements of a culture. Artifacts can be recognized by people not part of the culture. For instance, artifacts can be dress codes, furniture, art, work-space design, stories, work processes, organizational structures etc. The outsider might easily see these artifacts, but might not be able to fully understand why these artifacts have been established.

Values are the beliefs and behaviors normally expressed by the leading figures of a culture, usually the founders. Such values could be represented by philosophies, business strategies and organizational goals established by the leaders.

Assumptions reflect the shared values within the specific culture. These are often ill defined and not generally visible, but are frequently spoken about as the unofficial ground rules of the organization. It is not uncommon for these assumptions to become counter to the original values of the founders as a company grows and experiences both success and hardships.

Culture Meets Performance

An ounce of performance is worth a pound of promises.
~ Mae West

One more study will complete this short history of the beginnings of corporate culture. In 1992 two Harvard professors, John P. Kotter and James L. Haskett, published *Corporate Culture and Performance*, making one of the first real connections between the *'soft concept'* of culture and the hard economic realities of business performance metrics. They studied over 200 firms, including Hewlett-Packard, Xerox, ICI and Nissan, and concluded that adaptive cultures, those that are flexible enough to evolve with changing market conditions, tended to perform better economically than non-adaptive cultures.

By the mid-90's the concept of corporate culture was firmly established in the lexicon of international business and began to be taught in MBA courses as well as Advanced Executive Education workshops at Harvard, MIT, INSEAD, and other top business schools. It was around this time that the consulting profession discovered the growing and lucrative market for culture change projects and culture surveys, and the literature exploded with articles, opinion pieces, courses, trainings, books, studies and even videos on corporate culture. And it was during this explosive phase that consultants, academics and high-profile senior executives put forth their various definitions of corporate culture.

Definitions of Corporate Culture

One of the definitions of sanity is the ability to tell real from unreal. Soon we'll need a new definition.
~ Alvin Toffler

With the growth of the literature on corporate culture, the list of definitions has also grown, each somewhat skewed towards the biases of the author. Some are more behavioral, many psychological, others more operational, some academic and others merely colloquial in nature. The divide between Mythic and Academic has become permanently blurred.

The following are just a sampling of the many definitions of corporate (organizational) culture by the *'experts'*.

- *"The way we do things around here!"* (commonly attributed to Deal and Kennedy)

- *"Corporate Culture: those hard to change values that spell success or failure."*[10]

- Edgar Schein provides a classically academic definition: *Organization Culture: a pattern of shared basic assumptions learned by a group as it solved its problems of external adaptation and internal integration, which has worked well enough to be considered valid and, therefore, taught to new members as the correct way to perceive, think and feel in relation to those problems.* [11]

- Geert Hofstede looks at culture through the eyes of countries and nationalities, as well as businesses: *"Culture is the collective programming of the human mind that* distinguishes the members of one human group from those of another. Culture in this sense is a system of collectively held values."[12]

- "A blend of the values, beliefs, taboos, symbols, rituals and myths all companies develop over time."[13]

- "The shared norms and expectations that govern the way people approach their work and interact with each other. Such norms and expectations shape how organizational members believe they are expected to behave in order to fit in, get things done, and at times simply survive."[14]

- "Culture is the display of collective behavior. It is influenced by a set of shared norms and values. Every organization exhibits a culture. The departments within the organization have a culture. Anytime people work together for an extended period of time, a culture is formed. It's the force that guides and directs how people will interact with one another and deal with those beyond their group."[15] ~ John Schultz

- "Culture consists of group norms of behavior and the underlying shared values that help keep those norms in place."[16] ~ Professor John P. Kotter

- "Culture is an unwritten set of ground-rules on what is acceptable and what is not."

- "For me the evidence of culture is how people behave when no one is watching."[17] ~ Former Barclays Bank CEO, Bob Diamond

- "Corporate culture is revealed in an organization's behavior and structure. A hierarchical company may have individual offices, a formal environment and intricate rules regarding travel allowances and dress code. Companies emphasizing equality and innovation will demonstrate these values visibly too, for instance, Apple is famous for its casual dress and elegant product design. At Intel, which is known for its culture of face-to-face open discussions, everyone, including the top executives, works in the same size office cubicle and even senior managers fly economy class. Such symbols send powerful messages about a company's culture." [18] ~ Financial Times Lexicon

- "Organizational Culture is the behavior of humans who are part of an organization and the meanings that the people attach to their actions. Culture includes the organization values, visions, norms, working language, systems, symbols, beliefs and habits. It is also the pattern of such collective behaviors and assumptions that are taught to new organizational members as a way of perceiving, and even thinking and feeling. Organizational culture affects the way people and groups interact with each other, with clients, and with stakeholders." [19] ~ Wikipedia.com

- "Organizational Culture: The values and behaviors that contribute to the unique social and psychological environment of an organization. Organizational culture includes an organization's expectations, experiences, philosophy, and values that hold it together, and is expressed in its self-image, inner workings, interactions with the outside world, and future expectations. It is based on shared attitudes, beliefs, customs, and written and unwritten rules that have been developed over time and are considered valid. Also called corporate culture, it's seen in:
    - the ways the organization conducts its business, treats its employees, customers, and the wider community
    - the extent to which freedom is allowed in decision making, developing new ideas, and personal expression
    - how power and information flow through its hierarchy
    - how committed employees are towards collective objectives." [20]

- "Culture is the organization's immune system."

- "Culture is the DNA of the organization."

As you can see from these few examples of culture definitions, corporate culture is not one single thing, but a network or web of critical influencers to how an organization performs.

Curiouser and curiouser! ~ Alice in Wonderland

A Useful Synthesis

A very useful synthesis and overview on corporate culture comes from the insightful genius of Harvard professor Clayton Christensen (author of the famous studies on disruptive technologies) in a Harvard Business Review article : *What is an Organization's Culture?* (Aug. 2006). While just 8 pages, it is an excellent overall summary of culture from one of the most respected business thinkers and advisors. It's definitely worth a read [21].

JOHN R. CHILDRESS

Chapter 2: The Hijacking of Corporate Culture

*Looking for love in all the wrong places,
looking for love in too many faces . . .
~ Johnny Lee*

We Value Values

One of the noisiest and least productive sideshows in the corporate culture carnival is the obsession (by academics, behavioral scientists and most culture consultants) with values: cultural values, leadership values, shared values, values statements and so on . . .

In the mid-80's after the publication of *In Search of Excellence*, an army of consultants burst on the scene to help 'rudderless' organizations build mission and vision statements, which seemed to then require the need for values and value statements to guide the culture into alignment with the new vision. (Whew! I get tired of management speak).

Even Enron had printed values and lofty statements [22] which of course no one paid any attention to, (as is the case in most organizations).

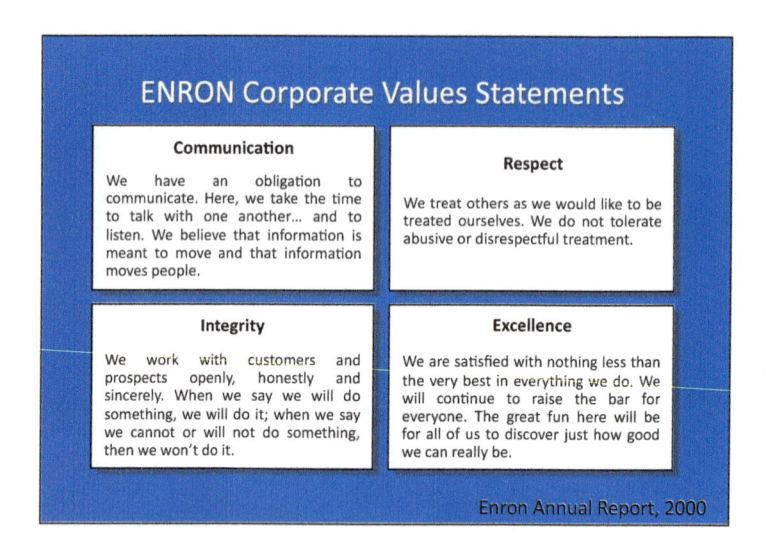

> **ENRON Corporate Values Statements**
>
> **Communication**
> We have an obligation to communicate. Here, we take the time to talk with one another... and to listen. We believe that information is meant to move and that information moves people.
>
> **Respect**
> We treat others as we would like to be treated ourselves. We do not tolerate abusive or disrespectful treatment.
>
> **Integrity**
> We work with customers and prospects openly, honestly and sincerely. When we say we will do something, we will do it; when we say we cannot or will not do something, then we won't do it.
>
> **Excellence**
> We are satisfied with nothing less than the very best in everything we do. We will continue to raise the bar for everyone. The great fun here will be for all of us to discover just how good we can really be.
>
> Enron Annual Report, 2000

Talk is cheap, except when Congress does it.
~ Cullen Hightower

You Show Me Yours and I'll Show You Mine . . .

I have asked dozens of CEOs and senior executives over my 35 years of work on leadership, culture change, performance improvement and business transformation if they have ever seen a value: *"Can you show me a value?"* They shake their heads in mild chagrin. I've also asked to see reports for Values KPIs and program management plans for improving corporate values. Nothing!

This obsession with values is not very useful to those business leaders trying to improve competitive performance and build successful and sustainable business enterprises. Values are abstract concepts of what is important and worthwhile. Flying the national flag on a holiday is a behavior that (in most cases) reflects the value of patriotism. Stating openly in a meeting that your project is behind schedule by three weeks is a behavior that reflects the value of *'accountability'* and *'open, honest communication.'* But these are behaviors, not values. We can't see, touch, nor can we manage values. And depending upon your upbringing and culture, the value of *'respect for others'* may look very different to a Japanese business person than one from Sweden. Value statements can be interpreted in many ways. Behaviors are much more binary and easy to observe.

We can begin to understand a corporate culture by observing the frequent behaviors displayed by employees in response to certain internal and external stimuli. Behaviors can be seen, understood and in many ways, managed to achieve an outcome. We can't even see, let alone manage, Values.

But somehow, the concept of corporate culture got mixed up with values. A recent search on Google turned up 78.3 million hits for the term "corporate values" and 44.3 million hits for the term "shared values", another of the behavioral scientists favorite expressions when defining corporate culture. These two Google searches also uncovered scores of colorful PowerPoint slides showing examples of corporate values statements and company values.

The management consulting firm, Booz Allen Hamilton, along with The Aspen Institute conducted a global survey in 2005 with 9,500 senior executives.

They found that 89% of the companies surveyed had written values statements. A chart from this research shows the frequency of values that appear in corporate values statements, annual reports and internal documents from companies across multiple industries.

The main reason values tend to be useless in business is that they are imprecise, vague and subject to multiple interpretations. Take the value *'Commitment to Employees'* from the chart above, which appears frequently in corporate values statements. Ask any 20 employees what this means to them, and in most companies you will get 20 different responses. To one it may mean paying top quartile salaries, to another it may mean access to training and professional development programs, to a third it may mean a

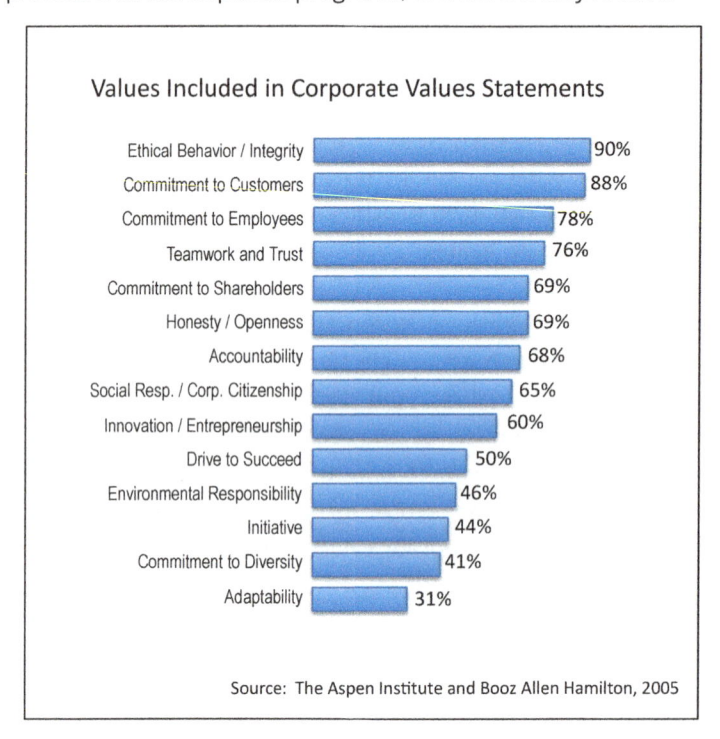

Values Included in Corporate Values Statements

Value	Percentage
Ethical Behavior / Integrity	90%
Commitment to Customers	88%
Commitment to Employees	78%
Teamwork and Trust	76%
Commitment to Shareholders	69%
Honesty / Openness	69%
Accountability	68%
Social Resp. / Corp. Citizenship	65%
Innovation / Entrepreneurship	60%
Drive to Succeed	50%
Environmental Responsibility	46%
Initiative	44%
Commitment to Diversity	41%
Adaptability	31%

Source: The Aspen Institute and Booz Allen Hamilton, 2005

commitment to work-life balance. These varied interpretations come from each individual's personal value system, not the company values. And to publish a set of company values and expect that they will be universally understood and internalized by 100 or 1,000 individual employees is just plain nuts!

Individuals have Values;
Corporate Cultures have Behaviors and Norms.

The Test

Life is a cruel teacher.
She gives the test first and the lesson afterwards!

When I give speeches to senior teams or audiences of senior executives, I almost always do this simple test with the group. I first ask: *"How many of you believe that values and value statements are important in running an effective organization?"* All the hands shoot up. I then ask them: *"How many of you work for an organization that has published their values or value statements?"* 90+% of the hands again go up.

Then I ask them all to pull out a piece of blank paper, grab a pen or pencil, and write down the exact values or value statements of their company. As you can imagine, there is a gasp and then a very awkward silence with much fumbling around and shifting in the chairs.

The results? Over the past 35 years the average has been that less than 50% of the audience can actually recall and accurately write down their company values or value statements. And these are the senior executives! I did this recently with a financial services organization in London, which had just 4 simple values. Only one of the 8 senior executives in the room got them all correct!

Why, if values are so important to running effective enterprises, are so few senior executives able to write them down, much less live them day-to-day? My friend Carolyn Taylor describes this difference between words and deeds in her book, *Walking the Talk*. (Taylor,
2005)

For many companies value statements are seen as a tick-the-box people requirement. The Corporate Communications department says: *"We should have a set of printed values, they look good on the wall and in the Annual Report."* But if you can't even remember your lofty value statements, how can you build and manage a corporate culture based on these values?

> *To write down, frame, and publish your corporate values is all about self-deceit and ego. It is almost certainly bullshit. ~ Barry J. Gibbons*

Human values are deep rooted and learned at an early age. Character, basic personality and values are molded by adopting the attitudes and behaviors of the influential people in our lives, whether they are parents, relatives or others. The frequent and habitual behaviors of our early role models and influencers determine in large part what will subsequently become our own most important beliefs and principles. In essence, our own values. And once formed, our deeply held values don't change easily. The failure of the criminal penal system has shown this fact time and time again.

And when an individual joins an organization, whether as an entry level employee or a senior executive, they don't easily change their values to fit those printed in the handbook, but they can and will adopt the behaviors and ways of working that are characteristic of influential groups within that organization. Culture is about behaviors, not values.

The concept of a culture being about personal values is not accurate nor very helpful to the CEO and business leader. Corporate culture is more easily understood as the behaviors and practices that become standard ways of working. And the adoption of those shared behaviors is powered by the human need to fit in and be accepted. Very few individuals are strong enough in their personal sense of self to not adopt the standard cultural practices and beliefs of the company they join. Most of those joiners who are *'counter-cultural'* in their behaviors either leave voluntarily or the culture *'spits them out'*.

> *People have values; cultures have behaviors. Cultures are less about VALUES and more about WORK PRACTICES. And people don't change their personal values when they enter into a new culture, but they can and will adopt new work practices and behaviors.*

A Case where Responsibilities can be of Value

Statements of business and individual responsibilities or a written business philosophy can have great impact on decision-making and performance. In the case of Johnson & Johnson, the core responsibilities set down in 1865 by founder Robert Wood Johnson, form the foundation of new employee orientation programs. The J&J Credo is also used as a lens for evaluating strategic decisions and business strategies, and is actively debated on a regular basis by executives and managers to make certain they remain current, relevant and well understood. Johnson & Johnson's quick reaction to the Tylenol poisoning crisis is a good example of how clear and well understood *Corporate Responsibility Statements* can be useful in making good decisions.

The J&J Credo is not just words on paper, but is brought to life through numerous behaviors by the senior team and middle managers on a regular basis and have, through openness, transparency, regular active debate and leadership role-modeling, evolved from words on paper into the genuine Johnson & Johnson culture.

> *I think that the only way we could have done what we did was to have all of the institutions that were affected by the Tylenol poisonings believe in us; whether it was the head of the FBI, the FDA or the people at the White House. There was no lack of trust about Johnson & Johnson* [23] ~ James E. Burke

In the case of Johnson & Johnson, the responsibilities laid down in 1865 were translated early on into clear and definable behaviors that have been nurtured and refined ever since.

Oh God! Not Another Mission Statement!

In a no-nonsense Harvard Business Review Blog titled: *If I Read One More Platitude-Filled Mission Statement, I'll Scream,* Stanford business graduate and Silicon Valley CEO Greg McKeown takes to task the ubiquitous trend of bland and meaningless mission statements (McKeown, 2012). The platitude-filled mission statement, another idea from the culture vulture consultants, is a way of describing the cultural and business aspirations of an organization. It is supposed to clearly communicate what the company is all about, but rarely does. Most mission statements are a useless list of vague, syrupy platitudes.

Here is a list of major global bank mission statements. Can you tell which bank is which?

1. *We strive to be the acknowledged global leader and preferred partner in helping our clients succeed in the world's rapidly evolving financial markets.*

2. *Our mission is to be the most respected global financial services company. Like any other public company, we're obligated to deliver profits and growth to our shareholders. Of equal importance is to deliver those profits and generate growth responsibly.*

3. *We want to be the best financial services company in the world. Because of our great heritage and excellent platform, we believe this is within our reach.*

4. *Proudly providing banking services for 5.8 million*

customers. We understand that earning your trust is key to our financial strength.

5. Our product: SERVICE. Our value-added: FINANCIAL ADVICE. Our competitive advantage: OUR PEOPLE.

6. We aspire to be one of the world's great specialist banking groups, driven by a commitment to our core philosophies and values .

Here's the key: 1. Bank of New York; 2. CitiGroup; 3. J P Morgan Chase; 4. Fifth Third Bank; 5. Wells Fargo Bancorp; 6. HSBC Bancorp.

Get any correct?

Nice words, but what is it really like to work inside these banks or be a retail or commercial customer? Based on the sorry state of the banking industry today, I would venture to say the mission statement and the reality are quite different, not because the mission isn't desired, but because most of them are just words on paper without any aligned internal business processes or daily leadership behaviors and role-modeling.

Here is the official Facebook mission statement: *"The Facebook mission is to give people the power to share and make the world more open and connected."* One of my clients came up with what she called a more honest Facebook mission statement: *"Help people pretend to be cool by having lots of Facebook friends."*

Is it any wonder why the CFO pulls her hair out when the culture consultant's invoice come across her desk? *"All this money for a bunch of platitudes that everybody rolls their eyes at. Employees must think we are idiots up here!"*

While most mission statements are bland and uninspiring and don't really say much about the company or the culture, a few exceptions stand out. One of them is the Lululemon Athletica mission statement, which they term their Manifesto. There is no question that this helps differentiate Lululemon from most other specialty retailers.

Here are just a few of the dozens of elements that make up the Lululemon Manifesto:

- Friends are more important than money.
- Do one thing a day that scares you.
- Listen, listen, listen, and then ask strategic questions.
- Life is full of setbacks. Success is determined by how you handle setbacks.
- Your outlook on life is a direct reflection of how much you like yourself.
- Dance, sing, floss and travel.

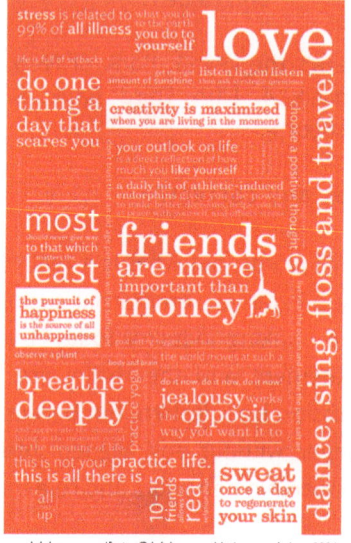

lululemon manifesto, © lululemon athletica canada inc., 2004

- The world is changing at such a rapid rate that waiting to implement changes will leave you 2 steps behind. DO IT NOW, DO IT NOW, DO IT NOW!
- Breathe deeply and appreciate the moment. Living in the moment could be the meaning of life.
- Sweat once a day to regenerate your skin.

A well crafted and focused mission statement can help employees and executives make decisions that are in alignment with the strategy and culture of the organization, but effective mission statements require at least three elements:

- **Clear, honest and direct language:** If it makes sense and is believable to the janitor and the night watchman, it's probably going to work for everybody.

- **A Specific Call to Action with Specific Metrics**: How much, by when and what behaviors are required?

- **An End Result People Can Understand:** Steve Jobs set a very clear mission statement for the iPod, *"We want to put 1,000 songs in your pocket."*

Cut Out the Crap and Get On With It

So, if you're going to really learn to use corporate culture as an effective business tool, then I suggest you scrap the old mission statement and corporate values, gather a diverse group from across the company and give them the task of building a few *'real world'* statements that tell the truth about who we are, our aspirations, and what this company is all about. The more honest and direct the better. Urge them to make it relevant for the shop floor and the night janitor and it will probably be perfect for everyone else.

"Our old mission statement was more eloquent, and dignified, but not nearly as effective."

You will be surprised, and very pleased, with the outcome. And the process of letting them have their say will go a long way in building the type of culture that is open, direct and honest, and productive.

Chapter 3: *'Seeing'* and Understanding Corporate Culture

I'll know it when I see it
~ Supreme Court Justice Stewart Potter's definition of pornography

In the UK retail banking industry the products, rates, reviews, credit checks and services are generally the same among all the London high street banks. Walk into any RBS, NatWest, Barclays, Santander, or Lloyds branches and the customer experience is pretty much the same as well, even after recent branch renovation schemes. You interact with a teller behind bullet-proof glass with little holes or a slit to speak through, manager offices are usually behind security doors, rarely does a member of staff approach you to provide assistance, and an unsmiling 'bouncer' guard is at the front door. Welcome to modern banking!

But walk into any Metro Bank branch and it becomes immediately obvious that this isn't UK retail banking as usual! No bullet-proof glass between you and a teller, people are dressed professionally in brightly colored branded outfits, they greet you openly and engagingly, the coin-counting machine is free (even if you are not a customer), they are open 7 days a week at hours that suit you, the customer, and they welcome dogs with water and biscuits. Same industry and same city, completely different corporate cultures!

If a picture is worth a thousand words, then an analogy or example speaks volumes.

An Analogy: 'Personality of the Organization'

> *Make no mistake between my personality and my attitude. My personality is who I am, my attitude depends on who you are.*

A person's personality can best be defined by how they routinely behave when interacting with the world around them. Some people have open personalities, others more defensive and closed. Some have inquisitive, risk-taking personalities, others cynical and risk averse. Some are highly analytical and detailed, others seem to live by the seat of their pants. Different personality types display characteristically different behaviors.

Larry E. Senn, in his 1970 doctoral dissertation, *Organizational Character as a Tool in the Analysis of Business Organizations* at UCLA, had the early insight that organizations have definable *'personalities,'* or characteristic ways of behaving, that impact their ability to deliver results and most importantly, to implement necessary change.

Some organizations, like IBM, British Telecom, Accenture, KPMG and Grant Thornton, have cultures that are formal and largely analytical in their approach to dealing with clients and solving business problems, even in their management consulting divisions. Others, like Virgin, BSkyB, Verizon or Zappos.com, have more daring, risk-reward cultures and are willing to try many different things, tolerating mistakes and failures as a part of the natural learning and improvement process to better understand and serve their customers.

And in the global airline industry, while all companies tend to have the same planes, fly from the same airports and go to the same destinations, there can be strikingly different cultures. Take for example the *'personality'* of Virgin Airlines and American Airlines.

As a frequent flyer (several million miles so far) I can tell you that the overall personality styles and behavior of the flight attendants and counter staff of Virgin Airlines is very different from that of American Airlines. I don't know this for certain, but I suspect Virgin has a specific hiring profile, looking specifically for those individuals who fit the *'personality'* of the Virgin culture. I would bet that American's hiring profile is definitely less rigorous.

And the *'company personality'* is blindingly obvious when you are boarding the airplane. Virgin flight attendants are upbeat, jolly, welcoming and engaging. American attendants seem to be going through the motions without any real passion or interest in the customer. Whenever I board an AA flight, I get the feeling the flight attendants just want to get passengers into their seats and buckled up as quickly as possible so they can get this boring flight over with!

What's the personality of your organization? How do employees behave when the boss isn't watching? If you want a real experience of your culture, go *'undercover'* within an area of your own company where nobody will recognize you. Be a mystery shopper. Be an *'average'* customer. File a complaint and see what happens. Talk to vendors and suppliers about what it's like to have your company as a customer. Walk around and read what's posted in the cubicles and what's written in the bathroom stalls. The personality of your organization is all around you.

Metaphors

Because of its holistic and complex nature, corporate culture is ripe for the use of metaphors as a way of better understanding what it is and how it functions. Here are just a few metaphors from the literature and consulting firms:

Corporate Culture as:
- Operating System

- DNA
- Compass
- Social glue
- Sacred cow
- Blinders
- Playing Field (Pitch).

Iceberg metaphor

A commonly used metaphor is the description of culture as an iceberg, with both visible and invisible (below the surface) elements.

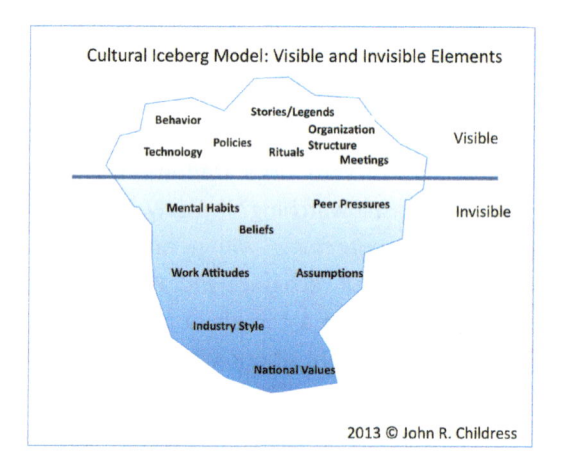

Cultural Iceberg Model: Visible and Invisible Elements

Visible: Behavior, Stories/Legends, Policies, Organization Structure, Technology, Rituals, Meetings

Invisible: Mental Habits, Peer Pressures, Beliefs, Work Attitudes, Assumptions, Industry Style, National Values

2013 © John R. Childress

When Henry Mintzberg, professor at McGill University and one of the world's leading management experts, was asked to compare corporate culture and organization structure, he replied:

> "Culture is the soul of the organization—the beliefs and values, and how they are manifested. I think of the structure as the skeleton, and as the flesh and blood. And culture is the soul that holds the thing together and gives it life force."
> (24)

LEVERAGE:

Another Way to Think About It: Culture as a Hologram

Things are only impossible until they're not.
~ Captain Jean-Luc Picard, Star Trek: The Next Generation

One of my favorite TV shows is *Star Trek: The Next Generation*. Now I did watch the original *Star Trek* with Captain Kirk, Mr. Spock, Scotty and Doctor McCoy almost religiously and loved every episode, but it went off the air, I went to college and it was 18 years before a new version hit television. *Star Trek: The Next Generation* episodes were less macho and portrayed leadership as more (dare I say) sensitive, more collegial and less '*all knowing.*' Captain Picard was the modern leader.

But what really hooked me on the new series was the Holodeck; a large room on the Starship Enterprise where the computer could create any location as a hologram environment such that the crew could live out their fantasies. They could have the computer create a program to simulate the wild west of the early 19th century and pretend to be small town Marshalls and outlaws, or create the illusion of sailing on a pirate ship. Great fun.

2013 © John R. Childress

The concept of a hologram is pretty interesting. I can't fathom the math or the physics, but one way to describe a hologram is to compare it to a photograph. If you take a photograph and tear it in half you get a left piece and a right piece, which when put together make the picture whole. Tearing the photograph into 4 pieces would give you four different parts of the original photo.

Now a hologram is a different kind of picture. If you could cut a holographic picture in half, each half would contain the entire original picture. Cutting it into quarters would give four complete original pictures, only smaller. And so on. You could cut the

51

hologram into a hundred pieces and each piece would be a complete version of the original picture, just smaller.

Corporate culture is more akin to a hologram than a two-dimensional photo. The Star Trek Holodeck isn't real, but corporate culture is. Whether you consciously create your culture or allow it to develop by default, culture impacts your company's ability to deliver on its business objectives.

Culture as Brand

Your brand is formed primarily, not by what your company says about itself, but what the company does.
~ Jeff Bezos, CEO Amazon

Brand is the company's promise made to customers through its advertising programs, websites, slogans, logos, stores or product design and packaging, as well as customer service. The company brand is reflected in everything the customer touches, sees and experiences.

The Apple brand signals *'cool, innovation, free expression with a slightly rebellious and audacious approach to life.'* Every Apple product gives the owner a distinct badge of identity and proud bragging rights. Apple products stand for the Apple way of doing things. The Apple way of living your life. Apple products are cool!

Harley Davidson, the iconic American motorcycle company, has created a brand rich in symbols and actions. All Harley Davidson products are engineered and designed to embody pride, craftsmanship, independence, passion, excitement and individualism. This is the essence of the Harley brand.

One way to think about culture is the internal brand of the company. Everything employees touch, see and experience while working in the company is a reflection of the culture.

When the brand promise to the customer does not deliver, more often than not you will find that the corporate culture is not aligned with the promised brand behaviors. For example, if treating customers as *'special guests,'* like the Disney experience, is the brand promise, then management needs to treat employees (and employees need to treat each other) as special. If internal management behavior or company policies don't allow employees to feel special, then how can they treat customers as special?

You can't give what you don't have! ~ Thomas D Willhite

The Real Picture: Culture or Climate

Another problem with so many *'experts'* writing about culture is the confusion between corporate culture and climate. The terms culture and climate (as in organizational culture and organizational climate) are often used synonymously. Is there a difference between culture and climate? In my readings and research I have found these terms often used to describe the same thing, and at other times to have very different meanings (another example of the very inexact *'science'* of corporate culture studies).

I am going to make a clear distinction between these two terms, **culture** and **climate**. Again, I am making this distinction so that the CEO and others can better understand their own organization's dynamics.

Think of it this way: **culture** describes the underlying elements that make up the way an organization performs. As an analogy, think of culture as the geology of the organization. If you have either visited or seen pictures of the Grand Canyon in the Southwest of the US, you gaze across the wide canyon and on the other side you can see all the various geologic layers with various colors, each laid down over a period of time and together they make up the whole beautiful phenomenon we call the Grand Canyon. Culture, like layers of rock, is laid down and imbedded over time.

Organizational climate on the other hand, is more analogous to the current weather report, or the morale or mood inside the company at any given time. Just as the weather can change from day to day (a storm in the afternoon and sunny the next morning), the organizational climate is changeable depending on certain internal and external events. Organizational culture, on the other hand, is deeply rooted and difficult to shift.

Many consultants offer an organizational climate survey or climate assessment and pass it off as "a description of your corporate culture." Not so! It's today's weather report of how employees are feeling. For example, at one point in time one of my defense clients was flush with business and long-term, highly profitable military contracts. A climate survey revealed a general sense of optimism and satisfaction about work and the organization. This was interpreted as a good, strong corporate culture.

Two years later, with the decline in US military spending and the impact of Congressional Sequestration finally taking hold, the same survey revealed a very different story. Optimism has been replaced with concern about jobs and a growing pessimism about the leadership capabilities of upper management. I predict that if another defense build up occurred tomorrow, that same climate survey would show a much different picture.

Over the short period of just two years, the climate (or mood) of this organization changed dramatically, but not the underlying corporate culture. They still approached work, each other, and customers in the same habitual ways of working.

So when you are approached by HR or a consultant to conduct a 'culture survey', make certain they will be really detailing the culture and not just giving you the current weather report! Embarking upon a culture change program, based on a climate survey, can be detrimental and with a high probability of failure attached from the beginning.

Culture as a Web of Interactions:

An integrated model termed the **Cultural Web** was put forth by Gerry Johnson and Kevan Scholes in 1992, to display the idea that culture was a set of interrelationships between key elements operating inside an organization. I have slightly revised some of the wording from their original model (Johnson and Scholes, 1992) to make this model as *'descriptive'* as possible.

- **Founders & Leaders** – The business beliefs, hiring decisions, work habits and vision of the founder(s) and early leaders has a great influence on how things get done inside the company.

- **Stories & Symbols** – The past events and people talked about inside and outside the company. Symbols are representations of the company and usually match with the stories told. Who and what the company chooses to immortalize in stories and symbols says a great deal about what is acceptable and what is not.

- **Rituals and Routines** – The daily behavior and actions of people that signal acceptable behavior. This determines what is expected to happen in given situations, and what is valued by management.

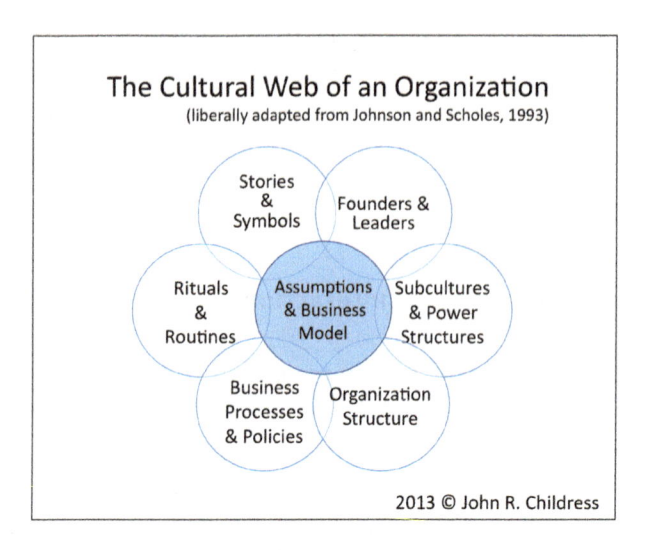

The Cultural Web of an Organization
(liberally adapted from Johnson and Scholes, 1993)

- Stories & Symbols
- Founders & Leaders
- Rituals & Routines
- Assumptions & Business Model
- Subcultures & Power Structures
- Business Processes & Policies
- Organization Structure

2013 © John R. Childress

- **Organizational Structure** - Includes both the structure defined by the organization chart, and the unwritten organization and how things really get done.

- **Business Processes and Polices** - The ways that the organization is controlled. These include financial systems, quality systems, and rewards

- **Subcultures & Power Structures** - The pockets of real power in the company. This may involve one or two key executives, a group of highly influential managers, or even a department. The key is that these people have the greatest amount of influence (formal and informal) on decisions, operations, and strategic direction.

When these six elements are interconnected and they all link to the central unifying element of the basic assumptions about the market, the strategy and the business model, the culture is considered to be in alignment with its overall purpose and as a result the culture works to support the organization's business goals and objectives. When one or more of the six elements of culture are out of alignment with the others, it weakens the ability of the organization to effectively deliver on its strategies.

LEVERAGE:

A Working Definition (if you really need one)

> *One of the definitions of sanity is the ability to tell real from unreal. Soon we'll need a new definition.*
> *~ Alvin Toffler*

CEOs and senior executives I have worked with find the following definition of corporate culture comprehensive and easy to understand:

> *Corporate culture is a combination of behaviors, beliefs, assumptions and business processes (formal and informal) that over time have become the common or "normal" approach management and employees use in solving business problems and interacting with each other, customers, clients and suppliers.*

Or in plain language: *"The usual way we go about solving business problems, interacting with customers and treating each other."*

Culture as Your Trade Secret

> *Anyone can copy your strategy, but no one can duplicate your culture!*

Jet Blue is a relatively new start-up US airline and like all start-ups who must win customers from the already established big players in the market (and the US airline market is highly competitive), it must have something different to cause travelers to break the loyalty habit and switch to a new airline. After all, planes are pretty much the same, all fly out of the same airports, overhead bins are all the same size.

As JetBlue CEO Dave Barger points out, a company's culture might be the only trade secret that can't be copied or commoditized.

> *"It has never been our goal to be the lowest cost airline out there. Our mission has always been to provide more value for a fair price," says Mr Barger. The carrier relies on its "award-winning brand, a strong route system, a fleet second to none in both fuel efficiency and comfort, a brand new terminal at JFK, solid strategic investors, outstanding business partners, a focused board of directors, a strong balance sheet and most importantly – a Culture and attitude that values winning in the marketplace".* [25]

A proprietary technology can be reverse engineered and a star performer can be recruited away by a competitor. But a successful culture? That's bigger than any single individual or innovation, and can survive them both.

The long-term success of Southwest Airlines is often ascribed to its unique culture in combination with its point-to-point business strategy. As of June 2012, Southwest celebrated 40 consecutive years of profitable operation, an unmatched record in the up and down world of airline transportation. So maybe there is a linkage between culture and performance.

Okay, Okay; But it Still Seems that Culture is Just a Soft HR Issue

> *If you don't understand your culture, you don't understand your business.*

Frequently I get asked the following question: *"Does culture really matter?"* Rather than answer this question, I usually respond with a question: *"Do you think the way your people treat customers and the amount of blaming and finger pointing when projects are off track has an impact on your business performance and profitability?"* Most often the response comes back quickly: *"Okay, I get it. Stupid question!"*

LEVERAGE:

In 1999, would you have invested money in an on-line, Internet-only shoe retailer? Probably not, especially in retail industry where everyone knows how important it is to physically try on the product, see how it looks and feels, and to be helped by a knowledgeable, experienced shoe salesperson. Besides, in 1999 the Internet and Internet retailing was still in its infancy, and very few people were comfortable giving up their credit card details over the phone, let alone through a computer keyboard. Not many Wall Street analysts and business gurus gave Zappos.com a snowball's chance in hell (good irony that they are headquartered in Las Vegas, Nevada).

But to Tony Hsieh, the guiding force and CEO of Zappos.com, the strategy was simple: build a strong corporate culture that will deliver excellent customer service. The definitive task would be execution, not marketing or product pricing strategies. And the challenge was how to sell lots of different brands of shoes directly to customers through the Internet while giving world-class customer service. While Tony and the team believed with all their body and soul that corporate culture needed to be the foundation of the company, they also knew they needed robust business processes that matched that unique culture in order to deliver consistent, world-class customer service. With these two principles in place, Zappos.com went from $0 in 1999 to $ 1 Billion in revenue in 2009, at which time they were bought by Amazon. That's right $0 to $1 Billion in 10 years!

Recently Zappos.com published a book about their culture titled: *Delivering Happiness: A Path to Profits, Passion and Purpose*. What I find interesting is that the culture doesn't come solely from a strict hiring profile. It is also built and sustained through a myriad of imbedded business processes (outsiders would call them people processes) that help perpetuate the unique Zappos.com service culture. For example, the Zappos.com order entry technology platform can turnaround a customer order in 8 minutes! That's from the time the customer hits the send button on the website to the order being ready on the shipping dock. And you don't think customer service is important?

Here's an actual customer quote: *"I can't believe how fast that Zappos.com was able to get an item to me. I ordered a coat for my daughter last night around 7:30 pm and it just arrived at 10:00 am this morning. It's hard to believe that anything could come that fast."* [24]

Culture, in alignment with robust business processes designed to fit the business strategy, create a potent competitive advantage. A strong culture with poor business processes leads to service breakdowns and broken brand promises, just as strong business processes and a weak or negative culture leads to inconsistent performance on all fronts.

Culture matters! Zero to $1 Billion in 10 years through the design and execution of a strong, customer-service corporate culture.

Culture as a Profit Center?

When asked to name their profit centers, few companies put corporate culture on the list! Especially in financial services. For an area to be a profit center, the return on investment needs to be concrete, and significant. Can investing in your corporate culture give a significant, and measurable return?

Robert W. Baird and Company [26] is a very unique financial services firm, with a focused mission: *"To provide the best financial advice and services to our clients and to be the best place to work for our associates".*

Based in Milwaukee, Wisconsin, this employee owned wealth management, capital markets, asset management and private equity firm has over 2,600 associates worldwide, annual revenues of over $900 million, a voluntary turnover of 4.7% (industry average of 16%) and manages over $105 billion in client assets. Every year since 2004 Baird has been listed on FORTUNE's Top 100 Best Companies to Work For®. In 2013 they ranked number 14.

If understood and managed, culture can be an important profit center.

An Insight from Saigon Traffic

> *If all the cars in the United States were placed end to end, it would probably be Labor Day Weekend ~ Doug Larson*

My first visit to Saigon, Vietnam (now called Ho Chi Min City) came as a rude shock. The smells, the colors, the noise, but most of all the traffic, and in particular, the waves of speeding motorbikes are overwhelming. And at least for me, particularly annoying is the honking and constant beeping from the motorbikes.

My first thought when stuck in the middle of this beeping frenzy was: *"How rude; honking at each other to get out of the way."* Based on my Western upbringing (culture), I interpreted the honking as rude and impolite behavior.

Over dinner one evening I asked our Vietnamese guide about this annoying behavior and expressed my disgust at how rude it was. My guide calmly explained that what I mistook for rude behavior to get people out of the way had an entirely different meaning in Southeast Asia. Honking is used to let others know that you are behind them so they are aware of your presence. It has nothing to do with telling others to move over or get out of the way, as it means in most North American cities.

Same behavior; very different meanings! To understand corporate culture it is important to look beyond the behaviors and the activities or artifacts and discover the real meaning behind the behaviors.

Corporate culture is not simply the behaviors within a company, but the meanings attached to those behaviors!

Here's another example of differences in meaning based on different cultures. HSBC runs an effective ad campaign at Heathrow Airport, which I frequent regularly. This one is about a cricket and goes like this:

> "USA—Pest. China—Pet. Northern Thailand—Appetizer."

> *I know that you believe that you understood what you think I said, but I am not sure you realize that what you heard is not what I meant.*
> *~ Robert McCloskey, U.S. State Department spokesman*

Chapter 4: The Missing Link: The Impact of Culture on Performance

Risk comes from not knowing what you're doing.
~ Warren Buffett

There is no denying the world of business is getting more risky. When global financial institutions and business icons like CitiGroup, AIG, JP Morgan Chase, RBS, Bank of America, Goldman Sachs, General Motors, Chrysler Corporation and Wells Fargo have to be bailed out to the tune of several trillion dollars of taxpayer money just to remain in business, nobody is immune from the growing risks of doing business in our fast changing, global economy.

A recent study on risk conducted by professors of the Cass Business School of the City University of London shows clearly the significant risks that modern organizations now face, and also the role played by corporate culture.

Eighteen high profile corporate meltdowns over the past decade were studied[27] (including AIG, Arthur Andersen, BP, Cadbury Schweppes, Coca-Cola, EADS Airbus, Enron, Firestone, Northern Rock, Shell, Societe General). The combined pre-crisis value of these companies was over $6 trillion; 7 of the 11 companies faced bankruptcy, of which 3 were rescued by Government; 11 Chairmen and/or CEOs lost their job; 4 senior executives went to prison. Most of the 18 companies suffered massive, uninsurable losses and extensive and long-term brand damage.

The study identified 7 key categories of risk that led to their subsequent corporate disasters:

- Inadequate board skills and inability of Non-Executive Directors to exercise control.
- Blindness to inherent risks, such as risks to the business model or reputation.
- Inadequate leadership of culture and values.
- Defective internal communication and information flow.
- Organizational complexity and difficulties with change.
- Inappropriate incentives, both implicit and explicit.
- Inability of Risk Management professionals inside the company to confront or point out risks emanating from the decisions and behavior of top management.

It's not hard to see the subtle yet powerful hand of corporate culture running through this list, particularly when the question of *"what are the risks?"* is replaced with *"why were these critical risks allowed to happen in the first place?"* The answer? The leadership culture (attitudes and mindsets of the leaders) deemed them acceptable or ignored the risk evidence all together.

A portion of the Cass study concludes by saying that many of these identified risks are inherent in every organization, but it is when risks are unrecognized, or worse yet, not allowed to be talked about or challenged, that they pose a potentially lethal threat to the future success of a business. As you will discover upon reading further into this guidebook, one of the biggest challenges of dealing effectively with corporate culture is that senior executives don't often see it clearly and honestly, mainly because they have become acculturated.

In the early 1980's I was asked to work with the new senior management team of GPU Nuclear, owner of Three Mile Island Nuclear Power Station. Following the accident and leakage of radioactive material on March 28, 1979 a new leadership team was put in place, consisting of former members of the US Nuclear Navy and NRC. Reading the report by the Nuclear Regulatory Commission on the TMI accident reveals the large part played by a dysfunctional corporate culture [28].

The purpose of my work was to help reshape the culture at TMI from one of interdepartmental rivalry, poor communications between departments and 'technical arrogance' to a culture where everything revolved around safety. And that we did, with TMI ultimately becoming one of the most productive, and safest nuclear plants in the world.

The recent crisis at the tsunami-hit Fukushima nuclear plant in Japan is another case of a dysfunctional culture, this time ascribed to the ingrained conventions of Japanese national culture [29].

> *Until I came to IBM, I probably would have told you that culture was just one among several important elements in any organization's makeup and success—along with vision, strategy, marketing, financials, and the like. I came to see, in my time at IBM, that culture isn't just one aspect of the game, it is the game. ~ Lou Gerstner*

JOHN R. CHILDRESS

The First Real Data on Culture and Performance

Culture can explain up to half the difference in operating income compared to similar organizations. ~ James Hazlett, Harvard Business School

After the frenzy caused by Peter's and Waterman's *In Search of Excellence*, the anecdotal descriptions of excellent or winning cultures exploded, but not much real data or solid evidence emerged on the relationship between culture and business performance. Employees liked working there, but was the company excellent in terms of real business metrics?

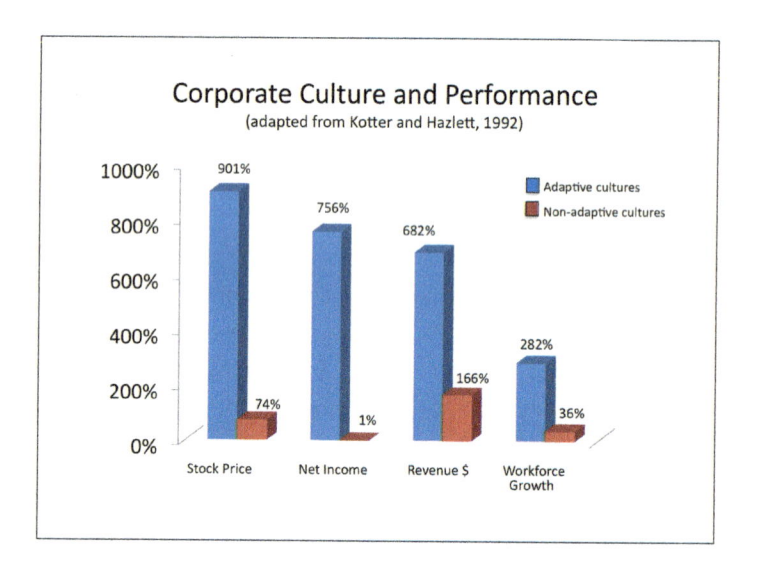

Corporate Culture and Performance
(adapted from Kotter and Hazlett, 1992)

Metric	Adaptive cultures	Non-adaptive cultures
Stock Price	901%	74%
Net Income	756%	1%
Revenue $	682%	166%
Workforce Growth	282%	36%

The first real evidence that culture matters to the bottom line came from the research of Harvard professors John P. Kotter and James Hazlett and published in their popular book, *Corporate Culture and Performance* (1992).

Using the term *'adaptive'* and *'non-adaptive'* to describe high and low performing cultures, they studied over 200 firms, including Hewlett-Packard, Xerox, ICI and Nissan, and concluded that adaptive cultures, those that are flexible enough to evolve with changing market conditions, tended to perform better economically than non-adaptive cultures.

> *Corporate culture can have a significant impact on a firm's long-term economic performance. ~ Kotter and Hazlett*

Since the original work by Kotter and Hazlett on the relationship between culture and company performance, many studies have shown the impact, both positive and negative, that culture can have on an organization's ability to perform. It is now well documented that elements of the corporate culture impact the ability of a company to execute on strategy and to deliver on major change programs. Culture can either propel or hinder strategic and business agendas. (*McKinsey Quarterly 2006, No 3; McKinsey Quarterly 2007, No.3, Childress, 2012*).

According to a 2010 Aon-Hewitt Associates study of more than 900 organizations globally, companies with high levels of engagement among their employees (read a strong culture of employee involvement and behaviors of accountability) outperformed the total stock market index, posting shareholder returns 19% higher than the average. By contrast, those companies with low employee engagement reported a shareholder return 44% lower than the market average.

This study tracks well with a 12-month Towers Perrin study of 50 financial organizations which found a strong relationship between employee engagement and business results. Those organizations with high levels of engagement outperformed the companies with low levels of engagement in three important measures of financial performance: operating income, net income and EPS. High-engagement companies saw a 19.3% increase in their operating income over the 12-month study, while low-engagement companies saw a 32.7% decline. Engagement in this case can be equated with corporate culture, since both are referring to the way employees engage with the organization on a repetitive basis, not just a one-time event.

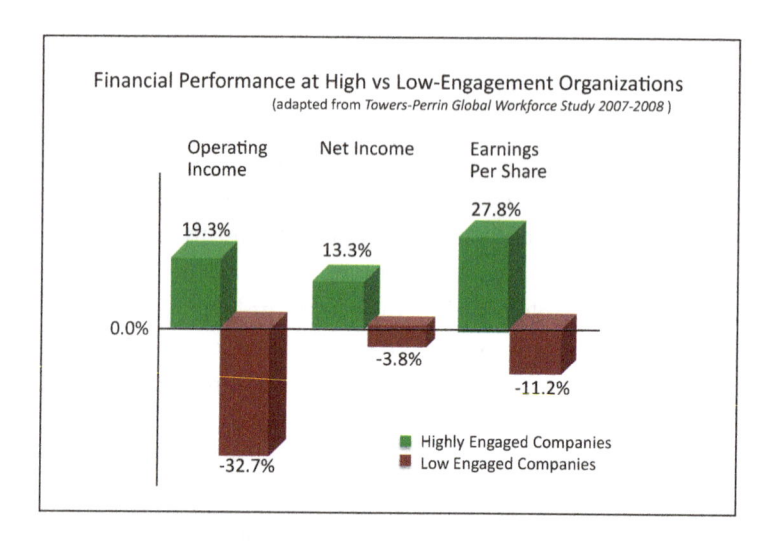

Financial Performance at High vs Low-Engagement Organizations
(adapted from *Towers-Perrin Global Workforce Study 2007-2008*)

	Operating Income	Net Income	Earnings Per Share
Highly Engaged Companies	19.3%	13.3%	27.8%
Low Engaged Companies	-32.7%	-3.8%	-11.2%

A 2003 Harvard Business School article, *What Really Works*, reported on a 10-year study of 160 companies, that just four out of 200 standard business practices had a significant impact on business performance and results. Those four were: Strategy, Execution, Culture and Structure. Additionally, a 2002 Corporate Leadership Council study, titled *Building the High-Performance Workforce: A Quantitative Analysis of the Effectiveness of Performance Management Strategies*, found that cultural traits such as risk taking, internal communications, and flexibility are some of the most important drivers of performance, and may also impact individual performance.

The Zappos.com corporate culture is our number one business asset. ~ Tony Hsieh, CEO

Impact of Culture on Sales Growth and ROI

Professor Dan Denison and his colleagues from the University of Michigan, developed a corporate culture assessment survey to clearly show the relationship between culture and performance. His study of 130 organizations between 2000 and 2010 shows a clear relationship between the Denison Culture Profile and performance metrics of Return-on-Assets, Sales Growth, and Market-to-Book Ratio (all standard business performance metrics). We will learn more about the Denison Culture Assessment model in Chapter 11.

Denison research study of 130 firms (2000-2010) using the Denison Organizational Culture Survey scoring for top and bottom performing companies		
	Companies Scoring in the Bottom 25%	Companies Scoring in the Top 25%
Return-on-Assets	2.3%	3.2%
Sales Growth	1.4%	23.1%
Market-to-Book Ratio	2.6	4.0

Anchor's Aweigh

The relationship between culture and organization alignment is easy to see with the understanding that *Strategy – Structure – Culture* are interlinked and for top performance, these three critical business elements must be in alignment. In simple terms, *"everyone knows where we are going"* (strategy), *"it's clear who does what in the organization"* (structure), and *"we all understand the ground rules for working together and for getting things done"* (culture).

In less turbulent times when the pace of change was slower, organizations were able to gain alignment between these three critical elements and as a result produced efficient performance and long-term growth. The era of public monopolies, such as the Bell Telephone System and Television Broadcasting are good examples of having the luxury of regulated stability so that Strategy – Structure- Culture could remain in alignment.

However, with the explosion of technology, rapid globalization, aggressive new competition and shifting regulation, companies today are often forced to develop and implement new strategies quickly. And there is often the need to reorganize in order to line up the organization to match the new strategy.

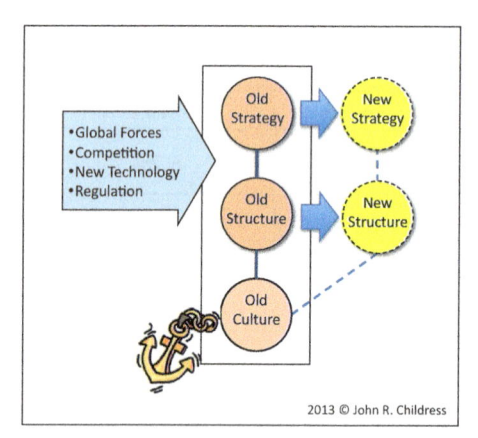

The problem is, that's as far as most senior teams take it; thinking that improved performance should naturally follow. Because most CEOs and senior executives are often insulated from the real internal culture(s) within their organization, it becomes difficult to see the link between culture and performance. It also becomes difficult to see when the existing culture is no longer aligned with the new demands of the business.

Unless there is work done to reshape corporate culture, the old culture can act as an anchor, slowing down and in some cases even stopping effective strategy execution. Therefore, to fully implement a new strategy or to rebuild your organization to be effective in a changed world, it is critical to reshape culture as well.

LEVERAGE:

The Return of Jaws . . .

You're gonna need a bigger boat.
~ Peter Benchley

Another good visual for understanding culture and it's impact on performance comes from the work by John Childress and Larry Senn and described in their 1999 book: *The Secret of a Winning Culture: Building High-Performance Teams*. Most of us are familiar with the 1975 thriller/horror film *Jaws*, which was so popular it spawned three sequels. Think of a negative and change resistant culture as the monster shark, Jaws!

When a major change initiative is introduced, unless steps are taken to gain employee buy-in and commitment, the old culture often acts as a barrier to the successful implementation. Cultural habits such as turf-wars, silo-focus, strong subcultures determined to resist upper management initiatives, blaming, poor communication pathways and little feedback can negatively impact the change effort, slowing it down and in some cases even blocking it all together. It's as if the change must pass through the *'Jaws of Culture'*.

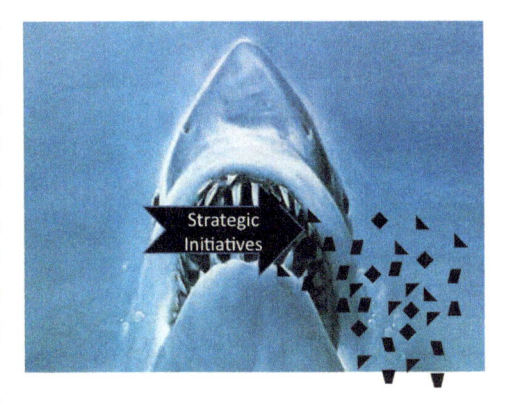

While this is a great visual analogy of how culture can impact performance, not all cultures are as obvious or as vicious as Jaws. In fact, the blocking and stopping of change initiatives by a culture is often extremely subtle. In most cases, I tend to think about the negative impact of a resistant culture as *'death by a thousand cuts'!* In non-obvious ways, the culture can block, frustrate and derail even the best prepared change initiatives. Behaviors such as *'malicious obedience,'* not returning phone calls until much later, making excuses for non-performance, stonewalling requests for information, *'accidentally* losing emails and slow email responses, all contribute to the attrition impact a resistant culture can have on change initiatives.

On the contrary, a culture that is open and flexible to change, what many in the literature today call an adaptive culture, not only supports new change initiatives, but can actually propel the delivery of the new initiative, acting more like a rocket launcher and less like jaws.

Corporate Culture and the Entrepreneur

There is much focus in today's business world about entrepreneurs and start-ups. The silicon valley stories of young people at a kitchen table ultimately creating global corporations is legendary, and appealing, since the barriers to entry for new businesses is at a historic low. Anyone with an idea can start a company these days, from apps to service companies to new technological breakthroughs.

And in the business literature and lore of start-ups, corporate culture is a much talked about ingredient for success. Joel Peterson, Chairman of Jet Blue Airways and Stanford Graduate School of Business lecturer cites the five most important reasons for start-up failures [30] :

- Liquidity; lack of enough cash.
- Inability to make good hire and fire decisions.
- Culture not aligned with business strategy (and culture ignored, left to drift).

LEVERAGE:

- Inability to deal with a founder whom the company has outgrown.
- Not willing to adjust the offering or product based on customer feedback or market changes.

With all the recent research and studies on culture and performance, it is quite disheartening to me to find numerous CEOs, senior executives and senior government officials who still either ignore, or actively dismiss the impact their corporate culture has on the ability of their company to deliver on its business and strategic objectives. One of the reasons for this inability to grasp culture as a business lever is perhaps the dubious reputation given to culture by the many culture vulture consultants, as well as the difficult readability of many the academic works on culture.

It is my hope this book will help all my readers understand, value and realize that culture matters, big time, and that it can be managed to support and even improve business performance.

Yikes!! Culture as a Legal Liabilty?

Corporate culture can also be cited as an explanation for injuries in a court of law. Recently in the United States the US Department of Labor Mine Safety and Health Administration levied a fine of more than $10.8 million on Alpha Natural Resources plus an additional $209 million as a Department of Justice settlement following the Upper Big Branch Mine disaster in April 2010. This was the largest fine in the history of this U.S. government agency.

> *While the investigation found the physical conditions that led to the coal dust explosion were the result of a series of basic safety violations at UBB, which PCC and Massey disregarded, the report cites unlawful policies and practices implemented by PCC and Massey as the root cause of the explosion --- including the intimidation of miners, advance notice of inspections, and two sets of books with hazards recorded in*

UBB's internal production and maintenance book but not in the official examination book. The investigation found that the operator promoted and enforced a <u>workplace culture</u> that valued production over safety, including practices calculated to allow it to conduct mining operations in violation of the law. — MSHA News Release 11-1703-NAT[31].

Got your attention, now?

LEVERAGE:

SECTION TWO: IT'S COMPLICATED . . .

Ants have the most complicated social organization on earth, next to humans. ~ Harvard Professor E. O. Wilson

Nearly everyone has heard the parable of the three blind men and the elephant. But in case you don't remember . . .

Once upon a time, there lived three blind men in a village. One day the villagers told them: "Hey, there is an elephant in the village today."

They had never experienced an elephant before and decided, "Even though we are not able to see it, let us go and feel it anyway." They went where the elephant was standing and each touched the elephant.

"An elephant is like a pillar," said the first man who touched his leg.

"Oh, no! It is like a rope," said the second man who touched the tail.

"Oh, no! It is like a snake," said the third man who touched the twisting trunk of the elephant.

Since they couldn't agree, they began to argue, each one insisting he was right. A wise man was passing by and heard the loud argument. He asked them, "What is the matter?"

> *"We cannot agree what the elephant is like."*
>
> *Each one of them told what he thought the elephant was like. The wise man calmly explained to them, "All of you are right. The reason each of you thinks differently is because you each touched a different part of the elephant. So, actually the elephant has all those features."*

It's no surprise there are so many and varied definitions of corporate culture, since people tend to define culture through their own training and points of view. The psychologists mostly focus on individual, group and subgroup behaviors. Consultants looking for work tend to focus on the elements of culture that inhibit business performance. Academics and business school professors define culture through research and statistics. Business analysts want to measure culture. Popular authors describe culture through fables and stories of excellence and customer service. All are true, yet none are the total (real) picture.

Culture is complicated and to understand culture better, in order to lead and guide it as a force for sustainable and competitive advantage, we need to understand not just what it is, but also where it comes from.

> *I can explain it to you again, young man,*
> *but I cannot comprehend it for you!*
> *~Mayor Ed Koch to a persistent reporter.*

Chapter 5: In the Beginning . . . Where Culture Comes From

In the beginning the Universe was created. This has made a lot of people very angry and been widely regarded as a bad move. ~ Douglas Adams

One of the things that frustrates CEOs and business leaders interested in learning more about corporate culture as a tool for business improvement is the fact the literature is filled with multiple culture definitions and articles describing what culture is, but very little on where culture comes from and how it is created.

How is culture developed? Can you design and build a culture or does it happen by default? What are the drivers and building blocks of culture? And which ones have the most influence on the development and sustainability of corporate culture? What are the critical culture change levers?

These are important questions, because only until we fully

understand the foundations of corporate culture and how a culture is developed and formed, can we begin to find the appropriate levers to build, manage and, when necessary, reshape corporate culture.

> *He who knows why will always win over those who just know how!*
> *~Thomas D. Willhite*

The Determinants of Culture: The Classical View

We can begin to explore where culture comes from and how cultures are developed by turning to the work and insights of Professor Edgar Schein of MIT. Schein postulates that sustainable corporate cultures develop by successfully adapting to three main influencing factors: external business pressures, internal processes and employee social needs.

To develop an ability to sustain itself in the competitive world of business, company cultures develop and persist because they help an organization survive and flourish. If the culture can successfully deal with the external pressures of competition, customer buying preferences, marketplace speed, etc., then it holds the potential for sustainability. A strong culture will guide people to respond appropriately on most occasions, avoiding the need to figure out responses every time a business situation arises.

At the same time, a culture must respond to the internal requirement of the business plus the internal needs of the people working there. In this case, internal practices of information flow, decision-making, reporting and metrics, and human relations policies are just a few of the internal business building blocks of the culture.

In respect to the social determinants, people joining the company quickly learn what is acceptable and what is not, and these then become codified into stories, formal and informal reward punishments, peer pressures and group dynamics. In a short amount of time, these elements come to be known as *'company groundrules'* or *'how to fit in and survive.'* Mostly they are not written down, but are informal, yet widely known and strongly held. They help to build and maintain group cohesion.

Tell Me A Story

> *Think twice before you speak, because your words and influence will plant the seed of either success or failure in the mind of another.*
> *~ Napoleon Hill*

Stories about the company and its people, as opposed to just facts, are some of the most powerful determinants of culture. Stories of heroic moments in the early development of the company, stories about good managers and bad managers, stories about employees who made breakthroughs and those who failed, all have a powerful influence on corporate culture.

We are social creatures and early on in the development of human society, long before the written word, stories were the way information vital to individual and group survival was handed down. Imagine the following scenario of early man:

> One village hunter says to another:
>
> *"Hey, Og, I have a great idea for getting us some food. What we will do is get a few guys together, sharpen some sticks, walk for days across the freezing tundra, sleep in the cold, find a giant Wooly Mammoth, stick it with the sharp sticks until it dies, cut it up and carry the meat back to the village while avoiding the wolves and Saber Tooth tigers. Voila! Food for a month."*
>
> The reply is pretty predictable: *"Are you nuts?"*
>
> Just reciting the facts is not a very effective recruitment or

survival strategy. Early man told stories instead:

> *"Hey, Og, you are one of the most clever men in the village, and one of the strongest. Remember the ancient story of the founder of our clan and how he killed a Wooly Mammoth and fed the village for months? Remember how all revered him, even to this day? Imagine how great a hero you would be if you brought Mammoth meat to the village? Your name would be praised for eternity. Your children would grow up strong and sing songs of your heroic deeds. The village would prosper and become a powerful clan. Your family would be revered throughout the land."*
>
> *"Now, Og, I have a plan about how to feed the village for a month and I need your help. And let's gather a whole bunch of us and do it together."*

These are the stories that turned into early cave drawings and lasted for thousands of years. Stories move people far more than just facts.

In the book, *Made to Stick: Why Some Ideas Take Hold and Others Come Unstuck*, the authors, brothers Chip and Dan Heath, tell a story about a class that one of them taught. (Heath and Heath, 2007) Students were asked to rank the effectiveness of each other's presentation about a certain business subject. Those who gave the best presentations showed lots of compelling charts with numerous facts, and were the most animated and professional in their presentations. They ranked at the top as rated by the class participants.

Several weeks later, the teacher asked the class to recall the presentations and rank them again. This time it was those who told vivid stories that ranked as the most effective, mostly because they were the ones the students remembered. Those who cited facts and showed lots of charts ranked near the bottom, mostly because the charts had quickly faded in the student's memories.

Stories get remembered about 13 times better than statistics. Facts tell, but stories sell!

Stories told by senior employees or supervisors to new employees about how to fit in and survive inside the company are far more powerful than the written policies in any handbook, and are certainly more powerful than printed culture statements. Stories stick because they help people fit in, which is one of the most critical requirements for a new employee. It takes a strong and self-assured individual to choose not to fit in with the group. Most employees who don't or won't fit in are literally '*spat out by the culture*' and often leave after a few weeks.

Cultures are built through the strong need by new employees and others to fit in and be a part of the group. And stories show the way.

Acculturation . . . Assimilation or Annihilation?

We are the Borg. Resistance is futile. You will be assimilated. We will add your biological and technological distinctiveness to our own.
~ The Borg Queen from Star Trek

One of the more fascinating and dangerous encounters by Captain Picard and the crew of the Starship Enterprise was with an alien collective called The Borg. The Borg functioned as an all knowing and all powerful collective. The Borg force other species into their collective and connect them to the '*hive mind*'; the act is called assimilation and entails violence, abductions, and injections of microscopic machines called '*nanoprobes*'. The Borg's ultimate goal through assimilation is '*achieving perfection*'.

The *Star Trek* episodes dealing with The Borg are intriguing and I always walk away with a deeper appreciation of how corporate cultures are developed. The assimilation analogies are scarily similar. The major difference being you can't resign or quit from the

Borg, and you don't get fired, you get annihilated!

Very little is written in the vast popular or academic literature of corporate culture about two of the strongest determinants of culture: peer pressure and the human social need to fit in. In my experience, these are extremely powerful, and yet frequently overlooked and under appreciated forces in the development of a company culture.

Here's the basis for how people easily become acculturated. A psychologist, Dr. Leann Birch, placed a young preschooler who hated peas (me too!) at a lunch table with three other preschoolers, all of whom loved peas. After just four days the pea-hater became a willing pea-eater, without any teacher or parental urging [32]. And the new habit stuck.

Human beings are hard wired to fit in!

Studies have shown that employees who work for the same corporation, no matter what their jobs, are 30% more likely to exhibit similar behaviors - defined as the way a person learns, deduces, envisions, engages, and executes - than people who do the same job but who work in different companies.

That is true even if the people from different companies work in the same industry or region. Consider, for example, an American engineer employed by Honda. The fact that she works for Honda tells you more about her behavioral work habits than the fact that she is an engineer or that she labors in the auto industry or that she is American. What's more, her ways of working will probably more closely resemble those of a Japanese purchasing manager at Honda than those of an American engineer at Ford [33].

In his insightful writings on organizational dynamics and behavior, former psychiatrist turned management advisor and business author Dr. Leandro Herrero is one of the few who point to the strength of peer pressure and the human need to fit in as critical components of corporate culture and the business change process. By understanding how these two forces operate inside organizations, Herrero has come up with a radical and highly effective approach to large-scale organization transformation and culture change.

His recent books *Homo Imitans* and *Viral Change™* are rapidly becoming classics among business leaders faced with the need for organization change. His small consulting group, *The Chalford Project*, have pioneered several successful culture change projects that harness the strengths of peer pressure and the human need to fit in. We will learn more about Dr. Herrero's approach to culture change in Section Six)

The Role of Founders and Early Leaders

Organizations are shadows of their leaders . . . that's the good news and the bad news!

It's no great secret that the values and business style of Sam Walton were instrumental in the development of the thrifty, innovative and competitive culture of Walmart. James Cash Penney, the founder of the J C Penney Company, was a firm believer in hard work and saving money and in 1940 at a store in Des Moines, Iowa, he trained a young Sam Walton on how to wrap packages with a minimal amount of ribbon. The teamwork, quality engineering and work ethic of partners Bill Hewlett and David Packard had a significant influence on the development of the early culture of technology giant, Hewlett-Packard.

Founders and early stage senior executives tend to stamp their beliefs and work ethics onto their organizations by their consistent behaviors, the stories they tell, and the coaching they give to employees. The Virgin companies are definitely a shadow of the anti-big business, consumer advocate beliefs of Richard Branson. The global growth and the gentlemanly culture of the early 1960's Chase Manhattan Bank was a direct shadow of the upbringing and personality of David Rockefeller.

It's easy to see how founders and early leaders can imprint their values and beliefs about business and people on the culture of an organization. In many cases they have almost complete control over the early hiring and firing of senior executives and tend to hire those who match their own beliefs, values and ways of working.

In addition to the important impact of the founder, the behavior of the senior executive team also signals what is desired and acceptable behavior for employees. When the senior team is aligned and displays effective team behavior, a culture of openness and teamwork tends to develop. On the other hand, if the senior team is somewhat dysfunctional, with hidden agenda, turf wars, blaming and lack of accountability, these behaviors also cast a significant signal to employees as to how to survive and get ahead inside the company.

> *What you are, Sir, speaks so loudly I can't hear a word you are saying! ~ Samuel Johnson*

It's not so much that the senior team consciously dictates the culture, but employees, most of whom desire to fit in and get ahead in the company, consciously watch the behavior of the senior team for clues as to what is '*acceptable behavior*'.

When the leadership team says one thing and then behaves differently, employees quickly figure out the real story. When a senior executive talks about the core value of respect and then promotes one of the most abusive managers, the real story of '*what is really important*' quickly gets around.

When members of the leadership team come into the building and head straight for their offices, head down, not interacting with anyone, that's the story that gets talked about in the canteen and the pubs, not the speech one of them gave on employee engagement and openness. The actions don't match the words.

If you want teamwork and collaboration on major customer business proposals as a core cultural behavior and business driver, it better happen at the top or you won't achieve it anywhere else, even with the best consultative selling training or cross-functional collaboration workshops.

If two senior executives won't support each other and instead openly bad-mouth each other (as is the case with the many co-head arrangements currently in fashion), you can forget about any meaningful support and cooperation between their respective departments, let alone intelligent collaboration on major client deals.

Internal Business Processes Foster Behaviors

After 35 years of working with senior teams on culture change, turnarounds and performance improvement I am convinced that corporate culture is significantly determined by the business processes the company designs and uses. Habitual behaviors (ways of working) are formed as a result of employees following specific business processes and work policies on a daily basis.

In essence, a business process, such as annual planning, departmental budgeting, expense reporting, billing hours and time keeping, or a management process such as the performance review or the promotion process have a tremendous impact on shaping first individual, and then collective behavior and ultimately the corporate culture. People can give lip service to a set of values on the wall or a fancy mission statement, but can't escape interacting daily with internal business processes. And those who don't adhere to the company business process are few and usually gone before too long. Except in big banks!

Processes have both business and behavioral outcomes, and it is the behavioral outcomes that most executives and managers don't understand. A new policy or process may be designed to improve business metrics (speed, quality, productivity), but it also causes people to behave in certain ways that become imbedded over time. And too often, the collateral behaviors developed are unintended and non-productive.

For example, it is not infrequent that processes for measuring sales productivity or sales performance can lead to various types of dysfunctional behaviors. Individual bonus schemes can drive results and at the same time risky behavior. This has recently been exposed in investment banking with the spate of trading losses and rate fixing scandals.

Plus, poorly designed business processes can do double damage by fostering '*malicious obedience*' and cynicism, while at the same time prompting time-consuming workarounds that hinder productivity and reduce performance. The annual bonus process in investment banking is an excellent example. Not only is the process based on a false assumption (that the only way to keep high performers performing and thus run a profitable institution is to pay them big bonuses) but an inordinate amount of valuable senior management time is taken up every year in seemingly endless meetings with '*important*' employees trying to find a compromise between individual expectations (and often demands) and the size of the overall bonus pool handed down from corporate. In this case the unwritten process (individual bonus negotiations) has definitely shaped a key part of the culture of banking.

I believe it makes good sense for senior executives to look closely at the business processes they are using internally. What I suspect you will find is that many of them are *'legacy processes',* developed some time ago when business conditions were different and might just be fostering a set of behaviors counter to the culture you now require.

The Big Three

Of all the internal business process adopted and used by an organization, some are more powerful at influencing the development of culture than others. And three stand out in particular as having a high degree of influence on corporate culture: **Hiring, Firing and Promotions**.

One of the most powerful determinants of corporate culture is the **hiring** process (new-employee selection process). Recent studies by Mark Murphy and his team at *Leadership IQ* have shown that more than 40% of new employees will fail within 18 months for reasons having nothing to do with skills. And 89% of those failures are due to attitudes and behaviors that don't fit the new culture. These people are failing because they weren't a good cultural fit with their manager or the team. (Murphy, 2012)

What if you could identify and hire individuals who fit not only the job requirements, but also the culture requirements? In other words, people who matched the culture you wanted to create, which in turn would best enable the delivery of your business strategy and objectives.

When employees hold the same core beliefs and values, you need fewer policies to control or manage work. Instead, your employees have an innate ability to deliver solutions and customer service that match your desired culture.

Think it's difficult to hire for cultural fit? Not really, and it is definitely worth the effort. Remember the rise to dominance by the luxury hotel chain, Ritz Carlton? The only hotel chain to win two Malcolm Baldridge Quality Awards! CEO Horst Schulz and his executive team decided to create a culture of exquisite service using two key drivers: focused metrics and focused employee selection. The key here is focused!

Early on they hired a Lincoln, Nebraska based psychometric research firm, *Talent Plus*, to develop an employee interview process that focused heavily on cultural fit. [34] Everyone from senior executives to chambermaids were interviewed this way. Nobody got hired at Ritz Carlton without the focused interview process. Their internal description of their culture: *"Ladies and Gentlemen serving Ladies and Gentlemen"* served as the starting point for the development of clear cultural behaviors and a focused selection process.

Ritz Carlton is not the only successful organization to use focused selection to match the culture. Focused selection has been a way of hiring at Walt Disney theme parks for decades. And for a more modern example, since its founding in 1999, the US based Internet shoe retailer Zappos.com has grown to be the largest online shoe store by focusing on superior customer service, driven by a clear description of their desired culture and hiring for cultural fit.

I wager that very few businesses use any type of focused employee selection for cultural fit. Why? At least two reasons; the senior team doesn't fully understand the importance of culture and employee behavior on business performance and secondly, if they have any cultural guidelines or written values, they are just that, written, not really lived.

Hiring profiles and *'hiring for cultural fit'* also comes with a potential dark side. Used unskillfully, a hiring profile can also be a subtle source of discrimination and possible biased or unfair hiring practices. When professionally developed and managed, this potential down-side risk can be effectively mitigated, giving fair treatment to all who apply.

Another hiring practice also has a significant impact on culture. The consistent practice of hiring outsiders for senior and middle management positions can send a strong message to employees about the company culture. In my interviews with employees and middle managers in many companies over the years it is not uncommon to hear the following: *"This company doesn't value internal experience or employee loyalty, they seem to consistently pass over existing employees and hire from the outside."*

When a defeatist attitude tends to grow in a culture, productivity and innovation are difficult to improve.

Whenever a **firing** occurs, it's not long before there is an unofficial story circulating throughout the company about the event. In the case of firings, companies rarely tell the truth about the event, opting for the politically correct; "*she decided to leave for personal reasons" or "he has resigned in order to pursue other interests."*

Employees are not stupid, and the stories that circulate are often powerful unwritten examples of what the leadership of the company really values in employee and executive behavior. When a manager leaves the company because he or she is outspoken in meetings about uncomfortable issues such as poor quality or engineering shortcuts, it soon becomes clear to all employees that speaking up, telling the truth or exposing issues is a career-limiting move.

And everyone talks about who got promoted and why!

The Hidden Cultural Influencers: Supervisors and Middle Management

Senior business executives don't spend much time closely watching the interactions between supervisors and employees and as a result a key determinant of corporate culture often goes overlooked and undermanaged. Middle managers and supervisors hold a key to your culture, and turnover.

The Gallop Organization surveyed over 1 million employees and over 80,000 middle managers to determine why employees quit or leave the company. While the study and subsequent book, *First Break All the Rules*, was about employee engagement, the results are important to our understanding of the power of culture (Buckingham and Coffman, 1999). Basically, their findings can be summarized in the following two statements:

- Employees leave managers not companies
- Talented employees leave, dead wood stays.

These two statements have a great deal to say about how corporate culture is formed and sustained, especially the second statement. While I wouldn't necessarily classify those who stay as "dead wood", I do think it is important to understand that employees who stay tend to either naturally fit or adapt to fit with their direct boss or manager.

Think about it. Middle managers oversee and directly influence more than half the organization and hold a great deal of influence over employees. More often than not, middle managers reward employees who match the attitudes, behaviors and work ethics they hold, not necessarily the values posted on the wall or written in the company handbook. Middle managers can energize or demoralize easily and quickly, and do so dozens of times a day without senior management even knowing what is happening. If you want a strong and aligned corporate culture, then hiring and developing middle managers to profiles that specifically fit the desired culture is critical.

Industry Dynamics as a Shaper of Culture

Most people don't realize the impact that industry dynamics have on shaping corporate culture. As an extreme example, consider the different work pace and rates of change in the fashion retail industry as opposed to the pharmaceutical industry. One is constantly changing and reacting to shifts in consumer trends and competitor discounting, the other is a long cycle business where new drugs may take years if not decades to be developed, tested and approved for use in the marketplace. Such industry dynamics tend to favor certain personality types over others. Big Pharma is not usually a good fit for someone who likes lots of new challenges and new activities on a regular basis, or someone who prefers dealing directly with customers instead of solving complex technical challenges.

Even in a similar industry, business dynamics may favor different personality styles. Retail banking is very different from investment banking in the types of personalities who succeed, which in turn helps to create very different cultures.

Company Rituals

In their book *In Search of Excellence,* Tom Peters and Bob Waterman put heavy emphasis on company rituals as a key determinant of strong corporate cultures. And those rituals which resulted in better customer service, helped build high-performance work habits, or fostered trust and teamwork are found more often in those companies considered excellent in relation to their peers.

Company rituals are often intermingled with '*perks*', the most famous of those being the Google employee benefits of day care, laundry and dry cleaning, haircuts, exercise facilities, open cafeterias, games rooms, on-site medical staff, and numerous others. Both rituals and perks together can have a powerful impact on building and keeping a corporate culture aligned with the company strategy and business purpose.

The most effective company rituals are those that magnify a key business success principle important to the competitiveness and performance of the company, involve lots of employees, and have tangible symbols that last beyond the end of the ceremony or ritual. The military has medals and campaign ribbons that are worn on uniforms. But what makes these bits of metal and fabric powerful symbols and strong elements of a shared culture is the ritual of presenting them in front of the entire squadron, and the recipient's family. These symbols can't be bought, nor are they given away for favors; they are earned and they symbolize, in the eyes of everyone in the company, that he or she is '*one of us*'.

Over the years many businesses have dropped the use of company rituals and symbolic awards, partially as a cost-containment measure, and sometimes from concerns by HR that company rituals don't recognize everyone and so are somehow '*unfair*' or '*politically incorrect*.' This is a big mistake. Company rituals help build a cohesive and aligned culture and as long as they reinforce the desired behaviors, they are great ways to build and sustain a strong corporate culture.

In my international management consulting firm we had a very important ritual whenever a new employee successfully passed their probation period and acquired the foundation skills and knowledge required to become a permanent member of staff, whether an in-the-field consultant or a member of the in-the-office team. At the appropriate quarterly meeting of all employees the successful individual would be presented with a 24Kt gold logo pin to either wear on their jacket lapel or as a necklace. And, it was presented by their 'buddy' (the person who was assigned to them upon entering the company as their guide, support system, helper, coach, confidant and friend). In addition, whenever we had clients attend one of our Quarterly Company Meetings to speak to the staff about our work and its impact, the senior consultant for that assignment would present one of our gold logo pins to the client, amid lots of clapping and appreciation.

Not long ago, well after I had retired, I ran into one of our former CEO clients in an airport, and she was still wearing her gold logo and talked animatedly about how much that symbol of excellence meant to her and her company.

Another company ritual that helped build our strong and aligned culture was our annual company holiday! The deal was simple, if we made our year-end company goals for sales and profit, we would arrange, in the first quarter of the following year, a big company holiday for all employees, their spouses or partners, plus children, for a full week of fun and togetherness somewhere exotic. No results, no trip. Simple rules.

Every year over the course of my time as a CEO, we closed the business for the week and took the entire company to places such as Hawaii, Cabo San Lucas in Baja California, the Caribbean, the Bahamas, Key West Florida, Palm Springs, and other warm, sunny places. Needless to say it was a large expense, but not only did they earn it, but it helped build a culture of teamwork, support and positive peer pressure to make our numbers, serve our clients, and reduce unnecessary expenses. Even the spouses were saying "*Get to work, we want to go on another trip next year!*"

Company rituals come in all shapes and sizes. They don't have to be expensive or exotic to be effective, but they must be transparent, honest and reinforce the behaviors you want in the culture.

Deck the Walls with . . .

Recently, Culture Decks have become popular with start-ups,

especially where the ability to attract and retain great talent is critical to rapid growth and long-term success. Many of these decks have come out of Silicon Valley (and other hotbeds of innovation) start-ups. Two of the most famous (for having been passed around via social media) are the culture decks from Zappos.com and Netflix, two companies who strongly believe that culture is one of their most important competitive assets.

A culture deck is a series of presentations or slides, usually in PowerPoint, that state the importance of culture to the success of the start-up and then go on, in great detail, to describe the culture in terms of phrases or statements, backed up by clear descriptions of the specific behaviors that the culture will be built upon. Some culture decks even go further and describe the specific work behaviors and practices that are not acceptable and will get you terminated.

Such decks are often used as proxies for the internal branding of the company but are mostly used during the recruiting process. The message is simple, if you don't like what our culture is, don't apply, and if you do apply, take the culture seriously!

Regional or National Cultures

You say "potato," I say "patattah" You say "tomato", I say "tomattah" Let's call the whole thing off!
~ George & Ira Gershwin

As businesses grow and become more global, regional and national cultures tend to impact the original corporate culture, creating additional subcultures. And cultures from one country don't always travel well or translate the same in another country. While English is the common language between the US and the UK, the national cultures are significantly different, from the meanings of words and phrases to the different meanings ascribed to the same behaviors. Many US companies setting up factories and operations in the UK and other predominantly English speaking countries like Australia and South Africa have been surprised at why they have such a difficult time gaining productivity or why morale lags.

The classic research and much of the writings on national cultural differences comes from the work of Geert Hofstede, a Dutch social psychologist. Professor Hofstede conducted one of the most comprehensive studies of how workplace behaviors (corporate culture) are influenced by national culture, gathering data from over 90 different countries. His work and interpretations on national and organization cultures are compiled in his classic book, *Cultures and Organizations: Software of the Mind* (Hofstede, 2004).

While there is too much information to go into any real detail in this guidebook, the figure below gives an excellent overview of how various national cultures differ from each other on five dimensions:

Power Distance is the extent to which the less powerful members of organizations (like hourly employees) and social institutions accept and expect that power is distributed unequally.

Individualism is the degree to which individuals are integrated into groups. On the individualist side a person is expected to look after her/himself and her/his immediate family. On the collectivist side people from birth onwards are integrated into strong, cohesive in-groups, often extended families (with uncles, aunts and grandparents) which continue protecting them in exchange for unquestioning loyalty.

Masculinity vs Femininity refers to the distribution of emotional roles between the genders. The women in feminine countries have the same modest, caring values as the men; in the masculine countries they are more assertive and more competitive, but not as much as the men, so that these countries show a gap between men's values and women's values.

John R. Childress

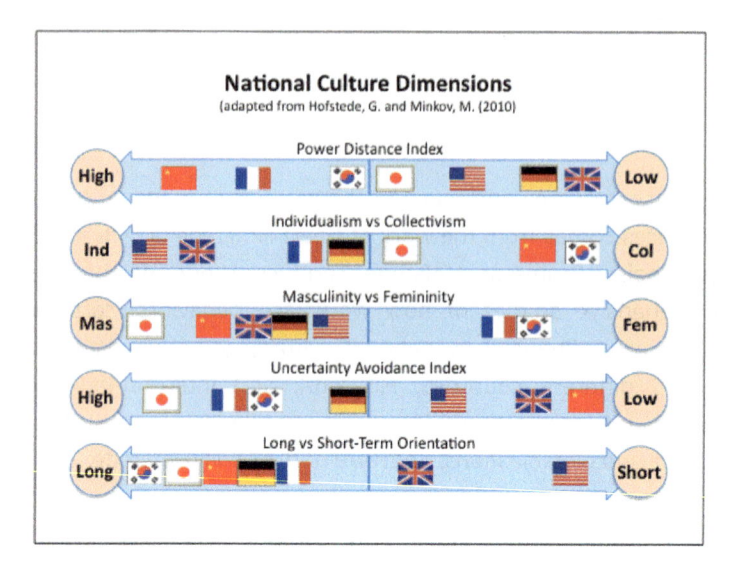

National Culture Dimensions
(adapted from Hofstede, G. and Minkov, M. (2010))

Power Distance Index — High to Low
Individualism vs Collectivism — Ind to Col
Masculinity vs Femininity — Mas to Fem
Uncertainty Avoidance Index — High to Low
Long vs Short-Term Orientation — Long to Short

Uncertainty Avoidance deals with a society's tolerance for uncertainty and ambiguity. Uncertainty avoiding cultures try to minimize the possibility of such situations by strict laws and rules. Uncertainty accepting cultures are more tolerant and try to have as few rules as possible.

Long-Term Orientation fosters pragmatic virtues oriented towards future rewards, in particular saving, persistence, and adapting to changing circumstances. Short-term oriented societies foster virtues such as national pride, respect for tradition, saving face and fulfilling social obligations.

In most cases, national cultures are much stronger than corporate cultures

We would do well as business leaders to better understand the dimensions of national cultural differences and the impact of national culture on corporate culture and performance as our organizations become more global.

National cultures are not always well adapted to the needs and requirements of modern business. For example, according to those involved in investigating the Fukushima Nuclear Plant accident, the ingrained conventions of Japanese culture were behind the crisis.[27] The accident at Three-Mile Island was due in large part to the national US culture of individualism, which resulted in poor teamwork between departments and internal competition. Decidedly not a safety culture.

> *In my youth, I travelled much, and I observed in different countries, that the more public provisions were made for the poor, the less they provided for themselves, and of course became poorer. And, on the contrary, the less was done for them, the more they did for themselves, and became richer.*
> ~ Benjamin Franklin

The Building Blocks of Corporate Culture

Corporate culture develops, whether we guide it or allow it to happen. Over the years I have made a list of the relative impact of certain elements that I consider to be the major building blocks of corporate culture. This chart is drawn from my own observations over the years as well as combing through the literature and talking with hundreds of CEOs and senior executives about corporate culture.

Determinants of Corporate Culture

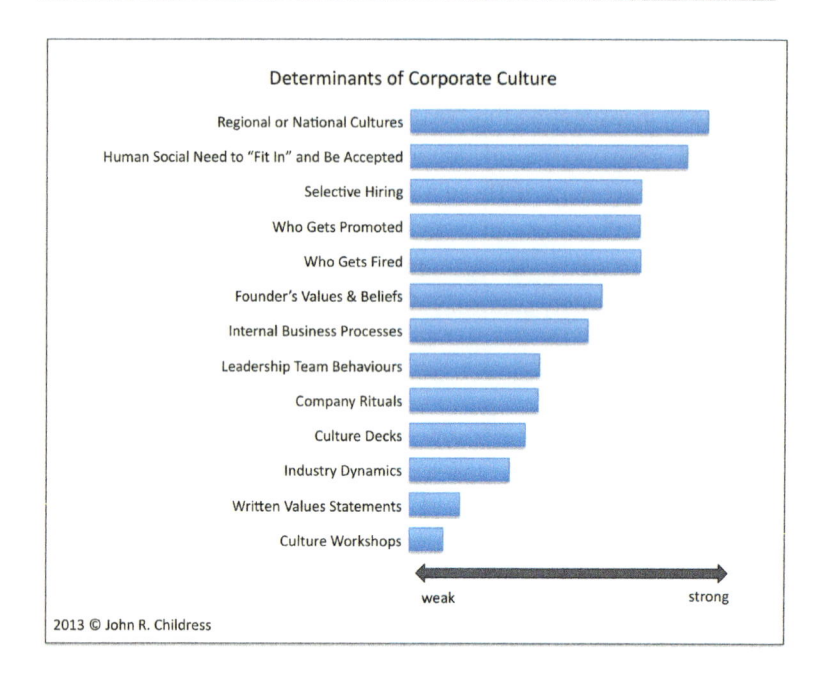

Factor	Strength
Regional or National Cultures	strong
Human Social Need to "Fit In" and Be Accepted	strong
Selective Hiring	strong
Who Gets Promoted	strong
Who Gets Fired	strong
Founder's Values & Beliefs	medium-strong
Internal Business Processes	medium-strong
Leadership Team Behaviours	medium
Company Rituals	medium
Culture Decks	medium
Industry Dynamics	medium-weak
Written Values Statements	weak
Culture Workshops	weak

2013 © John R. Childress

Difference of Opinion

Believe it or not, most employees don't leap out of bed in the morning ready to make more profit for the company!

A 2013 study on Core Beliefs & Culture by Deloitte Consulting surveyed over 1000 employees and 300 executives from large organizations about their views on culture and business performance. Not surprisingly there are some strong differences of opinion as to what are the key determinants of corporate culture between executives and employees. The important question coming out of this survey is, whose view of culture is the real culture?

Since executives tend to make the rules and set up policies and procedures, this information is insightful for those intent on gaining the leverage of corporate culture for improved business performance.

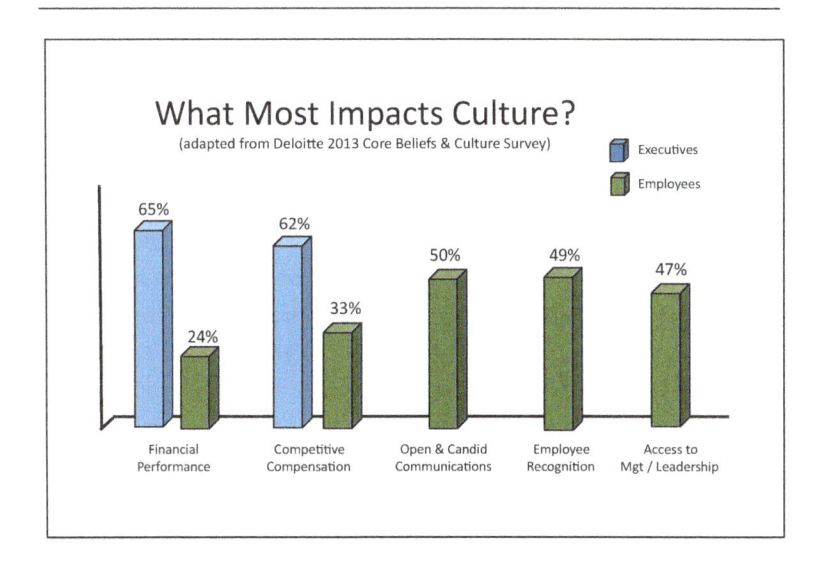

What Most Impacts Culture?
(adapted from Deloitte 2013 Core Beliefs & Culture Survey)

Category	Executives	Employees
Financial Performance	65%	24%
Competitive Compensation	62%	33%
Open & Candid Communications		50%
Employee Recognition		49%
Access to Mgt / Leadership		47%

Culture and the Time Warp:

> *First we shape our institutions and then they shape us.*
> *~ Winston Churchill*

Culture is not static and it doesn't spring up, fully-fledged at the beginning, but grows during the lifecycle of an organization. In most organizations, culture is allowed to develop by default and as a result, without the guidance of strong leadership committed to building a healthy, high performance culture, evolves in the following characteristic manner.

In the early start-up and developmental stages of an organization, culture is molded by the key business drivers and social influencers in the organization. The ***culture is dependent*** upon these elements and is shaped by them. Early successes, failures, leadership styles, decisions on strategy, operating principles, hiring, markets, HR policies and beliefs in how to motivate people, all leave a mark on the early culture. If you press your thumb into soft clay it leaves a shallow impression of your fingerprint. An early-stage culture is dotted with the fingerprints of early events and leadership behavior. **The organization has a culture, even if embryonic at this point.** Culture is a **dependant variable** and one of the many elements in the make-up of the developing young organization.

As time moves on and employees begin to celebrate 3-5 years with the company, patterns of habitual behavior begin to appear in how the leaders deal with employees, customers, competitors, each other. Subcultures or groups of employees with strong *'rules and roles'* begin to appear. If another location is added, the difference in cultures becomes palpable. If growth has been rapid, many new employees join, bringing with them cultural habits from other companies. People start talking about internal issues between departments, functions or levels of the organization and the term *'culture'* starts to be used to explain these difficult and sometimes contentious issues. The fingerprints are deeper and the clay is beginning to harden.

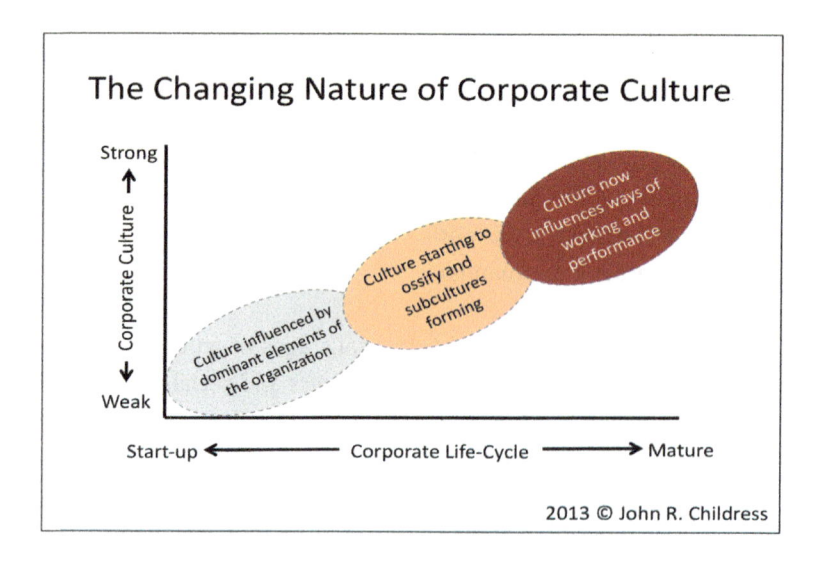

The Changing Nature of Corporate Culture

- Culture influenced by dominant elements of the organization
- Culture starting to ossify and subcultures forming
- Culture now influences ways of working and performance

Corporate Culture: Weak → Strong
Corporate Life-Cycle: Start-up → Mature

2013 © John R. Childress

After 10 years or so the leadership team has been diluted from exits and new additions, more ideas are introduced and there is talk of change. The subcultures and overall habitual behaviors and ways of dealing with customers and each other are codified in the *'unwritten'* ground rules and passed on from direct bosses and key influential employees to new employees coming in. Stories about a good or bad culture are told in the hallways and at the bars after work.

Everything that happens inside the organization is now heavily influenced by the culture. **Culture is now an *independent variable*** that has influence over everything that goes on in and around the organization. Even customers and suppliers are aware of the culture, as are competitors.

> *God grant me the serenity to accept the things I cannot change, the courage to change the things I can, and the wisdom to know the difference. ~ Reinhold Niebuhr*

Chapter 6: The Culture Continuum

Culture cannot be manufactured. It has to be genuinely nurtured by everyone from the CEO down. Ignoring the health of your culture is like letting aquarium water go foul. ~ Shaun Parr

Strong corporate cultures bind people together through shared objectives and aspirations, non-negotiable behaviors and ways of working that are supported through formal and informal reinforcement mechanisms. Some reinforcement mechanisms are as subtle as tacit approval and acknowledgement from a boss or respected key employee. Others are overt, such as awards and recognition in public. The clearer the required behaviors, the stronger the reinforcement mechanisms and the greater the 'pain' for violating them, the stronger the culture.

But can a culture be too strong? So strong that it overrides an individual's basic core values about right and wrong? Or so strong that the group's strength and focus overpowers the common sense of its individual members? So strong that it becomes toxic?

The answer is definitely yes. Examples of human atrocities inflicted on others is an extreme example all too real in the world today. In certain military, religious and sociopolitical organizations with heavy command and control policies, authoritarian leadership styles, strict behavioral norms and strong punishment for violators, it is easy to see how a toxic culture of wrongdoing can become tolerated or even accepted.

But what about the world of business and other non-military organizations? Was it a culture of greed and self-gratification among the leadership of Enron, Global Crossing and WorldCom that led them all to corporate bankruptcy and jail?

Fortunately, only a small fraction of organizations have such a negative, toxic corporate culture. Some, at the other end of the corporate culture continuum are classified as cult-like cultures. Just as a toxic culture does harm on many fronts, a cult-like culture is just the opposite and does good on many levels, for employees, for customers (usually called *'guests'*), and for shareholders in the case of publicly traded companies, and even for the environment.

The Continuum of Corporate Culture

At this point it is important to clear up some of the loose terminology used in the literature to describe corporate cultures. The following model and definitions are my own and have evolved over the years as I talked to more and more CEOs and diagnosed and observed hundreds of organizations.

Cultures don't just suddenly spring up. They develop slowly and can shift over time. Once highly functional cultures can shift, for a variety of reasons (poor leadership, marketplace or technological changes, or a combination of many factors) towards less functional and even toxic cultures. Corporate culture does not stand still.

Corporate culture is not static or frozen, but a living organism that responds to stimuli in certain and predictable ways.

In many ways, I see corporate cultures as residing on a continuum, along which they can, over time, shift left or right.

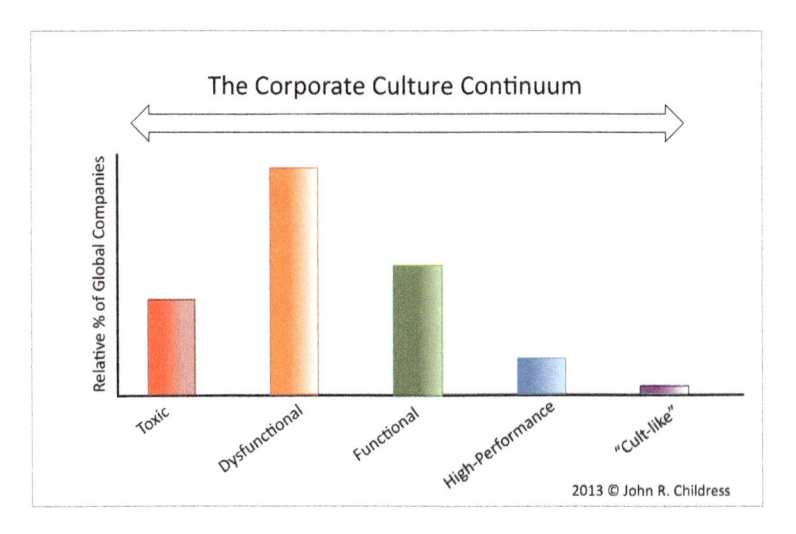

The Corporate Culture Continuum

[Bar chart showing relative % of Global Companies across: Toxic, Dysfunctional, Functional, High-Performance, "Cult-like". Dysfunctional is the tallest bar, followed by Functional, then Toxic, then High-Performance, with "Cult-like" being the smallest. 2013 © John R. Childress]

Functional Cultures work well for all stakeholders concerned and are characterized by a good degree of alignment between Strategy, Structure and Culture. Most employees know where the company is going and understand the company's competitive advantages. They know how to get things done with a minimal amount of time wasted, and are clear on the desired and required behaviors for fitting in and getting the job done with quality and timeliness. A functional culture is adaptive to shifting business and market conditions; people have a high degree of trust in upper management and generally feel the company is a good place to work and develop themselves. Functional cultures deliver average to good business performance.

People in Functional Cultures tend to focus more on the work and the benefits of the job than on the company culture. Often employees remain in these companies because they like their immediate boss and they like the work, and are willing to put up with minor frustrations. When asked about the company, most employees respond with "It's okay." Few employees go out of their way to introduce their friends into the company. The overall viewpoint of leadership seems to be one of: "*good products and good financials will build a good culture and employees can have a good career here.*"

Dysfunctional Cultures deliver erratic performance, sometimes posting good performance and at other times disappointing Wall Street and shareholders. Their performance profile can be classified as unpredictable. A dysfunctional culture is characterized by lots of blaming and excuses for poor performance. Turnover is moderate to high, depending upon the job market externally. Subcultures are strong and powerful and often display more loyalty to members of their group than to the company or customers. Management spends more time looking at and fixing internal problems than focusing externally on customers. Normally we see power and decision making concentrated at the top, with lots of meetings, most of which employees describe as a waste of time. Senior executives tend to focus more on their functions (silo focus) and their functional objectives than on cross-functional teamwork or the overall strategic objectives.

I believe that the majority of companies across the globe tend to fall into the dysfunctional culture category. This doesn't mean they can't turn out good products, grow, compete effectively or deliver on stated business goals. They can, but it takes more effort and hard work than is actually necessary since a large amount of energy is wasted on internal turf battles, politics, rework and redesign, workarounds, late shipment costs, daily crises and *'firefighting'*, not to mention the human toll of stress, emotional and physical abuse. Working in a dysfunctional culture is hard, like trying to sprint through molasses. When asked about the company, an employee will often reply, "I*t's not great, but it's a job*".

*When small men attempt great enterprises,
they always end by reducing them to the level of their
mediocrity. ~Napoleon Bonaparte*

Healthy, High-Performance Cultures In the more modern literature, high-performance cultures are often described as healthy organizations. There is also a strong and growing global movement to create a healthy, high performance culture by fulfilling the criteria for becoming a *Great Place to Work®*, which is based on research into what employees want and need in a healthy and productive workplace (Levering, 2010).

More than 100 studies have now found that the most engaged employees — those who report they're fully invested in their jobs and committed to their employers — are significantly more productive, drive higher customer satisfaction and outperform those who are less engaged. But only 20% of employees around the world report that they're fully engaged at work. [35]

*A great place to work is one in which you trust the people
you work for, have pride in what you do, and enjoy the
people you work with. ~ Robert Levering, Co-Founder, Great
Place to Work®*

High-performance cultures seem to have a solid foundation of trust. Employees trust management and their co-workers to act with credibility, respect and fairness. Trust is built and nurtured through progressive HR policies, caring and concerned leadership, selective hiring, recognition and rituals. The company produces goods and services that people can be proud of. They talk positively about their company to all who will listen. People really like each other and like working in these types of cultures and performance on all levels, growth, profitability, and share price is well above average. High-performance cultures are built from the inside-out.

Pushing the Envelope

At the extreme ends of the continuum are cult-like and toxic cultures.

> As far as I'm concerned, the first business leader who was able to establish a cult of personality around his tenure was Lee Iacocca. ~ Tom Peters

Cult-like cultures are fascinating to observe. I use the word '*cult-like*' here in a very positive sense (as opposed to the negative connotations of religious sects and other cults). These rare organizations are characterized by intense passion and devotion to the company shown by not only employees, but customers as well. Cult-like cultures literally attract employees and customers (as opposed to most other cultures which must use 'push and pull mechanisms' to find employees and customers). A cult-like culture was one of the fundamental attributes of the successful companies profiled by Jim Collins and Jerry Porras in their classic book *Built to Last*, regarded as one of the most influential business books ever (Collins and Porras, 2005).

A cult-like culture is usually built on a passion and devotion to a core ideology that enhances the well-being of its customers and staff in ways that other company products and services cannot. Cult-like cultures don't just happen, they are designed, nurtured and sustained by the founders and/or senior leadership, but are not dependant upon one or two individuals. It's the ideology, not the person that people are attracted to. Cult-like cultures often deliver superior performance at all levels; staff satisfaction, customer delight, sales per square foot, profits, growth and innovation.

One of the longest sustained cult-like organizations is the Walt Disney Company. Walt Disney invented a new language that would signal and reinforce the core ideology of the company. Instead of employees or staff, he called them *'cast members'*, and customers were *'guests'*. Roles and responsibilities were called *'parts'* in the Disney performance. He even helped implement an *'audition'* instead of the standard job interview and all those hired, no matter at what level, had to attend and pass the *'Disney Traditions'* employee orientation training, where they were indoctrinated into the real purpose of the company: *'to make people happy'*.

New on the scene, but growing fast into a global specialty retail powerhouse is the cult-like *lululemon athletica (NASDAQ:LULU)*, whose stores and on-line presence sell *"technical athletic apparel for yoga, running, dancing, and most other sweaty pursuits for people to live long, healthy and fun lives. By producing products that help keep people active and stress free, lululemon believes that the world will be a better place. Setting the bar in technical fabrics and functional designs, lululemon works with yogis and athletes in local communities for continuous research and product feedback."*[35]

While the clothing is designed for functionality and long life, it's in the stores and their customer service where the real cult-like culture shows up. Customers come into the stores just to hang-out, talk yoga or sports, share information and generally soak up the good vibes emanating from pleasant store design and up-beat, professional and motivated staff. And *lululemon* takes staff development seriously. All employees develop 1, 5 and 10 year personal goals, supported by the company through its own goal setting templates. As one staffer shouted: *"lululemon's not a place to work, it's a place to grow."*

And the numbers are impressive too. In 2012, *lululemon* (founded in 1999) had the third highest grossing retail sales per square foot ($1,936), behind only Tiffany and front-runner Apple, also a cult-like culture. The company had 2012 sales of $1.9 billion, a profit margin of 25+%, a market cap of nearly $9 billion and upwards of 200 retail stores, 38 showrooms and 5 outlets in North America, the UK and

Hong Kong, and have solid plans for upwards of 350 stores. Plus, they have no debt, all their expansion and product development being funded by free cash flow! [36, 37]

Toxic cultures are bad news for just about everyone; employees, customers, suppliers, shareholders, communities and often, the environment as well. A toxic culture has a single-minded focus on profits, often at any cost. They are characterized by posting highly erratic business performance numbers that are either superior or poor in their category, sometimes swinging from one to another over a short period of years, or quarters. They are full of *'flavor of the month'* improvement initiatives, usually around costs or sales, rarely around people development. They are often the company of last resort for customers and often win short-term business through special discounts and other incentives. Employees feel very little loyalty or love for the company; their main focus is on getting a paycheck. They are characterized by high turnover at all levels (before 1985 Continental Airlines had 10 CEOs in 10 years!).

Toxic cultures favor secrecy to openness and display poor internal and external communications. Rumors and the grapevine are the only conduits for news and information. Often we see toxic companies trying to acquire other companies to bolster their numbers, a tactic that only works in the short term. Unless culture is a priority at all levels, older companies can slide towards toxicity as they grow larger and ossify their bad habits.

A toxic culture is characterized by a specific set of behaviors that are commonplace [38].

- Widespread anger and frustration
- Common use of foul or abusive language
- The workplace bully is admired
- High degree of finger-pointing and blaming, "not my job" is a common phrase
- Dysfunctional relationships with low trust and respect

- Dysfunctional meetings
- Obvious hypocrisy where "rank has its privileges"
- Overly restrictive or controlling polices, procedures and systems
- Incompetent or powerless HR manager

Up until the successful 1985 turnaround led by Gordon Bethune and Greg Brenneman, Continental Airlines was a classic toxic culture organization. An amalgamation of 7 different airlines and with caustic leadership, employees would rip the Continental logo off their uniforms to avoid being hassled while in the airport or at the supermarket. People didn't just loathe the company, they hated it. Business fliers would go out of their way to fly another airline, even if it meant taking a non-direct route.

The old GM car manufacturing plant in Freemont was another toxic culture company, where employees would purposely put half-eaten sandwiches inside door panels that were then welded shut to get a semblance of revenge on Management. It was the worst performing, poorest quality, most-strike-ridden plant in GM worldwide. Another example is the corporate culture of Enron, which slid in a few short years from functional to toxic under the reign of new CEO, Jeff Skilling.

Both Goldman Sachs and Barclays Bancorp come to mind as classic toxic cultures in the financial services industry. According to a former Goldman Sachs executive, who sent the New York Times his resignation letter:

> *I believe I have worked here long enough to understand the trajectory of its culture, its people and its identity. And I can honestly say that the environment now is as toxic and destructive as I have ever seen it . . . The firm has veered so far from the place I joined right out of college that I can no longer in good conscience say that I identify with what it stands for.*[39]

In a recent study on why talented women leave corporate jobs, only 1% cited the glass ceiling. Most said they left because of toxic cultures of bureaucracy, back-stabbing, poor management, useless meetings, harassment and bullying. The costs to physical and emotional health, and their own personal values, was just too much (HCA Magazine, 2012).

A non-business example, but instructional none-the-less, concerns the 2012 Australian Olympic Swimming team. Australia has been a perennial winner in Olympic swimming, but in 2012 won just one gold medal. What went wrong?

Following their poor showing in London, a review (commissioned by an independent body, *Swimming Australia*) cited a failure of leadership and a toxic culture resulting from a lack of moral authority and discipline. The toxic culture involved bullying, the misuse of prescription drugs, getting drunk and breaching curfews [40].

Shift Happens

> *The way those outfielders shift against Ted Williams, I can't understand why he doesn't just hit to left field.*
> ~ Ty Cobb

In the early 1980's big changes were happening in the natural gas sector in the United States. Deregulation was sweeping multiple sectors: transportation, telecoms and then energy, and specifically, Natural Gas Pipelines. This led the way for price competition and cross border mergers and acquisitions. One such key player in the natural gas pipeline sector was Enron, the result of the 1985 acquisition of Houston Natural Gas by Omaha-based InterNorth Corporation. Following FERC Order 436 allowing for open access, Enron formed partnerships with other pipeline companies, making Enron the largest transporter of natural gas in the US, with gas flowing from Florida to California, and from Montana through

Illinois to Texas.

Integrating the operations into a cost effective organization fell to Ron Burns, CEO of Pipeline Operations. Ron was a former Northern Natural Gas executive and relocated to the new Enron Houston headquarters. It was when Ron took over as head of pipeline operations that we first met and I was hired to help him integrate the various cultures coming from the different acquisitions. Ron Burns was one of the few senior executives in the 1980s who truly understood and valued the importance and power of a high-performance culture based on open dialogue, shared vision, non-negotiable behaviors, ethical leadership and management development. Ron Burns was a great leader, a great client, and also a great golfer!

By 1991 the Enron Pipeline organization began to solidify its high-performance culture and productivity and profits were up, safety was world class and gas was flowing from coast to coast. Definitely a functional, high-performance culture. Then Jeff Skilling, a former McKinsey partner and consultant to Ken Lay, Chairman of Enron, became the company's new CEO, and according to Ron, things started to shift, and not for the better as far as culture and employees were concerned.

Skilling was no fan of his former McKinsey colleague Tom Peters and he ignored corporate culture in favor of diversification, earnings per share, online trading and revenue growth. Enron stock soared. Ron Burns resigned. I can still remember him saying something like: *"I don't care how high the stock price is, what they are doing just doesn't make good business sense."*

Ron was proven right. The Enron house of cards collapsed, the company went bankrupt, its auditors, Arthur Andersen closed up shop, and Skilling (along with others) went to jail. Ken Lay died of a heart attack from all the stress of litigation and the constant probing from the press. Just to show you how far the culture had shifted, the woman who first blew the whistle on the Enron illegal financial dealings got fired from the company!

A functional, high-performance culture shifted into a highly toxic culture of greed, lies, financial tricks, and an open disdain for employee welfare. Enron was once a good company, but shift happens!

A Few Key Questions for the CEO and Business Leader

- Why do companies become cult-like or toxic?
- How do they get that way?
- What causes a culture to shift over time?
- In what direction is the culture of your organization headed?
- What can you and senior team do to actively guide the culture?

These are important questions for the CEO and business leader to understand when seeking to build and harness the power of corporate culture.

Chapter 7: Culture by Design or Default?

This is not a trick question. It's actually very simple.
The answer is YES!

First of all, let me say it directly and clearly. Your organization has a culture, whether you know it or not, whether you like it or not, whether you want one or not, whether you designed it from the start, let it happen, or inherited it when you joined the company. All companies, large and small, start-ups or generations old, government or NGO, have a culture.

The real question is not whether you have a culture, but whether your culture is an enabler or barrier to competitive advantage, and whether you are actively shaping the culture or allowing it to develop by default.

John R. Childress

Culture by Design

> *Whether you like it or not, you're going to have a culture. Why not make it one you love?* ~ from the HubSpot Culture Code

Building a culture by design allows the founders and start-up team to align culture to the strategy and structure of the emerging organization and to imbed effective practices and behaviors right from the beginning. But this is not an easy task. It takes a fanatical commitment to three very critical cultural determinants: hiring profiles to find employees that fit the culture; business processes and practices that foster the right behaviors; and measures and metrics that track and help realign the culture.

The founders of Netflix, the online video rental and streaming mega-business, decided to use culture as the foundation for building their business. Their culture document, a 126 page PowerPoint deck, became their defacto business plan, against which all decisions were evaluated.

> *Let's make the company we always dreamed of.*
> *Let's create a company that will be a great place to be from.*
> ~ Reed Hastings and Patty McCord, Netflix

The Netflix culture deck, titled *Netflix Culture, Freedom and Responsibility*, published on the web (Hastings, 2013) has over 4 million viewings and Facebook likes. Sheryl Sandberg, COO of Facebook, called it *"the most important document ever to come out of Silicon Valley."*

Why? Because it is one of the first, and clearest articulations of the elements of a corporate culture by design. A culture-by-design, in contrast to a default culture, addresses several critical elements in building a competitive and sustainable organization: why a specific set of culture determinants are being established, who is expected to lead and promulgate the culture, whom it is intended to embrace, what it will mean in terms of aligned actions by all employees, when cultural change efforts should be made and how the cultural changes will be introduced, enabled, enforced, monitored and celebrated.

While the Netflix Culture document lists 7 important foundational elements of the emerging culture:

- Values are what we Value
- High Performance
- Freedom & Responsibility
- Context not Control
- Highly Aligned, Loosely Coupled
- Pay Top of Market
- Promotions & Development,

it is the meanings behind the words and rituals that have the real power in building and maintaining an aligned corporate culture.

Behind each of these seven cultural foundations are the rationale, clear descriptions of behaviors, and expectations for all employees. While many executives in traditional organizations tend to dismiss such culture decks as a manifesto to Generation Y, used effectively they are powerful in establishing cultural norms from the beginning in order to drive explosive growth.

After just 10 years Netflix delivered its 1 billionth video and is now beginning to dominate in video streaming. In an unprecedented move Netflix secured 14 nominations and three awards at the 2013 Emmy Awards for its own series, *Arrested Development, House of Cards* and *Hemlock Grove,* all original series developed and funded by Netflix.

At Netflix, we think you have to build a sense of responsibility where people are about the enterprise. Hard work, like long hours at the office, doesn't matter as much to us. We care about great work. ~ Reed Hastings

It takes a high-performance culture to build a high performing, fast growth company. And if everyone in the company keeps a maniacal focus on culture and listens closely to customer feedback, the organization has a good shot at delivering sustainable and superior performance.

Culture by Default

Few start-ups have such a maniacal belief in the importance of culture as Netflix, Zappos.com, Walt Disney Company, Apple, Google and lululemon athletica. For most organizations, culture is an afterthought with most of the attention of leadership being focused on products, processes and profits. As a result, culture develops on its own under the invisible influence of multiple forces and determinants. But culture is not a static or fixed element. Cultures shift, mostly slowly, as these invisible pressures grow or shrink in intensity. Shift Happens!

Pirate Stew

Soup and fishing explain half the emotions of human life.

Whenever we go on extended flyfishing float trips to wild Alaskan rivers, we try to take enough decent food (fresh, packaged and freeze dried) to give us a semblance of good eating. Needless to say we have fresh fish nearly every night as well. But, like the best laid plans, sometimes the food starts running low, or we tip over a raft in the rapids and lose a box of food. So, when it starts getting down to the end of the good grub, we improvise and create what we affectionately call, Pirate Stew!

Pirate Stew is a mixture of whatever we can find that hasn't spoiled or gone rotten, all cut up and thrown into the pot, along with some wine or vodka to kill the bacteria (and add some flavor). It does taste pretty good on a cold, rainy Alaskan evening by the campfire. It ain't pretty, but it does the job.

In many cases, corporate cultures inadvertently wind up like Pirate Stew, and while the diversity of ideas, experiences and agendas potentially adds to the ability to create and innovate, the dark side of having an excessively diverse corporate culture is the inevitable formation of subcultures that don't seem to work well together and often prove difficult to get moving all in the same direction to support business change or transformation.

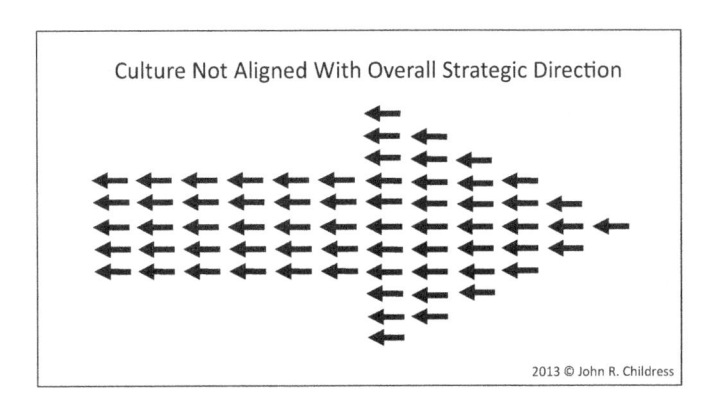

Culture Not Aligned With Overall Strategic Direction

2013 © John R. Childress

Here's what happens. Most organizations start out with a clear purpose and a set of shared values and ground rules about what is important and how we work together. The goal is clear, everyone knows everyone and has the same overall sense of purpose, usually something like *'do good for customers, be profitable and grow the business'.*

But as the company becomes successful and grows, new employees, new managers and new senior executives are added, bringing valuable new skills and experiences, but also their personal values and ways of behaving learned while working for other companies. In other words, the aligned culture and clarity of purpose starts to get lost as more and more people from other corporate cultures join. When clarity of purpose is lost, and conflicting ways of behaving start to clash, corporate culture begins to become a liability.

Consider the *Pirate Stew* cultures in today's global banking organizations. A very real example is Goldman Sachs, the full-service global investment banking and securities firm which provides merger and acquisition advice, underwriting services, asset management, and prime brokerage to its clients, which include corporations, governments and individuals. The firm also engages in proprietary trading and private equity deals, and is a primary dealer in the United States Treasury security market.

Goldman Sachs is huge. Thirty-three thousand employees and revenues in excess of $29 Billion, and is globally respected for its financial expertise. At one point Goldman Sachs was the elite financial services firm and regularly recruited the best and brightest from the top MBA schools.

But the elite reputation of the firm is now very much in question. The original corporate culture, based on its famous 14 Business Principles (with *'Our Clients' Interests Always Come First'* as the number one principle), has been transformed into that of a *'corporate pirate'* where greed and self-interest have replaced both personal and professional ethics. In fact, the common name in the industry for Goldman Sachs nowadays is the **'Vampire Squid'**, a nod to its blood-sucking greed and global reach.

Recently, a resignation letter by Greg Smith, former head of Goldman Sachs US equity derivatives business, which was published in the New York Times, brought to light the changes in ethics and corporate culture that have taken place over the past 20 years. The day after the publication, $2.5 Billion was erased from the firm's balance sheet. Greg Smith declared:

> *I knew it was time to leave when I realized I could no longer look students in the eye and tell them what a great place this was to work. When the history books are written about Goldman Sachs, they may reflect that the CEO, Lloyd C. Blankfein, and the president, Gary D. Cohn, lost hold of the firm's culture on their watch. I truly believe that this decline in the firm's moral fiber represents the single most serious threat to its long-run survival.*[39]

As Goldman Sachs grew and expanded, it recruited from many different cultures and didn't seem to understand that while they were gaining great talent and financial experience, they were also seriously damaging their original culture of excellence and principles. While Goldman Sachs is a big example, the principle of Pirate Stew happens to cultures of all sizes.

Cultural Drift

I clearly remember my second year in college sitting in a marine geology class and discussing the then revolutionary topic of continental drift. After decades of theories and much scoffing at the subject of plate tectonics by renowned scientists, in 1968 Geophysicist Jack Oliver published seismologic evidence supporting plate tectonics and continental drift. Massive areas of the ocean floor could move, although extremely slowly (geologic time), but small movements over millions of years have created our dynamically changing planet earth.

The analogy between continental drift and shifts over time in corporate culture is quite clear to me and needs to be also understood by business leaders.

Almost all early stage companies have some sort of foundation principles for how they will conduct business and how people should behave at work. While perhaps not as codified as the examples from Netflix, HubSpot or Zappos.com, never the less they helped to establish the early *'ways of working'* in the company and proved highly useful in establishing alignment between customers, employees and owners. So in some sense, all founding organizations had a culture by design, some stronger and more transparent than others.

Coming back to the Goldman Sachs example, in the very early 1980's, co-CEO John Whitehead penned their famous Goldman Sachs Business Principles. Here is an excerpt from his own story [41]

> There came a time when we were growing quite rapidly and I realized that if we grew at 10% a year and had a turnover of say, 5% a year, then 15% of our people every year would be new and in three years, 45% of our people would have been there less than three years. I wondered how our staff would ever be inculcated with the principles that defined Goldman Sachs.
>
> One day I wrote the principles down and called it a code of conduct. I didn't create the principles, my predecessors did. Goldman Sachs always stood for these principles. In the first draft, there were ten principles and somebody told me that it looked too much like the Ten Commandments, so I made it into twelve. I believe it's up to fourteen now because the lawyers got hold of it and they've changed a few words and added to it a little bit.
>
> In any case, I'm very proud of that. We got approval from the management committee and we sent it out to all the employees. We actually sent it to their homes, thinking that they might want to share it with their spouses and their children to show that they worked for a fine firm with high standards. So that was a good way to distribute it.
>
> At the time, we required all of our department heads to meet with their people to discuss just how that code of conduct fit with their day-to-day business and whether or not they might be doing things that were in violation of the code.

The problem with most organizations as they grow and change is that nearly everything gets managed, sometimes micro-managed, except the culture. Culture is often left to its own and as a result organizations experience *'cultural drift'* and can, over a fairly short period of time, wind up very different from how they started.

One of the prime reasons so many well aligned cultures shift out of alignment over time is that executives at the top don't fully understand or appreciate the importance of culture and most don't know how (and some don't care) to manage corporate culture. This lack of understanding and appreciation can lead to lost *'leadership moments'* that could have kept the culture in alignment.

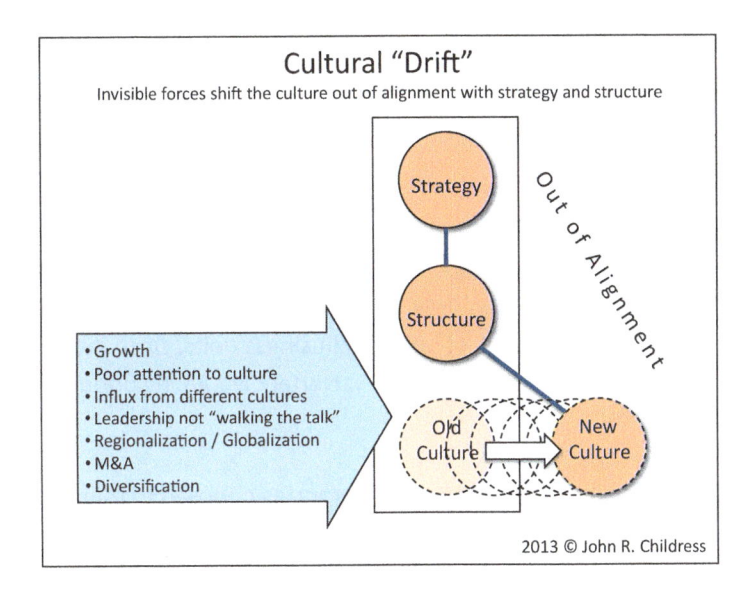

Cultural "Drift"
Invisible forces shift the culture out of alignment with strategy and structure

- Growth
- Poor attention to culture
- Influx from different cultures
- Leadership not "walking the talk"
- Regionalization / Globalization
- M&A
- Diversification

Strategy → Structure → Old Culture → New Culture → *Out of Alignment*

2013 © John R. Childress

As a result of culture neglect and unaware leadership, over time a culture will drift from aligned and optimal towards the median, or mediocre. And given the pressures of growth, mergers or acquisitions, sudden competitive challenges, or significant leadership changes, toxic corporate cultures and negative subcultures can and will evolve.

The Curious Case of the Culture That Went Missing

Nortel Networks Corporation began life in the 1880s manufacturing telephones, switchboards and equipment for Bell Telephone Company of Canada. At its height in the late 1990s, Nortel was a global powerhouse that accounted for more than a third of the total valuation of all the companies listed on the Toronto Stock Exchange, employing some 94,500 worldwide.

Nortel was the poster child for the Digital Age and the first company in its industry to deliver a complete line of fully digital telecommunications products. Starting in 1977, Nortel grew rapidly after the introduction of its DMS line of digital central office telephone switches, especially after the AT&T breakup in 1984. Northern Telecom became a significant supplier in Europe and China and was the first non-Japanese supplier to Nippon Telegraph and Telephone.

However, in January 14, 2009, Nortel filed for bankruptcy protection from its creditors in the United States, Canada, and the United Kingdom. In June 2009, the company announced it would cease operations and sell off all of its business units. Once the high flyer in a sexy and lucrative industry, Nortel died an inglorious and painful death.

What is fascinating about the Nortel story, as opposed to hundreds of other bankrupt companies, is the role played by corporate culture. For much of its early life the Nortel culture could be described as a *'large family'* where everyone knew each other, knew how things worked and who to call if they needed any support on a deal or information for a sales pitch. The *'informal organization'* was the way things got done. And speed to market with new products and services was a significant competitive advantage.

According to Gary Donahee, one of the key senior leaders during the rapid growth times at Nortel: *"we knew who the good guys were and just gave them a call when we really needed to get something accomplished, and it worked well".* The Nortel culture was strong and according to many during that time, a high-performance culture.

With a desire to grow fast, the company hired hundreds and hundreds of new managers, executives and employees who knew the official organization chart, but not the *'informal'* organization. And these new hires came with their own set of behaviors and attitudes about business and management. This rapid influx of outsiders, even though they had good experience and the necessary business, sales and technical skills, had the effect of diluting the original Nortel culture, creating in effect a cultural stew. It also muddied up the strong informal culture of getting things done quickly. There was lots of good diversity, but little cohesion around behaviors and attitudes towards work, customers and team members.

As a result, decision-making slowed down. Getting something through the system became more and more difficult until Nortel began losing ground to more agile companies. Then a significant number of experienced senior executives cashed in their stock options and retired. Nortel limped along, finally filed for bankruptcy, and subsequently died.

In essence, Nortel outgrew its original culture. In the end, it wound up with a weak and fractionated corporate culture full of subcultures and conflicting views on everything from customer service to business ethics.

Subcultures: Boxes Within Boxes

As companies age and the original culture begins to fade and get diluted, it opens up room for strong subcultures to emerge. And many of these subcultures are often developed around the need by small groups or departments for self-preservation and job security during times of change and business uncertainty. Here's an example.

When Dick Millman took over as CEO of Bell Helicopter in January 2007, the company was struggling to deliver to the sales demands on its commercial aircraft, and one of its biggest government development projects for the US Army was being threatened with cancellation due to cost overruns and schedule delays. Bell was on tough times and needed to focus on execution.

The new CEO went to work to fix the immediate major execution problems and stop the flow of red ink on the P&L, but also wanted to improve productivity and innovation, both of which had been floundering for some time. But that was more difficult than he had imagined. Metrics and measures were in place, training was in place, the people had the expertise, but productivity wasn't improving.

Dick was the fifth CEO in 12 years at Bell Helicopter, a place where the average employee age within the engineering and manufacturing ranks was around 50. People had worked at Bell for a long time, many being sons and daughters of former Bell employees. As he began to dig down into the ranks of middle management and supervisors, he discovered the *'We Be'* subculture.

'We Be' was a group of lower middle managers with long tenures in the company and a collective cynicism towards senior management and all the new initiatives and change programs. *'We Be'* was shorthand for *"we be here before you and we be here after you have moved on."* Needless to say their resistance to new initiatives and the collective strong peer pressure of this group of respected and influential managers had a considerable blocking affect on attempts to improve productivity and performance.

Most subcultures arise in older organizations with poor leadership and a poor understanding of the need to manage and sustain culture. Subcultures tend to form as a means of identity and self-preservation where peer group allegiance is stronger than allegiance to company or customer. It's not surprising that such subcultures tend to form in large bureaucratic organizations, especially within government bodies.

VanMannen and Barley, in a 1985 paper defined subcultures as *"groups of organizational members who interact regularly with each other, identify themselves as a distinct group within that organization, share the same problems, and take action on the basis of a common way of thinking that is unique to the group."* [42]

Task-Oriented Subcultures

Inside most organizations there are often 'task-oriented' subcultures. Professor Edgar Schein (2004) identifies three of them: **operator** (based on human interaction, high levels of communication, trust and teamwork), **engineer** (elegant solution, abstract solutions to problems, automation and systems) and **executive** (financial focus, lone hero, sense of rightness and omniscience).

Schein is adamant that in any organization, the alignment between these three subcultures is critical for effective performance. According to Schein:

> *Many problems that are attributed to bureaucracy, environmental factors or personality conflicts among managers are in fact the result of the lack of alignment between these subcultures.*

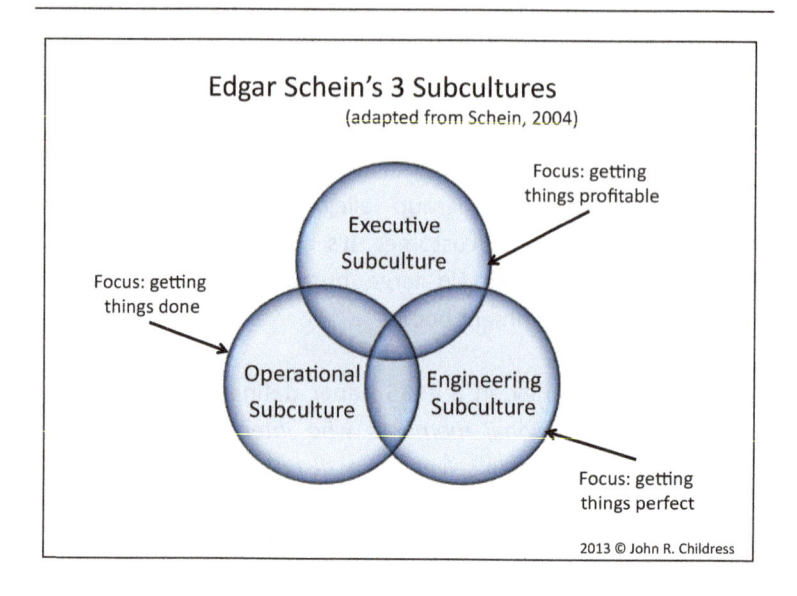

Edgar Schein's 3 Subcultures
(adapted from Schein, 2004)

- Executive Subculture — Focus: getting things profitable
- Operational Subculture — Focus: getting things done
- Engineering Subculture — Focus: getting things perfect

2013 © John R. Childress

Without alignment, these subcultures can often be working hard, but in different directions and with different motivations and objectives. Executive subcultures tend to focus on profit and costs while often missing the needs of the operator and engineer subcultures, which tend to focus on very different drivers and objectives.

And here's a scary reality. Most senior executives have no idea what the subcultures are within their company, how strong they are and how they impact performance! What is also critically important, as we will discover further on in this Guide, is why and how they are allowed to continue, and how they so often "ossify" into pockets of deep cynicism or resistance to change.

LEVERAGE:

SECTION THREE: LEADERSHIP AND CORPORATE CULTURE

The way management treats their associates is exactly how the associates will then treat the customers.
~ Sam M. Walton

Once there was a young boy who sold baseball style caps as a way to help his family earn money. He wandered the streets every day before and after school touting his brightly colored caps. His caps were hung on a line around his cart and made a colorful sight.

One hot day he parked his cart loaded with caps under a tree to rest and escape the hot sun. As he was sitting in the shade having a drink of water a troop of monkeys came down from the top of the tree and stole all his caps. They immediately began howling and chattering with delight at their success and hung all the caps on high branches.

The boy looked up. His caps were high up in the tree out of reach and the money to help his family seemed to be gone. In anger he picked up some rocks and started throwing them at the chattering monkeys.

> *Seeing the boy throwing rocks at them the monkeys gathered the large fruit from the tree and began to throw them down at the boy. One even hit him on the head. The monkeys roared with delight.*
>
> *The boy sat down by his cart, dejected and depressed. But as he relaxed and his mind calmed, no longer filled with thoughts of revenge on the monkeys, ideas began to occupy the space where angry thoughts once had been. Suddenly he had an insight.*
>
> *He stood up, yelled at the monkeys to get their attention, grabbed his own cap off of his head and threw it to the ground. Immediately the monkeys grabbed all the caps in the tree and threw them to the ground, laughing with delight.*
>
> *Calmly the boy gathered up his caps and moved on.*

This parable illustrates one of the key tenants of organizational culture. The monkeys were simply following the boy's example; first by throwing fruit after he threw rocks and then throwing the caps down to the ground like he did!

Employees watch the behavior of the members of the senior team to look for clues on how to behave, what is really important, and how to succeed in the organization. After all, if senior executives behave like that it must be acceptable behavior. And when senior managers talk about corporate values but behave differently, guess which employees tend to role model?

A fish rots from the head first!

Chapter 8: Shadow of the Leader

Organizations are shadows of their leaders.
That's the good news and the bad news!

Several years ago I was invited to attend a year-end sales conference by a CEO client. Imagine an upscale Florida convention center filled with happy employees who had just blown the doors off their revenue targets. Everyone was in a great mood and light-hearted laughter could be heard everywhere the attendees went.

On the final evening it was time for the closing ceremonies, gala dinner and a special guest entertainer. Sparing no expense, the event organizers had reached out to Las Vegas for a well-known stand up comic who was guaranteed to have them rolling in the aisles – just right for a year-end celebration.

After a great meal came the awards ceremony with recognition based on the six core values of the company. The Values Awards were given out by the CEO, who took the opportunity to stress the importance of each one of the company values. *"Our values help us produce excellent business results such as we've delivered this year,"* he said, *"but are also the foundation of our everyday behavior."*

Then it was time for the festivities. The lights dimmed and out walked the guest entertainer to thundering applause. It was obvious he had been briefed on the company and their stellar results since he started out with a few light-hearted comments about the products and some of the senior managers. Everything started out great.

But as he launched into his comedy routine, a wave of unease rippled through the crowd. The jokes were funny, but more suited for a *'boy's night out'* or a *'stag party'* than a corporate sales meeting. And with each passing joke the tension grew. People began to look around, wondering if it was okay to laugh – the jokes were crudely funny, but . . .

After a few more jokes the CEO stood up from the head table and walked up on stage. He motioned to the stunned entertainer for the microphone. By this time not a fork was moving. He turned to the shocked comedian and said: *"Thank you. You're services will no longer be required. You will receive your fee, but your act is finished, now!"*

He then turned to the audience. *"I apologize to you all. These jokes do not fit with our values of respect for all people. I am sorry and take full responsibility. I firmly believe our shared corporate values are more important than anything else – they are what make us a great company. I suggest for the rest of the evening we enjoy each other's company. That's the best entertainment I can think of."* He walked off the stage to a standing ovation.

The behavior of those in leadership positions casts an influence far and wide. In this case a simple act taking no longer than two minutes had a greater impact on the company culture than any speech, any memo, any poster on values or any training course. Because of the CEO's visible and clear action, everyone in the company realized that values were important. And even before he sat down the word was out on email to the rest of the company! The culture came to life that evening and the stories of *'that sales conference'* are still told inside the company.

The Impact of Leadership Behavior

Whether you like it or not, **YOU** cast a powerful shadow across your organization through your actions and behaviors. And actions speak louder than words! People watch the behavior of their leaders for clues as to what is accepted and what is not. When a leader says one thing and then behaves differently, employees quickly figure out the real story. And it's the real stories that build a culture.

Shortly after Allen Mulally became CEO of Ford Motor Company, instead of responding to an email in kind, he would walk into the person's office or call them, even lower level employees. Stories began to circulate about the new boss and his open communication style and his real interest in listening to ideas. Mulally's behavior was inspiring them. Through individual acts of reaching out and connecting with people, he built up the morale of a tired and insecure organization. Mulally became the Cheerleader in Chief, and people responded to his optimistic and direct style.

Then he went even further. He set up a weekly 4-hour meeting of all Ford senior executives around the world via videoconference and asked each to share their wins and problems and to highlight their weekly business results. Yes, weekly! And he never chastised anyone for poor results, but instead kept asking the same question, *"What do you need from us to get on track?"* And he recruited his new CFO, Lewis Booth, to model the same behavior.

At first, the old culture of *'never admit to problems lest you face a public humiliation'* kept people from asking for help. They needed support from other areas of expertise within Ford, but the real question was, could they trust the new leadership to support them? Over the next several months, a consistent pattern of new behavior by Mulally built the necessary trust and before long, problems and solutions were flying around the Ford global empire. The old silo culture had been broken by consistent and fair leadership behavior. Ford now had a plan, and leadership they could believe in.

When you come into the building and head straight for your office, head down, not interacting with anyone, that's the story that gets talked about in the canteen and the pubs, not the speech you gave on employee engagement and openness.

Here's an example of how leadership created a toxic and unproductive culture.

A number of years ago, during the heyday of the Mexican Maquiladora era, American companies set up factories just across the US border in Mexico. The objective was low cost manufacturing to make products competitively. However, rampant employee turnover among the Mexican workers, often as high as 800-1000% in some cases, negatively impacted the overall product costs. The American managers complained bitterly about the poor work culture and lack of accountability.

The high turnover, however, was inevitable! The American companies had only one purpose; to make stuff cheap. They had no real interest in Mexico or their employees. While they situated their factories close to the border for obvious logistical reasons, it was also well understood that the border hugging facilities allowed the American managers to retreat back to the US every night after work. Having executives and managers actually relocate to Mexico was not even discussed.

And so the Mexican employees developed one clear purpose; to make money. Sometimes just to put a few dollars in their pocket so they could cross the border and get a real job. Sometimes to build up cash before heading back to their Mexican hometowns to establish themselves. No one, neither Mexican or American, saw the work as their dream job or as a fulfilling career.

Turnover is the inevitable result when employers who want to pay as little as possible combine with workers who want to make as much as possible. The way the American managers and leaders behaved sent a clear signal about the work culture, and the employees behaved accordingly.

Another powerful influence on culture is cast by the senior team and how they interact with each other. If you want teamwork as a core cultural behavior across the organization, it better happen at the top or you won't achieve it anywhere in the company, even with the best teambuilding workshops.

If two senior executives don't support each other, you can forget about cross-departmental teamwork and cooperation. It was this type of poor leadership shadows that led to the nuclear accident at Three Mile Island and countless other examples of sub-optimal performance inside organizations.

The Stand Up Desks

In the early days of building my international management-consulting firm, I was the senior partner on a consulting project for a new client, the CEO of a large aerospace company in San Diego, California. The firm's history went back to the Ryan Aerospace Company who designed and built the Spirit of St. Louis, in which Charles Lindberg crossed the Atlantic in record time.

The CEO was a keen sportsman but, because of a chronic back

injury, couldn't sit for long periods of time, so he had a stand-up desk in his office, from which he conducted his work. And he often stood up for staff meetings as well.

When I first visited the company to conduct one-on-one interviews with the senior team and selected middle managers, I was struck by a curious thing. Five other executives had stand up desks in their offices. Was there an epidemic of bad backs in the San Diego area?

Again we see the subtle yet powerful impact of leadership on culture. I have also seen the same shadow or influencing phenomenon with cigar smoking among senior executives, or a penchant for fine Bordeaux wines!

Top Heavy

> *Mirror, Mirror on the wall, who casts the biggest shadow of all? ~ apologies to The Wicked Queen, Maleficent*

Several years ago we took a short holiday trip to Stockholm. Gracing the harbor of Stockholm is a museum housing the reconstructed 17th century warship, the 64-gun *Vasa*. Not only is the ship enormous and ornate, but the story of her demise illustrates an excellent principle of the relationship between leadership and culture.

The warship was built on the orders of King Gustavus Adolphus (1594–1632). One of the key requirements by the king was for the ship to be tall and imposing, symbolizing the might of the Swedish armada during the Thirty Years' War (1618–1648). It was arguably the most powerful warship of the time with a combined weight of shot that could be fired from the cannon of one side as 588 pounds (267 kg). However, there were two major design flaws. The ship was definitely top-heavy with a shallow draft, and it had insufficient space for ballast.

Here is where the story gets interesting and instructive. Gustav wanted the ship built quickly so it could support the war and as such he kept pressuring the architects and builders. They knew the ship was top-heavy and couldn't carry enough ballast, but were not willing to confront the king or tell him the bad news; they just kept trying workarounds. Finally the king ordered the ship to sail and just outside the harbor, less than a nautical mile into its maiden voyage, it rolled over and sank after encountering its first strong winds.

To me this illustrates several key business principles directly related to corporate culture. First is a culture in which people are afraid of speaking up or bringing *'bad news'* (otherwise known as the truth) to the leader (CEO or senior executives). When problems are watered down, minimized or hidden, they fester and eventually create even bigger problems. A culture of open and honest communication and celebrating problems is a culture where things get fixed, not swept under the rug.

Second is the principle of balance. As my mentor, Thomas D. Willhite used to say: *"balance is the key to power."* Being top-heavy without adequate ballast is definitely out of balance, with disastrous results. In the case of a leadership team, ballast refers to the key Guiding Business Principles which can help build an aligned culture that supports strategic and business goals. And the top-heavy analogy is pretty clear. If too many decisions are made by senior management then lack of accountability grows among middle management. *"Why should I stick my neck out when senior management is going to make the call anyway?"*

Next time you go sailing, or if you ever visit the Vasa Museum in Stockholm, think about the principles of ballast, balance and corporate cultures. You might be able to avert a disaster.

John R. Childress

Cultural Myopia

> *O would some power the giftie gie us, to see ourselves as others see us.* ~ Robert Burns

When I study and evaluate a company's culture, I usually spend a considerable amount of time observing the behavior, both individually and collectively, of the senior executive team and middle managers. During one-on-one discussions, attending staff meetings and other executive-led meetings I begin to see a pattern emerging. How they deal with poor performers and disappointing business results; how they give assignments; how well they listen to input and ideas from others; how they talk about the company and each other.

Based on the fundamental principle that *'organizations tend to be shadows of their leaders'*, cataloging the habitual ways in which the senior team interacts with employees, customers and suppliers gives a good start in understanding the corporate culture and the influence of leadership on the culture.

I am often asked why it takes an outsider to see the culture? Why can't we do this ourselves and save some time and money?

> *We don't know who first discovered water, but we are certain it wasn't fish!*

Most of us understand the concept of *familiarity blindness*. When we first move into a new house that is underneath the glide path for airplanes heading to the airport, the noise is noticeable and disturbing. But a few weeks later we don't register the noise anymore, it has become a part of the everyday milieu of our home life. It is only when visitors point out the airplane noise that we tend to take notice.

The same concept applies to senior executives (and all employees actually). When they first join the company, the culture and ways of working are very clear to them; more often than not the work behaviors are different and stick out vividly. But after a few months of back-to-back meetings, deadlines and numerous project reviews, they don't see the culture anymore. **They are the culture.**

They have become acculturated and their unconscious behaviors tend to conform, over time, to the norms and behavior standards of the rest of the organization. Many times they conform to the new culture and ways of working because it is easier than trying to change them, and other times it's the need to fit in and not make too many waves. Whatever the conscious or subconscious drivers, over time they become the culture!

It is always a revelation to the senior team when I point out their individual and collective behaviors and their role in establishing and perpetuating the corporate culture.

> *As ye sow, so shall ye reap. ~ St. James Bible, Galatians 6:7*

It Ain't All Leadership's Fault!

> *Someone once asked Slick Willie Sutton, the notorious bank robber, why he robbed banks. The question might have uncovered a tale of injustice and lifelong revenge. Maybe a banker foreclosed on the old homestead, maybe a banker's daughter spurned Sutton for another.*
>
> *Sutton replied: "I rob banks because that's where the money is."*

A great number of culture change gurus and corporate culture consultants tend to focus (and over-focus) on the impact the senior leadership team has on corporate culture. And there are some very interesting reasons for this.

First, the senior team does have an important role in establishing and perpetuating corporate culture (and in some non-obvious ways, as we will see further on in this guidebook). Second, equating the strengths and weaknesses of the company (and by association the corporate culture) with the behavior of the senior leadership team fits nicely with the current business infatuation with charismatic leadership and the perceived importance of 'rock star' leadership teams. And third, that's where the money is! By focusing on the CEO and senior team as the key influencers in culture and culture change, consultants are opening up the vault to more lucrative business down the line. The senior team has the keys to the vault!

As someone who has studied, consulted, coached and written about corporate culture and leadership for the past 35+ years, I do believe the senior leadership team has a significant influence on the corporate culture. In many ways, organizations are shadows of their leaders and the behavior of senior executives can set the tone for the culture going forward.

But the impact of leaders and the senior team on corporate culture is not uniform across time, and this is where the bulk of culture consultants get it wrong! In start-ups and early stage companies, the senior team, including the founder(s), tend to set the *'ground rules'* and even, in some recent instances, create and inculcate the Culture Decks. In small to medium organizations where employees have frequent contact with senior executives, the behavior of the leaders is of great influence in establishing the culture and the ways of working.

But things are vastly different in large or well-established companies. Here the impact of leadership behaviors tend to wane rather dramatically, being replaced by the significant influence of peer pressure, fuelled by the very real human need of employees to fit in with their workgroup and not be seen as an *'outsider'*.

Changing Influences on Corporate Culture

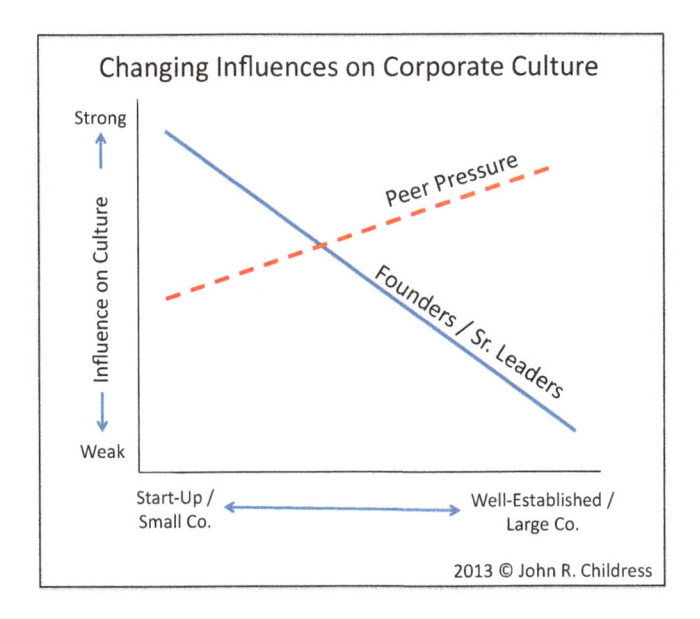

Chart axes: Influence on Culture (Weak to Strong) vs. Start-Up/Small Co. to Well-Established/Large Co. Founders/Sr. Leaders line declines from Strong to Weak; Peer Pressure line rises.

2013 © John R. Childress

This chart, based on experience and observations, describes the falling and rising influence of these two groups on establishing and sustaining corporate culture.

In many writings on corporate culture, the impact of the leader (CEO), and leadership team has been over exaggerated and as a result, many of those looking to understand corporate culture, how it is formed and how it is sustained have missed a very important and powerful cultural lever, peer group pressure!

However, when leaders join up with key employees who are respected by others and are also key influencers, the combination is a powerful catalyst in reshaping or realigning corporate culture.

Leadership as Cultural 'Glue'

Trust is the glue of life. It's the most essential ingredient in effective communication. It's the foundational principle that holds all relationships. ~Stephen Covey

Business leaders who understand the importance of culture realize they have another job, along with all the other demands of leading a business. They have to make a special effort to keep the culture from fragmenting and drifting out of alignment with their business strategies and the needs of employees, customers and the community. If leaders ignore the culture then strong internal and external forces can pull the culture apart.

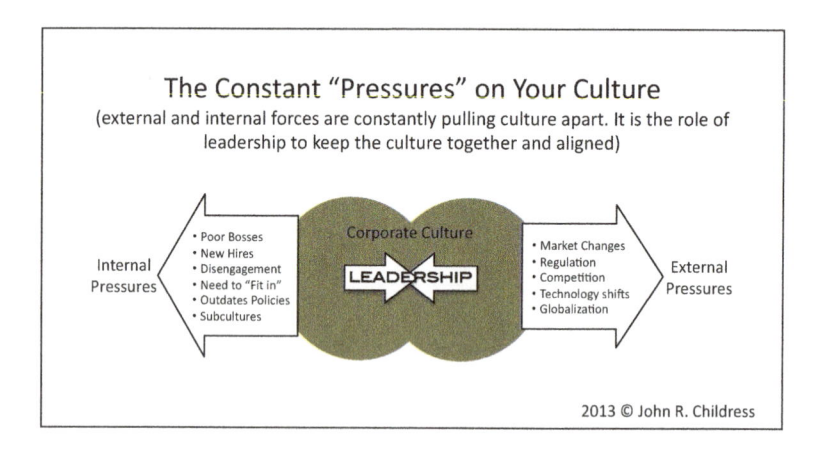

The Constant "Pressures" on Your Culture
(external and internal forces are constantly pulling culture apart. It is the role of leadership to keep the culture together and aligned)

Internal Pressures
- Poor Bosses
- New Hires
- Disengagement
- Need to "Fit in"
- Outdates Policies
- Subcultures

Corporate Culture — LEADERSHIP

External Pressures
- Market Changes
- Regulation
- Competition
- Technology shifts
- Globalization

2013 © John R. Childress

The external pressures of market changes, shifting regulation, growing competition, new technologies and the challenges of globalization are strong and frequently in play. The CEO and business leader needs to foster and lead a continuous dialogue within their organization about the relationship between the external environment and the corporate culture. Everyone needs to understand and be aware of these forces and understand the importance of an adaptive culture. Either we adapt our culture to the external changes by choice and thoughtful maneuvering, or our culture can begin to become a liability instead of an asset for competitive success.

And at the same time, internal pressures are trying to reshape the culture, again often in ways that are not conducive to high performance. Without conscious attention to the forces and demands of subcultures, outdated internal policies and procedures, the influx of new hires from other cultures, weak middle management and other elements leading to employee disengagement, a culture over time can be pulled towards becoming more and more dysfunctional. Again, leadership must actively engage with all levels of the organization in acknowledging and discussing these forces and how important an aligned culture is to everyone for job satisfaction, job security and growth opportunities.

The executives at Johnson & Johnson Company regularly engage in company-wide discussions and debates on the culture and the J&J Credo (the embodiment of their culture) to keep the culture from being pulled off course by internal and external forces. Keeping culture at the forefront of every meeting was a big factor in the return from near bankruptcy of Lycoming Engine Company, whose turnaround was orchestrated by its new General Manager, former Marine helicopter pilot and Harvard MBA, Ian Walsh.

Alan Mulally, the outsider from Boeing who took over as the CEO of Ford Motor Company, made leadership behaviors and culture a standard topic at his weekly executive business review meetings. Up until Mulally arrived the entire focus of the Ford executive group was on costs, market shares and other important financial issues to the point where the Ford culture had been seriously pulled out of alignment with the market and its people.

Some Disturbing News about Culture and Leadership

Not only is the world becoming more complex and more interconnected, it is also becoming more litigious. Most litigation is centered around finding fault and making restitution, and there is a growing trend in business focusing on who's to blame for employee health problems. And the target in the bull's eye is leadership, management behavior, and the corporate culture.

Several recent research studies are beginning to show causal linkages between poor leadership and management behavior and employee distress and illness. More than thirty studies over the last 15 years have clearly shown that leader behaviors do affect employee health.[43] The overall research shows that certain types of behaviors from leaders and bosses can increase heart disease, promote musculoskeletal pain, foster sick leave, increase anxiety and depression, as well as, lead to stress or even burnout. Literally they are implying: *"Your boss can make you sick!"* Positive leader behaviors, on the other hand, can reduce sick leave, increase attendance and reduce anxiety, depression, stress and burnout.

And a whole new field of litigation is opening – lawsuits against *'bad'* bosses and the organizations that negligently allow them to supervise.

And if corporate culture is determined by the repetitive and habitual behaviors of its leadership and employees, then it won't be long before *'toxic'* or *'dysfunctional'* corporate cultures will be cited in more and more employee health lawsuits, just as it has been cited in lawsuits about industrial accidents and poor safety practices.

Case in point. Recently, brokerage firm Merrill Lynch settled a lawsuit for $160 million that claimed the company culture was *'toxic'* for African Americans.[44]

Another good reason to put corporate culture on your business and strategic agenda, now!

Chapter 9: You Get The Culture You Allow

You cannot escape the responsibility of tomorrow by evading it today. ~ Abraham Lincoln

Ignoring Customer Feedback... The Road to Ruin

A few years ago I purchased an HP Officejet Pro 8500A "All-in-one" wireless printer. So many neat capabilities; fax, print in B&W or color, double-sided copying, scan, copy, and best of all, work either through a network cable or Wi-Fi. What's not to love about all of those? And Wi-Fi was the real sales clincher.

All the features worked really well, except the Wi-Fi. It seems that there is a bug in the internal software of these models that when the machine is not used for a little while it goes to sleep, thus dropping the Wi-Fi connection. Okay, sounds reasonable to save energy. But it is supposed to wake up when sent a signal by the computer and get into the act of printing. Only thing is, it doesn't wake up. Nothing.

After an hour of trying to find the problem, I resorted to rebooting both my computer and the printer. It worked. Wi-Fi connection restored and printing successful. Only the next time I wanted to print something over the Wi-Fi, the same time consuming and laborious process was required. Reboot in order to wake up the printer!

Basically, the claim of this being a Wi-Fi printer was false; it didn't work. Now I could very easily have put in an Ethernet cable between computer and printer and go direct, but then the other two computers in my household couldn't print.

Okay, it sounds like I've got a bad machine and need to swap it out for a new one. Things happen during the manufacturing process and not all quality checks are successful. I get that. But after surfing the Internet looking at reviews by users, I found about a gazillion comments on how this HP printer model drops the Wi-Fi connection and doesn't pick it up again. The basic sentiment? These users will never buy another HP printer again!

And, here comes the real interesting part, not one response or comment from HP can be found on the Internet. Total silence. No communication to customers who paid real money to purchase this model on the strength of the offering and the positive brand equity of HP.

> *You don't drown by falling in the water; you drown by staying there. ~ Edwin Louis Cole*

I find the behavior of HP in this case not only appalling, but somewhat sad. And here is the saddest part, HP used to be one of the organizations held up as a role model for its innovative, team oriented and customer attentive corporate culture. And Bill Hewlett and David Packard were examples of great leadership. The founders of HP established a revolutionary corporate culture that actually became the antecedent of many Silicon Valley and technology companies for decades.

The HP Way - an example of corporate culture for a whole industry [45]

From the beginning the two founders of Hewlett-Packard developed a management style which had never occurred in a large company before. They coined a new type of corporate culture, "*the HP Way*."

HP renounced the traditional 'hire and fire' mentality, which meant to employ many workers for a single big order and to dismiss them afterwards. Instead, the company offered its employees job security. Even in 1974, when the U.S. economy was in a profound crisis and many people were unemployed, HP avoided layoffs with a four-day workweek, which was a unique measure in corporate America.

The two founders trusted in the individual's own motivation to work and treated their employees as family members; hence the custom to call each other by the first name - even the two chiefs were only known as Bill and Dave.

The HP workers participated in the company with stock options and were even paid additional premiums when HP was successful - today known as profit sharing. These measures served to identify the employees with their work and to encourage them. Moreover, the HP way included extensive employment benefits such as scholarships for the employee's children.

At the end of the 1950s Bill and Dave decided to write down the company's objectives, which were to serve as guidelines for all decision-making by HP people, since the company had grown ever larger. They cover as follows: Profit, Customers, Fields of Interest, Growth, Our People,

> Management, and Citizenship. And these objectives were to be achieved through teamwork.
>
> The HP Way continues to be seen as model for (a strong and aligned) corporate culture in many countries. The roots of many subsequent companies are located in HP, e.g. Steve Wozniak, who worked at HP and later co-founded Apple. HP pioneered the establishment of a new corporate culture in Silicon Valley and many firms have tried to imitate the HP way and adopted measures such as stock options, innovative work rules, teamwork, and profit sharing.

But HP is now, and has been for some years, in turnaround mode, and the Wall Street jury is still uncertain whether the sentiment is Hold or Sell. But it's definitely not Buy.

And hiring three high-profile CEOS in a row, Carly Fiorina, Marc Hurd and Meg Whitman, isn't the answer. The answer doesn't lie in a grand new strategy or balance sheet magic. The answer lies in listening and responding to the customer, fixing issues, openly acknowledging problems and making them right, treating employees with respect and dignity. Getting the culture right is the real opportunity for the future success of HP. And it's nearly impossible to revive a culture without leaders who are passionately committed to an enduring set of core cultural principles and behaviors (values if you like) of *'how we will work together and treat customers.'* The lessons contained in the original *'HP Way'* would be a good start.

That's not new technology. That's not M&A. That's not dancing to Wall Street's short-term, maximize quarterly earnings tune. That's not the sexy part. That's not frontpage news. That's not Davos invitation material. No, that's just good business conducted by good management and engaged employees under the thoughtful eye of good leadership, based on a set of non-negotiable behaviors. That's what a strong corporate culture is all about.

LEVERAGE:

When HP decides to abandon the quest for charismatic and high-profile executives and gets back to the business of shaping a culture that is committed to fulfilling customer promises and making things that work like they are supposed to, the stock and fortunes of a once great brand will begin to recover.

What's so hard about fixing a Wi-Fi problem in a very popular printer?

> *The measure of success is not whether you have a tough problem to deal with, but whether it is the same problem you had last year. ~ John Foster Dulles*

The Coachable Moment

When I started out in business in 1975, Hewlett-Packard was one of the top brands and was also lauded for its strong corporate culture. Today it's on the verge of irrelevance. It's the little things that eventually make the biggest difference. A strong and aligned corporate culture is a collection of many little things, all focused on one or two overriding objectives. With HP it used to be engineering excellence and customer satisfaction. Not any more.

How did HP loose its way? I have a theory.

And it is one of the key lessons a CEO must internalize in order to build and/or sustain the corporate culture required to survive and thrive.

> *Most corporate disasters are crimes of ambivalence, not crimes of passion.*

One method by which business leaders, executives and managers influence corporate culture, either positively or negatively, is subtle and often goes unnoticed. It's called *'the coachable moment.'*

John R. Childress

Funny thing about the word leadership, it has the word '*lead*' right at the beginning. Leaders are supposed to lead and there is no leading without fully engaging with others; peers, direct reports, bosses, and everyone else who works inside your organization, as well as external stakeholders. Leadership is a contact sport! Avoiding leadership responsibilities when it comes to building, sustaining and shaping corporate culture is akin to handing out free passes for a jailbreak!

A coachable moment is as follows:

> a company VP passes the open door of a manager's office. Inside several managers and staff are gathered. She overhears the following: *"I'm really upset. Those morons in Purchasing have messed up my customer order again. They just don't care down there. Next time they want help from me they can just forget it!"*

This is definitely a coachable moment. Choice time. She is late for a meeting called by her boss. She has a million things to do today. It's not even her department.

No suspense about the outcome. What really happens is easy to predict with a high degree of certainty.

She walks on past, muttering under her breath about the lack of accountability, poor teamwork and making a mental note to talk to her peer who manages that department (which she never does, of course, because the pressures of day-to-day work crowd out the good intentions, and besides, he's not very open about criticism of his area).

> *The hardest thing to explain is the glaringly evident which everybody has decided not to see. ~ Ayn Rand*

Most leaders and managers will intervene in cases of truly bad behavior, but when it comes to conversations or behaviors that don't fit the culture, they hesitate and more often than not don't take the opportunity of the *'coachable moment.'* Oh, they will grumble about such poor behavior, usually to their peers, but rarely will they take a stand, talk to the person, explain that such behavior or attitudes are not useful or helpful in this company and ask if there is a reason they are behaving that way? More often than not such a firm and direct dialogue uncovers some level of frustration, either personal or about the company. An issue that needs attention.

Complaining about attitudes and behavior is not leadership, taking a stand on behalf of the few non-negotiable behaviors that define the company culture is one of the most important roles of leadership. Most executives fail the test, and the culture drifts towards more and more unproductive behaviors by employees.

Leadership is not a title or position, it is a set of behaviors!

How many *'coachable moments'* have you walked right by? Does your management team understand it is their job to engage and redirect behaviors?

And you think coachable moments are few and far between? Here is statistic from the 2013 Deloitte Core Beliefs & Culture survey of over 1000 employees and 300 executives [46]. Basically (and on this they agree) both executives (81%) and employees (86%) believe that declared cultural behaviors are not upheld inside their organizations. That means to me a significant number of behaviors and actions not in alignment with the desired culture are either ignored or tolerated.

You get the culture you tolerate! You reinforce the behaviors you ignore. You build the culture you want through engaging in *'coachable moments'*. And building and sustaining a culture is everyone's job!

The Blackberry Backstory

I admit it! I was addicted to my Blackberry. What a great little device that was. I remember when they first came out; a business revolution was born. Instant messaging and emails on the road, anytime, 24/7. As a result, my business life got another notch faster, but a whole lot easier and more responsive as well. And in 2003, the Blackberry Smartphone was released with push email, mobile telephone, text messaging, Internet faxing, Web browsing, a camera and other wireless information services. Almost overnight Blackberry owned the business market and made significant inroads into the personal market as well. Many of my colleagues had two devices, one for work and one personal. The Personal Digital Assistant (PDA) market was owned by Blackberry.

Fast forward just 10 years and Blackberry is a failed company. In early September 2013, Blackberry announced it would eliminate 4500 positions, 40% of its operating staff, and reduce its product line from six to four models.[47] At its trading high in 2008, shares were close to $150. The stock price chart looks like the 'Death Drop' roller coaster of my childhood; dramatic climb and rapid plummet.

The Blackberry post-mortem will go on for quite a while and I predict the rise and fall of Blackberry Ltd. will become a favorite B-school case study for many years. But recently I ran across the hint of an interesting backstory [48], which details a *'leadership culture'* of senior executive infighting, the resignation of the former co-CEO in protest, and angry boardroom clashes over strategy and product decisions. Lack of alignment at the very top can have a profound impact on performance, especially when strategic decisions are concerned.

Culture and Cynicism

> *Cynicism masquerades as wisdom, but it is the farthest thing from it. Because cynics don't learn anything. Because cynicism is a self-imposed blindness, a rejection of the world because we are afraid it will hurt us or disappoint us. ~ Stephen Colbert*

On almost every executive team I have worked with over the past 35 years there seems to be at least one hard-core cynic. We all recognize the cynic: the person who is not only a pessimist about new ideas, but also has the ability to discount other people's success and good fortune. There are many definitions of cynicism:

- A person who believes all people are motivated by selfishness
- A person whose outlook is scornfully and often habitually negative

Most of us don't enjoy being around the cynic for very long and they definitely aren't inspiring and motivating. I've never found cynicism on the list of the behaviors that define leadership. There are numerous popular books on leadership, such as *Leadership Lessons from Genghis Khan*, *The 21 Irrefutable Laws of Leadership*, *Leadership Lessons from the Navy Seals*, *Leadership Lessons from the Godfather* and so on. But I've never seen: *Leadership Lessons from Cynics*!

So, I have a question. How do cynics get into senior management in the first place, and why are they often tolerated by others on the team? And how does a cynic on the senior team impact the culture?

Mostly I have to fault the CEO for allowing cynics to rise up into senior management.

Let's start with those who promote the cynic in the first place. One of the reasons the cynic gets promoted is because most managers believe that technical skills or business acumen are the most important criteria for promotion. Behavioral traits seem to be far down the list. Yet it is often the behavior of the cynic that does more damage than can be compensated for by their technical or business skills. For example, they are often the worst at developing young talent, either technical or managerial. They are also poor team builders, believing that good work is all that matters and all that motivational '*kumbayah*' stuff is simply new age rubbish.

And then there is the belief, erroneous in my view, that the cynic is much like the devil's advocate and their presence is necessary to help overcome group think and to bring in different points of view. A big difference between the devil's advocate and the cynic is that the former brings up alternative ideas and other points of view that actually help expand the thinking about the problem or situation. The cynic, on the other hand, offers no advice or useable ideas, instead being content with contempt!

Another major culprit in why cynics are allowed into senior management ranks is corporate culture. Many cultures are weak and lack clear and meaningful behavior guidelines or guiding principles. Such weak cultures tolerate cynics because no one has the courage nor the mandate to confront them and their negative behavior.

Too often cultures have informal rules such as:

- *don't critique others, they might start in on you,*
- *it's not your job to coach or comment on the behavior of peers,*
- *those who point out bad behavior aren't part of the team but just trying to get ahead.*

Cultures that allow unproductive behaviors to go unchecked rarely deliver high performance. When you find a company with a sick or weak culture posting excellent results, you can bet it's more about a favorable economy than great leadership.

For those CEOs with the commitment and courage to confront and ultimately remove the cynics from the organization, a clear signal is sent far and wide that negative and cynical behavior will not be tolerated. Professionalism, yes; cynicism, no!

And what about the cynic themselves? What is behind this destructive behavior? The following quote seems to ring true for me in my dealings with teams and cynics.

> *Inside every cynic there lies a wounded romantic.*
> *~ Glenn Beck*

Toxic Behaviors, Vampires and Corporate Culture

One of the most common ways that CEOs and senior executives inadvertently create a culture that inhibits high performance is by ignoring toxic behaviors in favor of business results! On numerous occasions I have had long drawn out conversations with a CEO about an individual senior executive and his toxic behaviors with employees and customers. More often than not the CEO will shake his head, acknowledge that the individual's behavior even bothers him, but then is quick to add: *"But he consistently delivers results to the bottom line, and besides, this is a business, not a country club."*

Only when this type of behavior finally begins to drive away customers or talented employees will most CEOs become concerned and begin to get involved. Most of the time it is too little too late as the early *'coachable moments'* have long passed and the toxic behavior has ossified over time.

> *The toxic impact of countercultural senior executives is not a big bang affair, it's more akin to death by a thousand cuts. The company culture slowly dies before your eyes and the good people exit quietly. ~ Aerospace CEO*

155

Such tolerance of toxic behavior in favor of results most often stems from beliefs about business and people, ingrained in many of us, that results trump behavior and that it is really an either-or choice; good behavior or good results. Exploring this deeper tends to unearth other connected beliefs, like *'good results have to be driven hard'* and *'it's important for someone to be the bad guy to keep others from slacking off.'* Whatever the internal belief system operating, the fact is, toxic behaviors toward employees and customers is eventually toxic to business results!

Most of those who believe in using such toxic behavior are open to coaching and changing their behavior, if approached early in their tenure with the company during *'coachable moments.'* And it is imperative upon the CEO when hiring a new senior executive to be clear during the interview process and even clearer during on-boarding and orientation, about which leadership behaviors are acceptable and which are not. As we will see later in the chapter dealing with culture change, a small number of 'non-negotiable' behaviors relentlessly managed have a dramatic and rapid impact on shaping and aligning corporate culture.

In a recent HBR blog article by Eric C. Sinoway, *When to Fire a Top Performer Who Hurts Your Company Culture,* the author and his partner describe a way to begin to think about toxic behaviors in relation to management staff (Sinoway, 2012). It's a simple 4-box model with "delivers results" on one axis and "behavior aligned with desired culture" on he other. This model seems to be similar to one developed by Jack Welch during his time as the CEO of General Electric and is also used by the Ken Blanchard Company, a well-known leadership training company.

- **Stars** are the employees who perform well and do so in a manner that supports and builds the desired organizational culture.

- **High potentials** are those whose behavior matches the culture but whose skills need further development and maturation. With training, time, and support, these people could move closer and closer to the Star quadrant.

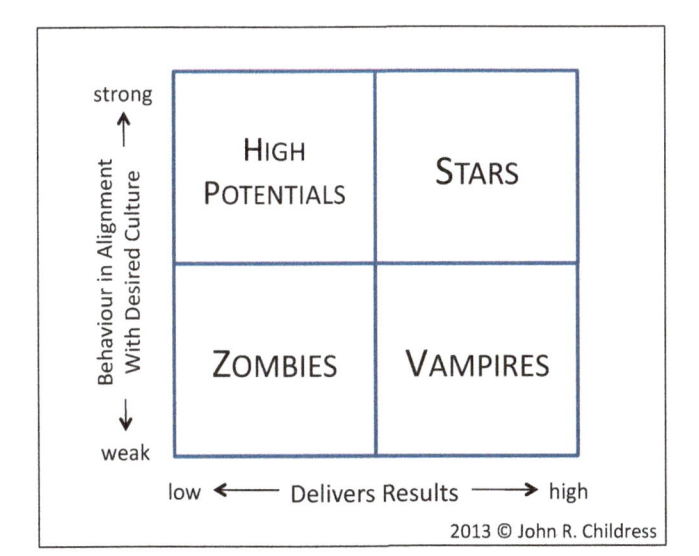

	low ← Delivers Results → high
strong (Behaviour in Alignment With Desired Culture)	HIGH POTENTIALS | STARS
weak	ZOMBIES | VAMPIRES

2013 © John R. Childress

- **Zombies** fail on all dimensions. Their behavior doesn't align with the desired culture and performance is average at best. Many cultures refer to these as '*dead wood.*' What is interesting about Zombies is that they actually do little business harm since they lack internal credibility, but when they are tolerated by management their presence tends to signal that the culture is more about longevity and loyalty than excellence.

- **Vampires** get business results, they deliver, but with behavior that is not in alignment with the desired culture. They have influence, and often become informal role models, especially if they are praised and promoted. But Vampires do the most damage to the development and sustainment of a high performance culture by showing that the cultural values are meaningless and not nearly as important as bottom line results and *'making your numbers.'*

Thinking about your direct reports and key staff using this model (or the Jack Welch version) starts the process of looking at leadership through the dual lens of both performance and culture.

> *If you aren't fired with enthusiasm, you will be fired with enthusiasm. ~Vince Lombardi*

Section Four: Strategy and Corporate Culture

We tend to think we can separate strategy from culture, but we fail to notice that in most organizations strategic thinking is deeply colored by tacit assumptions about who they are and what their mission is. ~ Edgar Schein

Recently *Fast Company* magazine published an article by Shaun Parr entitled *Culture Eats Strategy for Lunch.* The article, quoting the phenomenal success of such companies as Zappos.com, Starbucks, Whole Foods and a host of others was intended to be a vindication of corporate culture, taking it out of the realm of '*soft issues*' and the backwaters of HR and thrusting it to the top position of the ingredients for sustainable business success.

While the author does cite some very good examples from cult-like cultures, he thoroughly and naively misses the point about the relationship between corporate culture, strategy and strategy execution. That's not surprising, however, since most people don't really understand culture beyond what they observe through surveys and anecdotal observations of behavior. *"This company has a culture problem and a lack of accountability"* or *"That company has a win-lose culture."* Descriptive and colorful, but not very helpful.

There are two fundamental points that are important in understanding the relationship between culture and strategy. And it is a very tight relationship, since they are mutually inclusive when it comes to the overall performance of a business.

First, a great strategy without a supportive culture is doomed to struggle with execution and more often fails miserably. Second, even the best corporate culture cannot make up for an uncompetitive strategy. Both are vital for sustained competitive performance, yet they are not one and the same.

> *Strategy tells us how to get from A to B and culture determines how we behave during this journey.*

This is a bit like the relationship between horse and carriage; you can't have a functional mode of multi-person transportation without both. In the case of the relationship between culture and strategy, it's 1 + 1 = 3.

However, while they are both required elements for business success, they are not equally on par with each other. For long-term sustainability of the business, especially with major changes happening at an ever-increasing rate (global markets, technology advances, customer preferences, regulation, growing competition), of the two, culture is the more important in the long term. A good example is Apple, which has had many different strategies over the years but one overriding sustaining culture.

Instead of culture eats strategy for breakfast, we should be saying:

> *a high-performance culture aligned with the appropriate strategy for the marketplace are the key ingredients in the breakfast of champions.*

Chapter 10: Culture and Strategy: Paper, Rock, Scissors

The important thing is not having a strategy, it's getting it implemented ~ Jack Welch

One of the games we used to play as children was paper, rock and scissors. It's a game of whose choice overrides the others'. Basically, both players make a fist, count to three and then make the appropriate pattern with their hand. Paper covers rock, but scissors cut paper, and rock breaks scissors. One out of two chances to win the round (both having the same choice is a tie). A fun way to occupy time on a boring road trip with parents and an equally good way to *'psych-out'* my little sister by telling her I could read her mind!

The point of this little game is to win by adapting your strategy to keep your partner off balance and at the same time to be one step ahead of their decisions. Beginning to sound like competitive strategy doesn't it?

Sticking with the same strategy in the paper, rock and scissors game is a design to lose, just as a rigid, non-adaptive corporate

The CEO's Lament: Execution, Execution, Execution

All businesses require a strategy. In essence, a strategy is a defined set of actions to achieve success against competition. To be effective, the strategy needs to be forward thinking, based on deep insights into opportunities and capabilities, and a product of clear thinking, honest assessments and effective decision-making. **But most importantly, to be effective the strategy must be executed in a way that achieves the desired results.**

Unfortunately, the statistics on effective strategy execution are universally dismal. The fact is most companies have a poor track record of strategy execution:

- In an article by Mark Nadler, he cites a 2004 survey of 276 senior operating executives by *The Economist* found that 57% of the companies had been unsuccessful in executing on strategic initiatives over the previous three years.[49]

- In a 2006 survey of more than 1,500 executives by the American Management Association and the Human Resource Institute, only 3% of respondents rated their companies as very successful at executing corporate strategies, while 62% described their organizations as mediocre or worse.[50]

- In a recent survey of 200 FTSE 1000 companies, 80% of directors said they had the right strategy, but only 14% thought they were implementing them well.[51]

- A survey of 400 companies found that 49% of the leaders reported a gap between their organization's ability to formulate a strategy and its ability to deliver results. Shockingly, only 36% of leaders who thought their company had an execution gap had confidence in their organization's ability to close the gap.[52]

- In a recent *McKinsey Quarterly* survey of 2,207 executives, only 28% said that the quality of strategic decisions in their companies was generally good, 60% thought that bad decisions were about as frequent as good ones, and the remaining 12% thought good decisions were altogether infrequent.[53]

- In another McKinsey & Co study of 197 companies, despite 97% of directors believing they had the right "strategic vision", only 33% reported achieving "significant strategic success."[54]
- 70% of CEOs who get fired do so not because of bad strategy, but because of poor execution.[55]

In a recently published book, *FASTBREAK, The CEO's Guide to Strategy Execution*, I discussed the major, invisible factors that cause poor strategy execution, beyond the obvious lack of funding and misreading the marketplace. As you can see from the list below, many of these barriers to execution have a significant element of corporate culture in them (Childress, 2012):

- Execution is usually an afterthought rather than an integral part of strategy formulation.
- Lack of clearly defined accountability for strategic initiatives and overall objectives.
- Poor alignment at the top and heavy silo focus leads to sub-optimization and resource conflicts, wasting valuable management time.
- Many initiatives are not directly linked to key strategic objectives. Too often we see *'pet'* projects buried inside departments, thus wasting resources on *'Disconnected Initiatives'*.
- Less than 14% of employees have seen or understand the strategy.[56] Without understanding of the company strategy, employee engagement and new ideas for improvement are limited.

- Teamwork, openness, risk tolerance and innovation are required for effective strategy delivery.

- Disciplined governance of strategic initiatives is notoriously lacking and day-to-day operations problems often hijack the attention of the senior team away from strategic issues. Recent studies have shown that less than 5% of the senior team's time is spent on strategic issues. [57]

- Too often the strategy is developed by an outside consulting firm (after interviewing executives, of course), delivered to management in a dazzling presentation and a thick deck of slides, but with little real 'ownership' by those left behind to implement it. Commitment is lacking from the beginning and only diminishes as difficulties are encountered.

Cultural 'Adaptability'

> *A corporation's culture can be its greatest strength when it is consistent with its strategies. But a culture that prevents a company from meeting competitive threats, or from adapting to changing economic or social environments, can lead to the company's stagnation and ultimate demise.* ~ Business Week

The relationship between culture and the ability of an organization to execute a new business strategy is more easy to see with the understanding that **Strategy – Structure – Culture** are interlinked and for top performance, these three critical business elements must be in alignment.

When an organization is aligned both internally and with its marketplace, *"everyone knows where we are going"* (strategy), *"it's clear who does what in the organization"* (structure), and *"we all understand the ground rules for working together and for getting things done"* (culture).

In less turbulent times when the pace of change was slower, organizations were able to gain substantial alignment between these three critical elements and as a result produced efficient performance and long-term growth. The post-war years (WWII) in the US represented such a time of relative stability, predictable growth, growing markets in most sectors, optimism for lending, and favorable regulation supporting business.

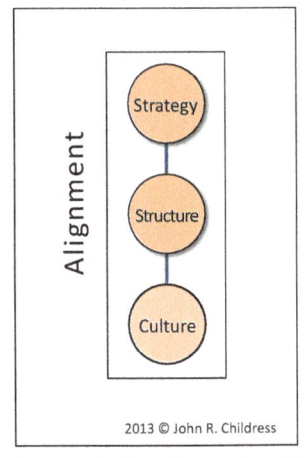

During this time, between 1950 and 1980 the relative stability allowed many businesses the luxury of gaining alignment between strategy, structure and culture. The Bell Telephone System expanded, IBM grew to be one of the largest companies and a Wall Street bellwether, the Big 3 US automakers achieved global dominance, and nuclear power plants sprung up. Everything worked, and everybody was working.

However, with the explosion of technology, rapid globalization, aggressive new competition and shifting regulation, companies are often forced to develop and implement a new competitive strategy. Along with a shift in strategy comes the need to reorganize (new structure) in order to line up the organization with the new strategy.

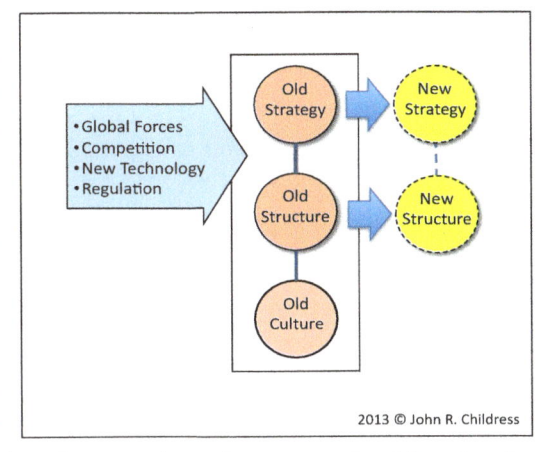

The problem is, that's as far as most senior teams take it; thinking that improved performance should naturally follow. Because most CEOs and senior executives are often insulated from the real culture(s) within their organization, it becomes difficult to see the link between culture and performance. It also becomes difficult to see when the existing culture is no longer aligned with the demands of a new business strategy.

Unless there is work done to reshape corporate culture, the old culture can act as an anchor, slowing down and in some cases even stopping effective strategy execution.

A good example of culture hindering the execution of a new strategy is the attempt of the venerable retail brand, J.C. Penney, to implement a new strategy to capture the younger, hipper, cash rich youth market segment. Other examples abound.

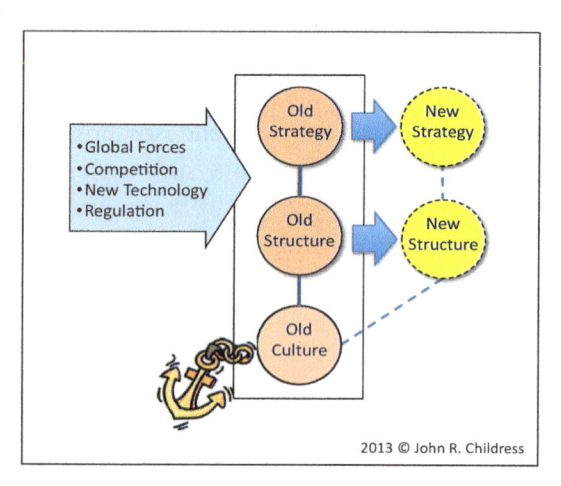

If you spend as much time on corporate culture as you do on the balance sheet, you will run a very successful organization.

Strategy, Innovation and Adaptive Cultures

Another great business insight about culture and strategy to come out of the minds at Harvard Business School is the work done over the past 20 years by Dr. Clayton Christensen and his colleagues. Clayton Christensen is the Kim B. Clark Professor of Business

Administration at Harvard Business School and is widely regarded as one of the world's foremost experts on innovation and growth.

Christensen is the bestselling author of a number of books: his classic work, *The Innovator's Dilemma* (1997) received the Global Business Book Award for the best business book of the year; *The Innovator's Solution* (2003); *Seeing What's Next* (2004); *The Innovator's Prescription* (2009) examines how to fix the US healthcare system; and *The Innovators' DNA* (2011). In 2011 Dr. Christensen was named as the World's Most Influential Management Thinker.

I doubt if there are many CEOs in the world who haven't read about Clayton Christensen's seminal study on disruptive strategies and the growth of Nucor specialty steel mills. Basically, the steel industry was for a long time dominated by big mills which kept acquiring other mills under the strategy that size increased efficiency of scale, helped reduce product costs and increased competitiveness. This was the standard *'wisdom'* in the steel industry. Problem was, to achieve these efficiencies they systematically abandoned specialty steels as being too low volume and too expensive to produce.

Seeing that small could be profitable with the right market and with the right culture, Nucor began turning out the specialty steel the market required but weren't available to buy from the big steel makers any more. As they grew and became more profitable at the lower end of the market, Nucor then began making other steels that the big mills were dropping in their search for efficiency of scale. In a few decades, NUCOR became one of the largest steel producers in North America, equal is size to US Steel, but much more profitable.

What's even more interesting about the success of Nucor is the role played by its own unique corporate culture. The Nucor Culture[58] has five core elements:

- decentralized management philosophy,
- performance based compensation,
- egalitarian benefits,
- customer service and quality,
- technological leadership.

Underlying these elements is the fact that none of Nucor's plants, whether built from scratch or acquired, are unionized. The company has never laid off an employee due to a work shortage.

Basic message? The Nucor culture was adaptable, the US Steel culture rigid and controlling in its policies and treatment of people. Without an adaptable culture, shifts in strategy are difficult to execute. Think of culture as a giant magnetic force, either holding you back or drawing you forward! As I reread the original work of Kotter and Hazlett in their book, *Corporate Culture and Performance,* I am amazed at the prescience and insight of these two professors to talk about adaptive and non-adaptive cultures nearly 20 years ago.

Chapter 11: Good Culture, Bad Culture

When I'm good, I'm very good, but when I'm bad, I'm better.
~ Mae West

A culture isn't good or bad in and of itself. Cultures develop by design or default, as we have seen earlier in this guidebook, based on numerous causal factors. When people say this company has a *'bad'* culture or that company has a *'good'* culture, they are usually describing the culture in relation to something else. Perhaps it is in relation to employee engagement or overall morale. This is the common connotation used when most people talk about good or bad cultures. But for the CEO and the success and sustainability of the company, another important comparison is between the culture and the business strategy.

Corporate culture either supports and empowers the strategy, or acts as a barrier. While strategy determines the direction the company takes across the competitive landscape, culture supplies both the fuel and the constraints. A culture well aligned with the strategy provides alignment between actions and objectives and offers little constraint. A culture aligned with the strategy can, in most cases, provide significant leverage for effective strategy execution. A culture out of alignment with the strategy adds multiple constraints and significantly slows down the process of strategy execution.

A strategy can only be effectively deployed if the culture supports it. And yet a strong culture will not make up for a weak strategy. *"They may be aligned, but they're headed in the wrong direction!"*

Southwest Airlines is a classic example of an effective, and designed, relationship between strategy and culture. Southwest turns a plane (the time elapsed from parking to unloading, loading, and pushing back) faster than any other airline, a product of a culture designed with the customer in mind, as well as the bottom line. They delight passengers and they make money, every quarter for the past 40 years! The combination of a high-performance, customer-focused culture in conjunction with a focused business strategy of point-to-point destinations and only one type of aircraft is simple, focused and profitable.

More often than not the difference between a '*good*' culture and a '*bad*' culture is visible in where executives spend their time, focus and energies. At the two extremes are internally (process) focused cultures and externally (customer) focused. Southwest is a good example of a customer focused culture. Most other big US airlines are more internally focused, with a myriad of rules and schemes to get more passenger dollars. Even the common phrase in the airline industry, '*bums on seats*', says a great deal about the culture. Many dysfunctional cultures spend far more time on internal meetings and internal process than on listening to and satisfying the customer.

The Culture – Strategy Matrix

A useful way to characterize the important relationship between culture and strategy is on a Culture-Strategy matrix. With one axis measuring strategy from weak and unfocused to robust and competitive, and another axis measuring culture from toxic to cult-like, a simple 4-box matrix can be developed.

Having a Good Time Going Broke: An organization with a high-performance or cult-like culture, yet a weak and unfocused strategy in relation to its marketplace is usually not sustainable.

A good example of organizations in this lower right quadrant are the Dot.com failures of the late 1990s and also many of the current technology-driven start ups.

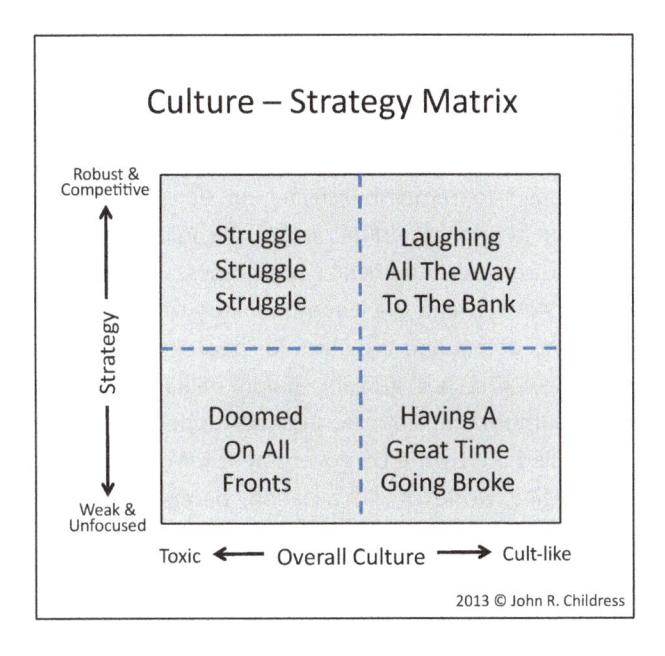

Culture – Strategy Matrix

	Toxic ← Overall Culture → Cult-like
Robust & Competitive (Strategy ↑)	Struggle Struggle Struggle | Laughing All The Way To The Bank
Weak & Unfocused (Strategy ↓)	Doomed On All Fronts | Having A Great Time Going Broke

2013 © John R. Childress

They make a big splash, raise lots of money, build a strong cult-like culture, produce lots of positive PR in the early days, then quickly go out of business, often by burning through their cash without bringing in adequate revenue. In this case, the strategy is usually more focused on the product or the technology than the customer or marketplace dynamics. They have a good time and wonder why they failed!

Doomed on all Fronts: Organizations in the lower left quadrant, with toxic and dysfunctional cultures and weak, unfocused strategies are doomed on all fronts and usually either go bankrupt or are acquired, but not without damaging the lives of many employees along the way and disappointing shareholders. Many such examples can be seen over the past several decades.

Both Kodak and Polaroid developed hugely bureaucratic, inward facing cultures and rigid strategies that focused more on internal operations than changing technologies or shifting customer preferences. Bethlehem Steel, Kaiser Steel and US Steel are examples where toxic cultures fostered militant unions and poor productivity, along with a weak strategy based on commodity costing and economies of scale.

I am old enough to remember flying on Pan American World Airways, the first global airline and an iconic symbol of the expanding power of American businesses. Known as the *'businessman's airline'* and the leader in luxury travel, Pan Am flew everywhere and dominated the skies for decades with the largest fleet of jumbo 747s. But growing union militancy and policies fueled by an authoritarian culture, an underfunded pension liability (eventually bailed out by the US government for over $800 million) and the changing world of globalization, deregulation and anti-American sentiment spelled doom for Pan Am.

These organizations didn't start out with the intention of being doomed, but through poor leadership and unrealistic views about their strategic capabilities and the marketplace, over time they drifted into the *'doomed'* quadrant.

LEVERAGE:

Struggle, Struggle, Struggle: Most organizations seem to struggle to remain competitive and profitable, and wind up in the upper left quadrant having a robust and competitive strategy but a mostly dysfunctional culture characterized by high stress, long hours, endless time in meetings, poor hiring and costly turnover, significant rework, mediocre quality, poor employee engagement and average productivity. In these cases, leadership is more focused on the P&L than culture and fails to realize the significant drag a dysfunctional culture can have on business performance.

In an effort to improve performance, they resort to hiring high flyers from the outside in the hope of finding a superstar rainmaker, go on the hunt for acquisitions to bolster the balance sheet and add revenue growth, and diversify into other markets in the hunt for improved results. It's like a speed boat with plenty of gas and a calm sea, but dragging the anchor. Lots of noise and excitement, but slow progress. Many times I have sat in the CEO's office and heard the same words: *"I don't understand why we can't seem to gain traction!"* To paraphrase a famous quote during the Clinton Presidential era; *"It's the culture, stupid!"*

All The Way to the Bank: Those few organizations in the upper right quadrant have both a robust and focused competitive strategy plus a high-performance culture. They are firing on all cylinders. Many of the organizations detailed in the Collins and Porras book *Built to Last* fall squarely into this quadrant.

The 18 companies profiled in *Built to Last* all met a stringent set of requirements: a premier institution in its industry, widely admired by knowledgeable business people, made an imprint on the world, had multiple generations of CEOs, had multiple product/service life cycles, and were all founded before 1950. The likes of Walmart, American Express, Boeing, Disney, Ford, General Electric, Johnson & Johnson, Marriott and Nordstrom populate the list. The full 18 companies, over the period from 1926-1990, outperformed the stock market by 15 times. All the way to the bank!

While few on this list can be described as having a cult-like culture, with the exception of Disney and perhaps Nordstrom, all have strong and highly functional cultures. You might argue that some, like GE, are tough cultures with clear non-negotiable behaviors and an in-or-out policy when it comes to performance, but they also are clearly tops at developing executives and leadership. And while employee engagement may not be cult-like in every case, these are not the typical layoff and rehire types of companies, and productivity is traditionally high.

For those with cult-like cultures, lululemon athletica, Netflix, Southwest Airlines, Facebook, Apple, Google, Starbucks, their performance in the marketplace rests squarely on the close relationship between strategy and culture, and how their culture allows them to do things, like change quickly to adapt to market trends, that less functional cultures don't.

> *It's hard work focusing on both strategy and culture at the same time, yet that's what is required for sustainable success.*

The Case Where Strategy Eats Culture!

> *You're not getting a refund so p**s off. We don't want to hear your sob stories. What part of 'no refund' don't you understand? ~ Michael O'Leary, CEO Ryanair*

Ryanair was the undisputed king of Ultra Low Cost (ULLC) airline travel in Europe, flying more international passengers that any other airline. Ever since the current CEO, Michael O'Leary took over in 1990 and adopted the single aircraft, point to point, no frills strategy based on his visits to Southwest Airlines, Ryanair has been profitable every year and passenger miles and total revenue have grown steadily (except for the global economic crash in 2008).

However, Ryanair departs from the Southwest Airlines model in two fundamental ways.

First is the relentless focus on cost cutting (to keep reducing fares) and the pushing of ancillary revenue based on in-flight sales (phone cards, train passes, duty free shopping, in-flight meals, rental car reservations), plus charging for passenger extras, such as luggage, additional charges for oversized or overweight luggage, charging for ticket printing (if you failed to print your online eTicket), charging for early boarding and seat selection. According to O'Leary, a significant amount of revenue can be generated from these extras, a bit like the Las Vegas casino hotel strategy, where hotel room rates are minimal but customers spend money at the gaming tables, go to shows and have elaborate dinners, bringing in additional high-margin revenue.

The second departure from the Southwest Airlines successful formula is its culture of *'no customer service'*. In general, passengers hate Ryanair and the way they are treated by staff and gouged for extras. Forget to print your boarding card at home? £60 charge! Charging £50 extra for a bag that was 1 millimeter too large! Flight attendants who chat to each other about their dates and relationships all through the flight while virtually ignoring passengers, and charging outrageous prices for plastic wrapped sandwiches.

> *You are not a fee paying passenger; you are cattle in a box car being shipped to the slaughter house! ~ an angry Ryanair passenger*

Trolling the Internet will reveal dozens of websites set up for people who hate Ryanair and their stories of abuse and poor customer service are tragic.

The airline people love to hate, yet they still fly it! Why?

O'Reilly admits that the culture of *'indifferent'* customer treatment comes directly from him and his cost cutting, no frills attitude towards everything. He even refuses to purchase ballpoint pens for the office staff, insisting that they pocket them from hotels and other places that give away free pens. In his mind, an ultra low-cost ticket price means no frills or niceties. Take it or leave it. And it seems that for students and families on a budget holiday, the ultra low prices are worth the abuse.

Here we have an example where a culture of poor or indifferent customer service, fostered by internal policies, is perfectly aligned with an ultra low cost strategic business model that works for a significant segment of the travelling public. People will put up with a *'crappy experience'* when the price is right, and the flight not too long!

Enter the Ultra Low Cost Competition

Another ultra low cost European airline using the Southwest Airlines model is Easyjet. Founded in 1995 by Stelios Haji-Ioannou, son of a Greek shipping magnate, he also made the pilgrimage to Texas to learn from Southwest Airlines. While Easyjet's main strategy is low cost, single point routes, one type aircraft, and selling ancillary services, Stelios believed in finding a way to balance low cost, no frills and still provide compelling customer service. Their staff are well trained in their own training academy, they spend money on branding and have developed policies focusing on being able to give excellent service to customers, while in the back ground continuing a relentless drive for cost reductions and therefore fare reductions.

Compared to Ryanair, a vast majority of European passengers prefer the Easyjet experience of travel. In almost every customer service category voted by passengers, Easyjet trumps Ryanair, even though Ryanair ranks first in on-time take offs and landings, and other airline industry customer service metrics.

Here is a quote from one Internet airline comparison website:

> *I have experienced Ryanair's flights twice, once without the family and was shocked to see people running for seats and barging people out of the way to climb the stairs, the second time with the family and all 5 of us (3 kids) were scattered around the plane, not an experience I will be paying for the privilege again. As for the excessive costs for baggage don't even get me started on this!*

The YouGov® brand perception tool, *BrandIndex*, is a way of understanding how consumers regard both brands based on six key measures of brand perception. Between April and June, 2013, Easyjet significantly outranked Ryanair, and the trend has been consistent. [60]

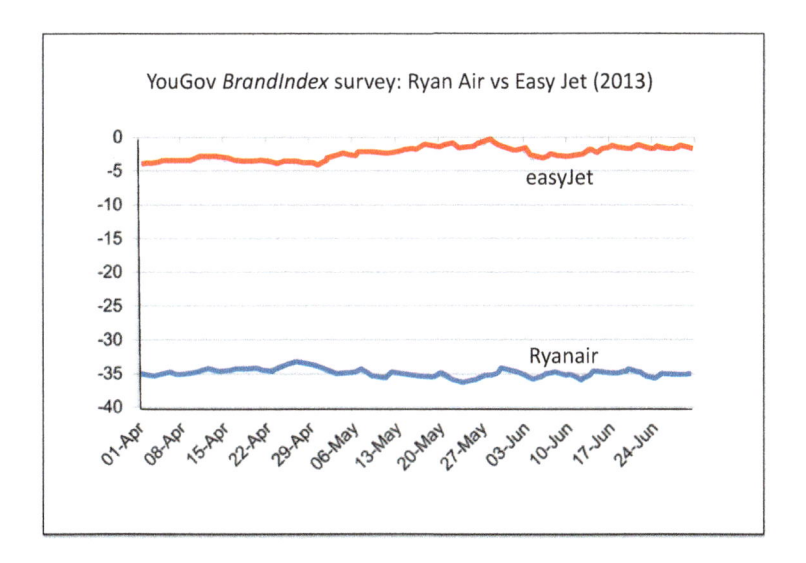

YouGov *BrandIndex* survey: Ryan Air vs Easy Jet (2013)

So, what can the CEO and business leader learn from this example about strategy, culture, customer service and performance?

177

First, let's look at each organization's strategic focus [59, 60, 61].

Ryanair, as a result of being maniacally focused on cost reduction, continues to grow by delivering lower fares, better punctuality, and fewer lost bags, which results in high profit margins. Ryanair's fundamental strategic belief is that low fares and point to point convenience will generate increased passenger traffic, which coupled with a continuous focus on cost-containment and operating efficiencies will lead to continued growth in passenger numbers and larger EBIT returns.

The strategic drivers for Ryanair are defined as:

- **Low cost fares**
- **Customer service (= convenience),** being measured as punctuality, fewer lost bags and fewer cancellations than all of the rest of its peer group in Europe
- **Frequent Point-to-Point Flights on Short-Haul Routes**
- **Low Operating Costs** (including using third party organizations at ticketing counters, gate operations and baggage handling)
- **Drive customers to use the Internet** as much as possible when organizing travel
- **Commitment to safety and quality maintenance**
- Enhancement of Operating Results through **Ancillary Services**
- **Expanding its footprint** and market access

Easyjet, in reviewing its strategic drivers in 2010, assessed the dynamic changes of the European travel marketplace and decided that their strategic drivers have been tried and tested and remain appropriate.

- **Safe and sustainable:** We will never compromise our

commitment to safety, which is always the first priority for all our people, and we continually strive to improve our sustainability.

- **Focus on customer**
- **Network development:** We are focusing on improving our routes, slots and bases to build on our leading presence across Europe.
- **Improving our customer's experience:** We are focused on improving the travel experience for all our passengers.
- **Operational excellence:** We focus on maintaining a strong operation that delivers convenience for our customers.
- **Where people make the difference:** We are committed to ensuring high employee engagement levels across the business.
- **Financial discipline:** We are committed to improving shareholder returns whilst maintaining a strong, liquid balance sheet.

Charting the performance of Ryanair and Easyjet (total passengers carried and profit margin) since they became publicly traded tells an interesting story. It seems that the customer service and employee satisfaction focus of Easyjet is an added expense that, in the case of a low cost ticket strategy, doesn't seem to have a significant return.

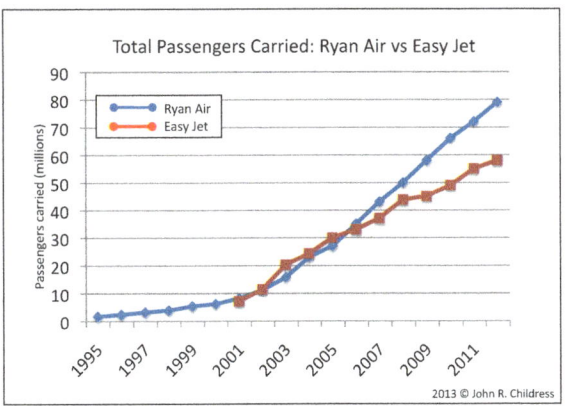

Total Passengers Carried: Ryan Air vs Easy Jet

Ryanair delivers a poor customer experience and has often been described as having a *'bad culture'*, yet still delivers significant financial performance. Here we see the limitations of the culture vulture's dogma that culture trumps strategy and that a strong culture means focusing on positive human values of respect, trust and fairness. Some business strategies don't require a *'people positive'* culture, but instead a culture that is in alignment with the strategy.

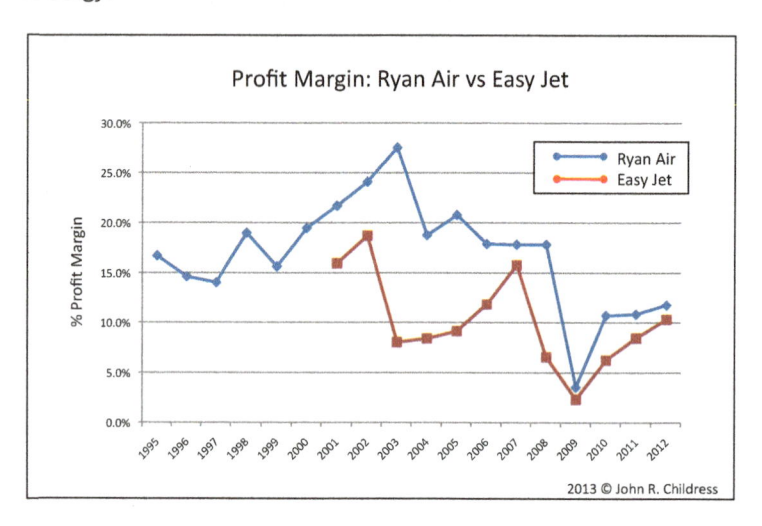

Profit Margin: Ryan Air vs Easy Jet

I believe strongly that culture must match the business strategy and not be developed based solely on psychological or *'values'* principles. In the case of both Ryanair and Easyjet, their corporate cultures are in perfect alignment with their slightly different strategic drivers.

The Next Chapter?

The Ryanair and Easyjet battle for customers and sustainable performance is only beginning, as both airlines are just under 20 years old. As the low cost air travel market matures, the crucial differentiator may shift away from low fares alone and towards low fares **plus** a healthy customer experience. In fact, we may already be seeing this inflection point.

At the 2013 Ryanair Annual General Meeting, angry shareholders, hearing of a profit warning and slowdown in forecasted bookings (as opposed to the robust forecast of Easyjet), chastised the CEO, Michael O'Leary about the abusive and "macho" Ryanair culture. That same week Ryanair was voted the worst of Britain's 100 biggest brands [62].

Responding to shareholder concerns that poor customer service issues were negatively impacting sales, O'Leary replied:

> *"I am very happy to take the blame or responsibility if we have a macho or abrupt culture. Some of that may be my own personal character deformities. A lot of customer service elements don't cost a lot of money and we will try to eliminate things that unnecessarily piss off customers."*

As the market and customer demands change, strategy and culture must shift as well.

LEVERAGE:

SECTION FIVE: MEASURING CORPORATE CULTURE

*Not everything that can be measured counts,
and not everything that counts can be measured.*
~ Albert Einstein

A CEO client asked me pointedly one day:

> "I don't see the value of having my corporate culture mapped and classified into some academic's 4-box model? That's about as useful as someone telling me I'm lost in a forest at exactly Map Section 16, Grid 45 when what I really want to know is, which way do I go! I want a roadmap, not a grid coordinate."

I can sympathize with this CEO's frustration about employee surveys, and culture surveys in particular. Since not even the academics and culture consultants can agree on a definition of culture nor the elements that make up culture, how the heck can anyone really measure or accurately assess corporate culture? And can surveys, assessments and culture models really show the CEO how to improve performance?

Believe it or not, there are currently around 70+ culture assessment tools and culture survey instruments, all different!

And they range from simple and anecdotal all the way to complex and statistical. Some are designed by sociologists, statisticians and psychologists, others by business professors and academics, many by culture consultants, a couple by cultural anthropologists, and a few by HR professionals.

How is the CEO, concerned about her corporate culture and its impact on performance, to decide which assessment to use, if any? They may be statistically valid, but are they really measuring culture? And what useful insights will they provide?

The following chapters in this section give a brief overview of the most widely used culture assessment tools, along with my personal comments after years of advising and supporting CEOs and senior executive teams on understanding and reshaping culture to better support their business strategies, their people and their marketplace objectives.

I see, said the blind man to his deaf wife.

Chapter 12: Culture Surveys and Assessments

A few are useful, all are curiously interesting, some are crap.

How it all started

It's like giving the fox the keys to the henhouse.

During the explosion of interest in corporate culture in the early 1980s, many researchers, academics and consultants built a *'model'*, based on their point of view and understanding, to visually describe culture. And since we all know different companies tend to have different cultures, these models most often took the form of plotting the different cultures along a continuum based on one or more obvious characteristics. And to make the model more interesting, they usually used two different characteristics in the form of an X and Y axis, thus coming up with a 4-box model. On this matrix you could position and assess (either qualitatively or quantitatively) the various types of cultures observable in real companies.

As the interest and discussions about culture grew in the literature, more complex models, based on 3, 4, 5, 6 or more axes were developed since the two axes models were deemed too simplistic, especially for the academics.

It seems to me that in most cases, the models came first (made up from either experience and observation of real businesses, or a theoretical construct), then an assessment or survey was subsequently designed to fit the model.

The main rationale for developing and using a culture assessment survey initially involved the search for a way to understand and describe corporate cultures. The models and surveys were designed to map and describe a company's particular culture in relation to other possible cultures. While this was interesting, an even more interesting question quickly emerged: *"Is my culture positive or negative?"* Which actually means: *"Is my current corporate culture helping us drive performance or acting as a barrier to reaching our strategic and business goals?"*

To use the culture models and surveys to answer these questions, the next step in the development of culture surveys was to correlate various culture *'positions'* or *'scores'* with performance data from similar companies in similar industries, or at least with industry average performance criteria. Thus was born the concept of a positive correlation between culture and performance.

The next question in the evolution of culture surveys is fairly obvious: *"What are the elements of a 'desired' or 'better' culture for my company?"* And this is where, for me at least, the whole process gets very dubious and highly suspect. If you ask people inside a company, who are already a product of the current culture, what the best cultural elements should be, how do they really know what is better? Are they experts in organizational dynamics? I don't really think so, since most are more focused on their jobs and current responsibilities than on characteristics of excellent companies in their industry. It seems to me that when they answer the questions about *'desired culture'* they are answering from some ideal based on personal values and beliefs about a *'good'* culture. And *'good'* could mean anywhere from *'a nice place to work'* to *'hard-nosed business fundamentals'*, depending upon the individual.

But that seems to be what the culture assessment industry has done. Many culture assessments and surveys have two parts to each question: *"What is the current culture?"* and *"What is the desired culture?"* These two scores, when combined with all the other characteristics used in the survey, form a simple Gap Analysis between current and desired. Which of course is a perfect lead-in to a large consulting assignment to help a lackluster company change its culture and become a great company!

Another major flaw in most culture assessments is that they often ignore the power of subcultures (departments or segments of departments) by lumping all the data from one division or company together. Some do break down their culture scores by level (executive, middle mgt, supervisor, hourly, etc.) and/or by function (HR, Operations, Engineering, Finance, etc.). And again I find the same problem with this approach; *'desired culture'* may mean very different things to the HR department than it does to the Engineering or Outside Sales groups!

And lastly, another reason I am suspect about culture surveys and assessments is that whatever the characteristics measured in order to pinpoint your culture, all have equal weight and everything seems to be averaged to get a *'culture score'*. Not every ingredient of culture has the same impact on business performance! Some are trivial while others may have a significant impact.

Recent advances in modern genetic mapping have shown that the DNA difference between a human and a chimpanzee is about 1%. Now I would argue the genes that make up those 1% have a critical weighting that is greater than the other 99%. One percent means the difference between a human being and chimpanzee.

Which are the business and behavior characteristics that separate a cult-like culture from a toxic culture? There seems to be no effort made to add a weighting factor to any of the assessment methodologies. What you get is the average, and with something as complex and as important as culture, I think those developing and pushing their culture surveys should do better. We need to know which factors carry the most weight in shaping different corporate cultures.

But, my concerns notwithstanding, culture surveys are a significant part of the current business landscape, a big part of the culture change process, and if designed and executed well can, under the right circumstances, can be a useful tool for the CEO and business leader.

The Great Divide

My good friend and former business partner, Blackburne Costin, once owned, along with several college friends, a bar in the rustic ski town of Crested Butte, Colorado, named *The Great Divide Saloon*. It was a raucous place and over the years we had great fun there, but sadly it closed and we all had to grow up (most of us anyway). However, there is still a great divide occurring in the world of corporate culture assessments (doesn't the saloon sound much more fun at this moment?) between whether the way to measure and assess culture is through Individual Values or Business Characteristics.

Here's the debate and it's important for us to understand since a whole raft of corporate culture models and assessments have sprung up around each of these two camps.

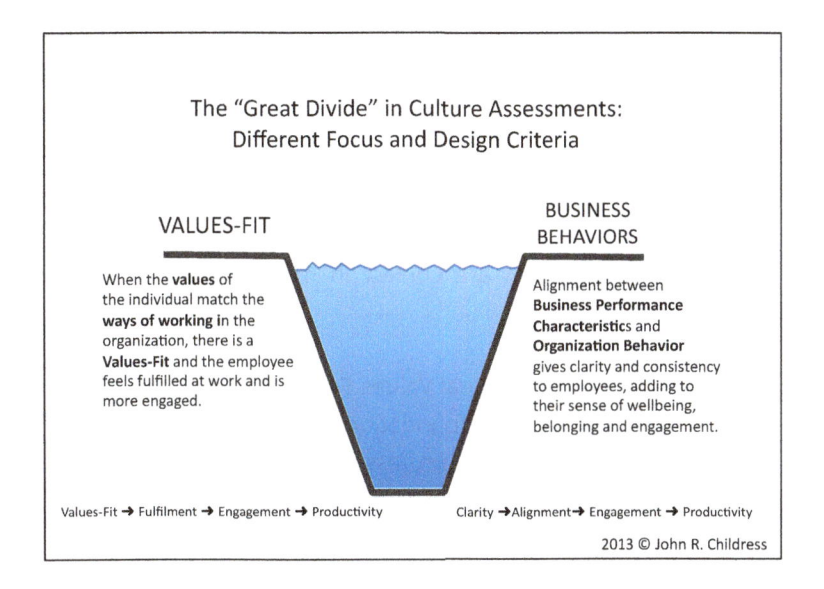

> **The "Great Divide" in Culture Assessments:**
> **Different Focus and Design Criteria**
>
> **VALUES-FIT** | **BUSINESS BEHAVIORS**
>
> When the **values** of the individual match the **ways of working** in the organization, there is a **Values-Fit** and the employee feels fulfilled at work and is more engaged.
>
> Alignment between **Business Performance Characteristics** and **Organization Behavior** gives clarity and consistency to employees, adding to their sense of wellbeing, belonging and engagement.
>
> Values-Fit → Fulfilment → Engagement → Productivity   Clarity → Alignment → Engagement → Productivity
>
> 2013 © John R. Childress

Those in the Values-Fit camp believe that business performance has a strong link to how well an individual 'fits' in the organization and fit has a lot to do with a match between how the organization works and the deeply held values of the individual. People who hold deep personal values that don't align with how the organization works become disenfranchised and rarely give their best effort. They are not fully engaged. However, when there is a match between personal values and how the organization behaves (culture), the 'magic' of employee engagement occurs and the employee feels they can make a difference and are (theoretically at least) capable of high productivity and engagement.

Across the divide, the Business Characteristics camp is populated with those who believe that high-performance cultures are built when there is clarity and certainty around the business behaviors and policies required for success in a given industry. Therefore culture can be best measured by assessing whether or not employees see the organization behaving in ways that are in alignment with these specific characteristics for business success.

When the organization's culture (policies, procedures, leadership and management) habitually behaves in ways that are out of alignment with the required business characteristics, performance suffers. When the culture is in alignment with these characteristics of business success, performance is enhanced.

First of all, both groups are correct in many ways, but not in absolute ways.

My problem with the Individual Values-Fit belief is two-fold. First, it seems to ignore one of the foundation laws of social psychology, developed by Kurt Lewin, MIT professor and widely acknowledged father of Social Psychology and Group Dynamics[63]. The classic formula is: $B = f(P,E)$. Basically, this states that Behavior is a function of both the Person (values, experiences, habits, beliefs) and the Environment (organizational constraints, business processes, etc.). Those pushing the individual values-fit approach tend to ignore the impact of the environment (organizational constraints) on individual behavior.

My second concern is that employees nowadays come from many diverse backgrounds and national cultures. Even an IT employee or retail staff born in the UK and thus a UK citizen may have more of their ethnic and/or religious values imbedded in their beliefs and behavior than the traditional UK national values. And for those organizations with a diverse employee base, it is impossible to match all these values, let alone to match the values of one individual.

Organizations, by nature are imperfect and governed by the practical constraints of cash flow, cost pressures, time pressures, customer preferences, competition and technology changes, just to name a few. The culture must take into account these constraints, and not just the personal values of employees. Bringing the two closer together is a good goal, but what is really required for high performance is common sense, tolerance and flexibility on both sides.

My problem with the other side of gap, the Business Characteristics focused culture assessment, is that an organization is not a machine; it is a complex entity of emotions and human dynamics as well as P&L statements and process efficiency improvements. To reduce it down to 13 or 15 business characteristics is not fully accurate and to ignore human values and motivations is giving an incomplete picture.

> *One machine can do the work of fifty ordinary men. No machine can do the work of one extraordinary man.*
> *~Elbert Hubbard*

A Time and a Place

In my discussions with several academics and those consultants knowledgeable in the realities of business performance, there is an interesting twist to this great divide between individual Values-Fit and Business Characteristics.

Most of us pretty much agree that in an early stage organization and/or a high growth environment where the culture is not yet fully ossified and where new employees are constantly coming into the firm, the Values-Fit assessments are of great value since they can help define an organization-employee fit model for selective hiring. Hiring-for-fit is an excellent way to build the culture you need and avoid a culture developing by default.

In later-stage organizations where culture has not been closely managed, the business characteristics assessment models may be more helpful, since the organization is already filled with individuals from various backgrounds, experiences and with different Values foundations. Expecting all individual employees to align around a set of core values is going a little far. Employees can adapt their behavior, but not so easily their individual values.

Over the past decade the trend as to which group is winning has shifted. Currently I would say that the values-fit group is rapidly gaining popularity, mainly due to the growing clamor for greater employee engagement during tough economic times, and the strong promotion of employee engagement measures by the Gallup organization (and others). Also swinging the tide is the business and popular press with articles and headlines citing statistics such *as "only 30% of US employees are fully engaged at work"*[64]. Good headlines, and I fully agree that employee engagement is very important, but I'm not sure that the Values-Fit culture models are the only way to improve employee engagement. Employee engagement depends on many factors other than the personal values of the employee.

A Quick Review of Culture Assessment Instruments:

There are basically two formats used to describe and measure culture: **'*Type Assessments*'** and **'*Profiles'*.**

Type-Assessment models of culture tend to classify a culture into two or more descriptive categories. These models, and their surveys, tend to be from the earlier years in the development of the concept of corporate culture, although that does not make them any less useful and informative.

As the academics and psychologists got interested in culture, the instruments and models started to become more complex (they would say more accurate). Instead of trying to find a *'type'* of culture, they began to assess culture by assembling a set of culture characteristics or dimensions and using a **profiling** methodology.

This basically means that for each culture characteristic (remember these are made up from either observation, research or best guess), such as Communication, Leadership, Decision-Making, Teamwork, Motivation, etc., the respondent was asked to rate their culture along a continuum, say from 0 to 5, where 0 means *'definitely not like our culture'* and 5 means *'our culture is exactly like this'*. Scores could be placed anywhere on this 0 to 5 continuum which the respondent believed best described their company culture.

Most **Profile** assessments contain multiple characteristics (dimensions), sometimes 4-15 or more, with multiple questions about each characteristic. All the scores would be tallied, the average taken and a description, either as a bar chart or a circumplex, would then describe the highs and lows of your culture. Usually a dominant theme would emerge around two or three of the characteristics, signaling (theoretically at least) areas of either significant cultural strength or significant areas of concern about the culture.

> *Don't measure yourself by what you have accomplished, but by what you should have accomplished with your ability.~ John Wooden*

Examples of Type Assessments

Wallach Culture Assessment: An early culture model to have a corresponding culture assessment comes from the work of Ellen Wallach (1983), where she uses three characteristics to describe an organization's culture: bureaucratic, supportive and innovative. Using a series of nine different questions for each characteristic dealing with observable behaviors and scoring them simply from 0 (strongly disagree) to 3 (strongly agree), one of the three culture options tends to have the highest score.

An interesting use of this simple culture model plotted performance against SLAs (Service level Agreements) for four departments within a South African Life Insurance Company, Liberty Life in 2006 [65]. The results showing that an innovative culture creates better performance than either supportive or bureaucratic on adhering to SLA times. While this analysis tells a business leader that a department with an *'innovative culture'* performs better, it leaves us with the question of what is the cause of the cultural differences between these four departments and how to go about improving performance. But for the leader concerned with performance, this culture tool is simple to use and begins to point the way to understanding performance deviations.

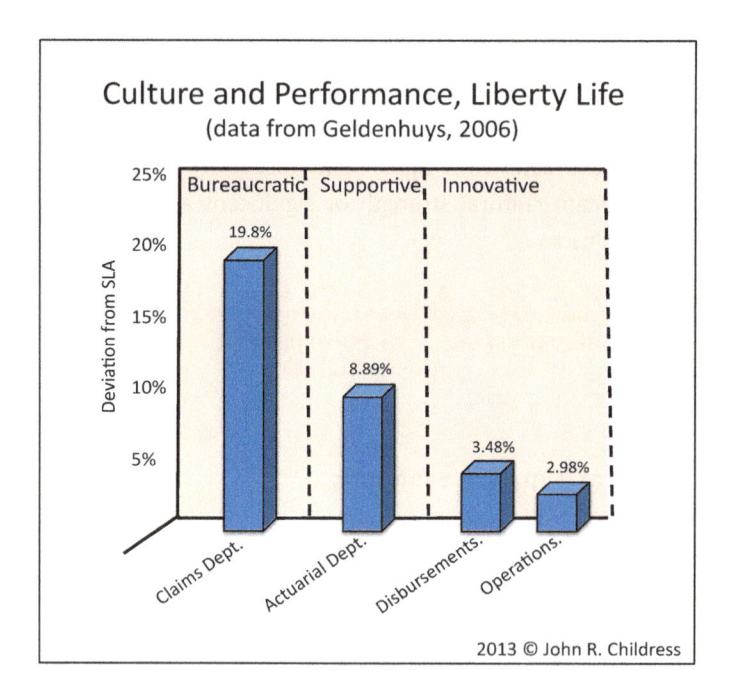

Culture and Performance, Liberty Life
(data from Geldenhuys, 2006)

Department	Category	Deviation from SLA
Claims Dept.	Bureaucratic	19.8%
Actuarial Dept.	Supportive	8.89%
Disbursements	Innovative	3.48%
Operations	Innovative	2.98%

2013 © John R. Childress

Very few people use the Wallach Culture Assessment anymore due to its simplicity – only three types of organizations (somehow equated with not accurate) and prefer instead more complex models.

Deal and Kennedy Model: The model put forth by Terrance Deal and James Kennedy in their 1982 book, *Corporate Culture: The Rites and Rituals of Corporate Life*, is based on two dimensions, Speed of Feedback from the Marketplace, and Degree of Risk.

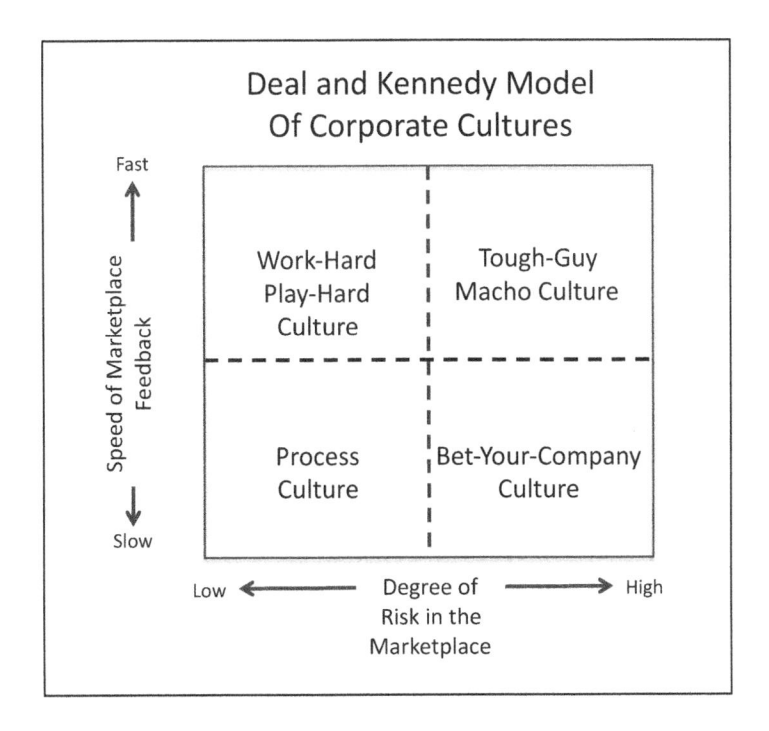

```
                Deal and Kennedy Model
                 Of Corporate Cultures
         Fast
          ↑
                 Work-Hard      | Tough-Guy
                 Play-Hard      | Macho Culture
                 Culture        |
          ---------------------- ----------------------
                 Process        | Bet-Your-Company
                 Culture        | Culture
          ↓
         Slow
              Low ←——— Degree of ———→ High
                       Risk in the
                       Marketplace
```

Speed of Marketplace Feedback

The 4-quadrant model is based on their belief that the biggest single influence on a company's culture was the business environment in which it operated. As a result, they used the term '*corporate culture*' to refer to the business aspects of how an organization behaves, as opposed to the more academic term, '*organizational culture.*' In their book they provide their own version of a culture assessment questionnaire, however this assessment seems to have gone out of fashion.

JOHN R. CHILDRESS

OCAI®: Organizational Culture Assessment Inventory®

One of the most widely used of the Type Assessments for measuring corporate culture is a model and inventory first developed by Kim Cameron, John Rohrbaugh and Robert Quinn, business professors and academics, which they called the Organizational Culture Assessment Inventory (OCAI®)[66]. This model is based on the Competing Values Framework and has been named as one of the fifty most important models in the history of business. It is a four-quadrant type model with two major axes.

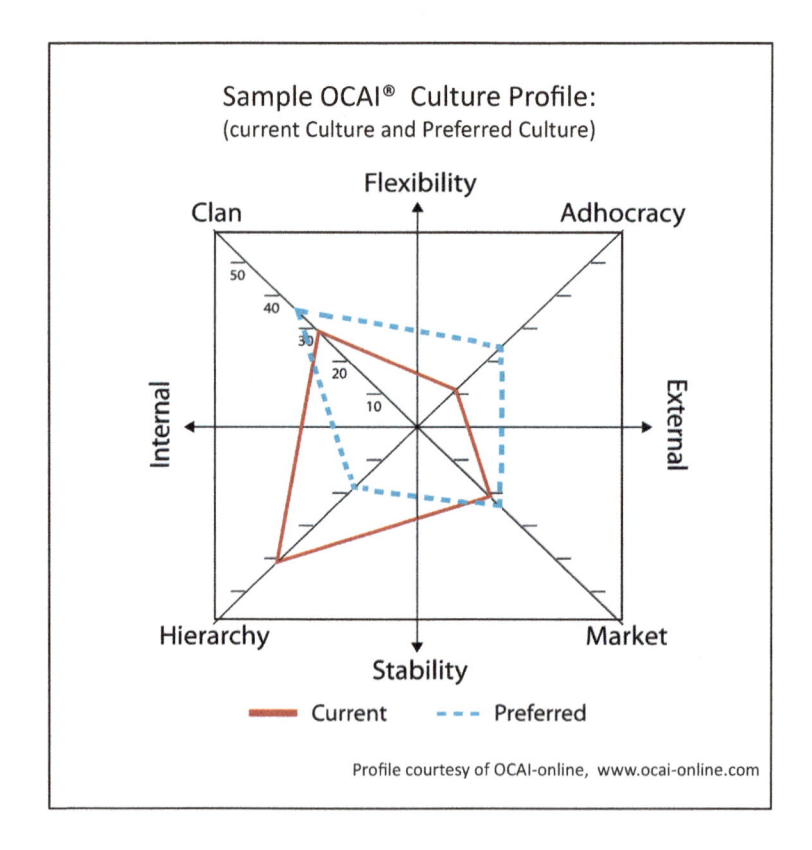

Sample OCAI® Culture Profile:
(current Culture and Preferred Culture)

Profile courtesy of OCAI-online, www.ocai-online.com

One axis (dimension) of the model differentiates an orientation toward flexibility, discretion, and dynamism at one extreme from stability, order, and control at the other. The second perpendicular axis differentiates an orientation toward an internal focus and the integration and unity of processes, from an external focus on opportunities and competitive differentiation. The four resulting types of cultures have been labeled with descriptive names: the Clan Culture, the Adhocracy Culture, the Market Culture and the Hierarchy Culture. No one type is better or worse and there are highly successful organizations of all four types.

The OCAI® assessment has been used on over 100,000 managers and 10,000 different organizations and has amassed a large amount of industry norms and comparative data. Slightly modified versions of the OCAI® are also available that use a colorful circle instead of a 4-quadrant model, but for all intents and purposes they are the same.

I have two concerns about this assessment, and its many similar offshoots. First it is a model and assessment based on the personal values-fit concept instead of business behaviors. And secondly, this assessment asks for two views from respondents, *current culture* and a *preferred culture*. I have concern about the ability of employees inside an organization to accurately state what is the preferred culture for business success.

Profile Models and Assessments

Many consultants and academics complain that Type Models of culture are too narrow and limiting, giving only 3 or 4 choices for describing something as complex as corporate culture. As a result of further academic research into corporate culture, profile models and assessments began to be developed and now are gaining in usage. Profile models do not attempt to characterize culture, but to identify and map its core characteristics, the overall picture telling a story about the culture.

The Organizational Culture Questionnaire (OCQ) is a profile model that describes an organization's culture from choices across thirteen different dimensions. A core product from the psychometric measurement and consulting firm, *Human Factors International*, whose *"distinctive competency is a deep and extensive knowledge of psychology coupled with experienced understanding of the business environment."*[66]

The thirteen dimensions are: *Individual Performance, Leadership, Customer Focus, Organization Structure, Communication, Conflict Management, HR Management, Participation, Decision Making, Innovation, Professionalism, Goal Orientation, Fun.*

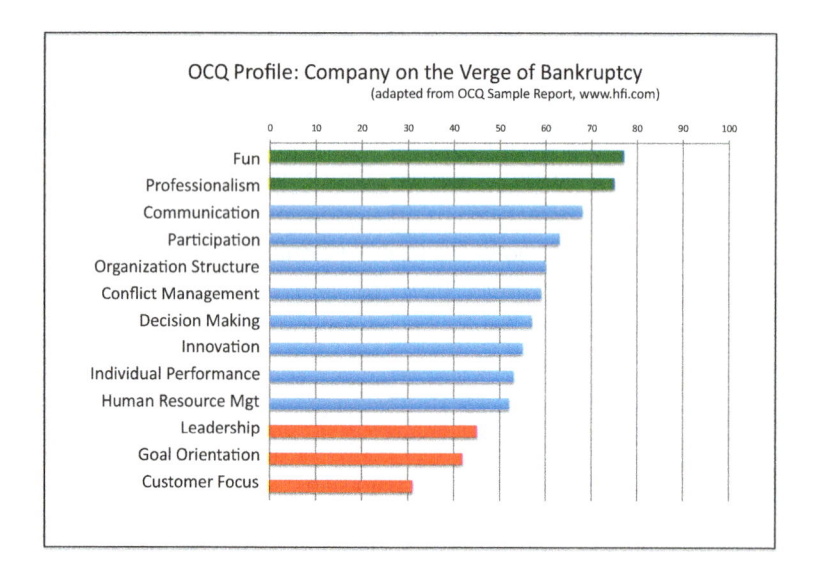

OCQ Profile: Company on the Verge of Bankruptcy
(adapted from OCQ Sample Report, www.hfi.com)

Dimension	Score
Fun	~75
Professionalism	~75
Communication	~65
Participation	~60
Organization Structure	~60
Conflict Management	~60
Decision Making	~55
Innovation	~55
Individual Performance	~50
Human Resource Mgt	~50
Leadership	~45
Goal Orientation	~45
Customer Focus	~25

Several behavioral questions have been developed for each dimension, which are then scored on a 0 to 100 basis and the averaged results are presented in a graph format.

While the OCQ culture assessment is based on Business Characteristics, not Values, and avoids the mistake of asking respondents to score their thoughts about a preferred culture, it is still questionable whether their 13 dimensions are the most important ones to describe culture.

What I like about this assessment is the amount of normative data that has been collected since 1983 and their commitment to avoiding giving advice, but instead to provide evidence based justification for why a culture is either failing or exceeding its performance objectives. They too are mainly a psychological measurement and diagnostic group and license their models out to other consultants to use with their clients.

Organizational Culture Inventory® (OCI®)

Widely regarded as *"the most widely used and thoroughly researched survey for measuring organizational culture in the world"*, the OCI®, developed by Drs. Robert A. Cooke and J. Clayton Lafferty, *"provides an assessment of the operating culture in terms of the behaviors that members believe are required to 'fit in and meet expectations' within their organization"* (Cooke & Szumal, 2000).

In 1971, Lafferty founded *Human Synergistics*, an organization specializing in quantifying personal and leadership development concepts based on his own research. In the 1980s, Lafferty engaged Cooke, at the time a research scientist at the University of Michigan's Survey Research Center, to further develop and validate the Life Styles Inventory (LSI), which was based on a "circumplex" model of interpersonal styles. While working on the LSI, Dr. Cooke began developing the OCI® which measures culture in terms of the strength of norms and expectations for the twelve styles arranged around the circumplex.

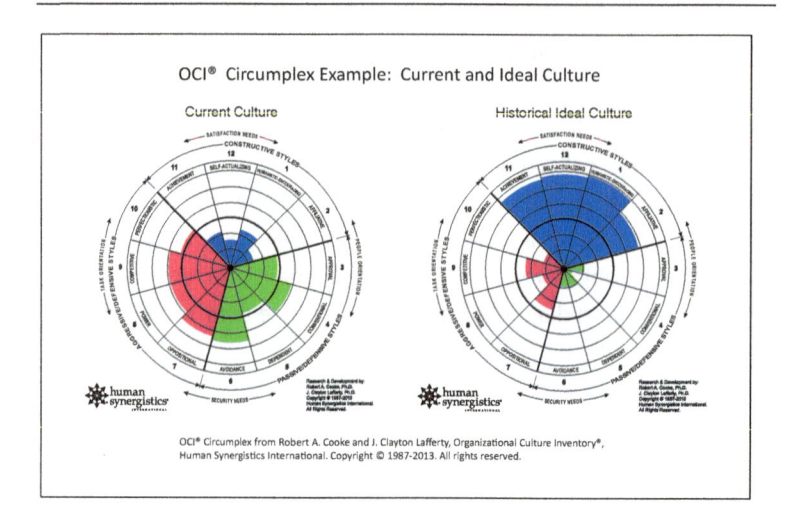

OCI® Circumplex Example: Current and Ideal Culture

OCI® Circumplex from Robert A. Cooke and J. Clayton Lafferty, Organizational Culture Inventory®, Human Synergistics International. Copyright © 1987-2013. All rights reserved.

The OCI can be used to assess both current and ideal culture in terms of 12 behavioral norms (characteristics).

The results are displayed on a circumplex model, organized into three types of cultures: *Constructive*, *Passive/Defensive*, and *Aggressive/Defensive*.

Each cluster contains four styles or behavioral norms. Research shows that the Constructive styles are related to effectiveness while the Defensive styles detract from organizational performance.

Human Synergistics is a measurement and assessment organization; the *Life Styles Inventory*® (LSI) and *Desert Survival Situation*™ are their original flagship products. Over time, the firm has developed an Integrated Diagnostic System--a suite of circumplex-based assessments focusing at the individual, group, and organizational levels. They provide assessments, simulations, consulting, and Accreditation and Application Workshops for developing individuals, managers, leaders, teams, and organizations. Their instruments are used by internal and external consultants and coaches, human resources and organization development professionals, and academic researchers and instructors.

Again, what concerns me about this culture diagnostic is the use of current and preferred scores, but otherwise, this is a well validated and researched model focusing on behaviors.

Denison Organizational Culture Suvey (DOCS): *Denison Consulting* was founded by Dr. Daniel Denison and William S. Neale in 1998 and is headquartered in Ann Arbor, Michigan, USA. Denison Consulting *"provides research-based solutions and consulting support to help build high performance business cultures"*[67]. Dan Denison is a firm believer that culture is best understood by assessing validated business drivers and organizational behaviors. This is **definitely not** a values-fit or individual psychometric model, but deals firmly with what Denison and his researchers describe as accurate and validated drivers of business performance.

At the core of their products and services is the Denison Model, which is based on over two decades of research linking twelve dimensions of culture to business performance outcomes and metrics. The 12 dimensions are grouped into four categories: **Mission** (Strategic Direction & Intent, Goals and Objectives, Vision), **Consistency** (Core Values, Agreement, Coordination & Integration), **Involvement** (Empowerment, Team Orientation, Capability Development), and **Adaptability** (Creating Change, Customer Focus, Organizational Learning).

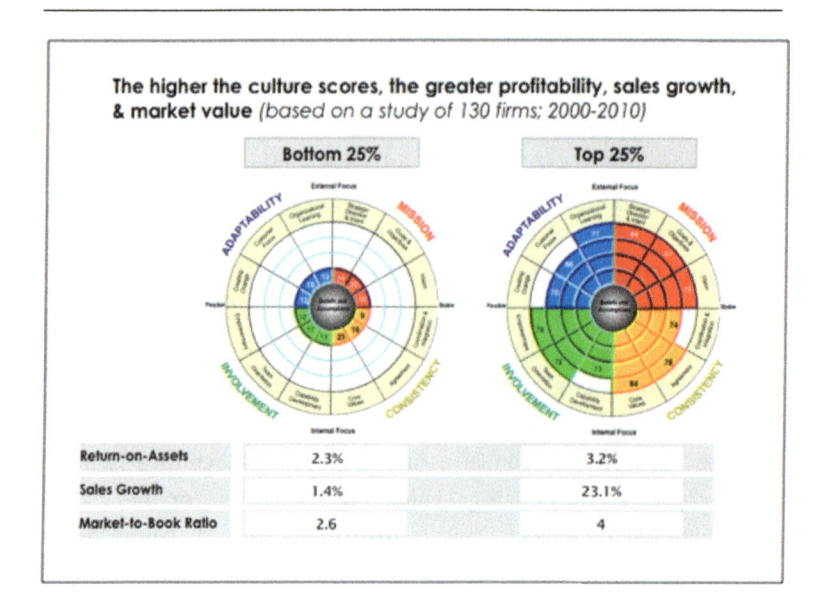

The higher the culture scores, the greater profitability, sales growth, & market value *(based on a study of 130 firms; 2000-2010)*

	Bottom 25%	Top 25%
Return-on-Assets	2.3%	3.2%
Sales Growth	1.4%	23.1%
Market-to-Book Ratio	2.6	4

Using a circumplex to visualize the data, it is relatively easy to see differences between organizations. What is somewhat unique about the Denison approach is that they have been able to survey over 7,000 organizations in a variety of industries and come up with
very compelling correlations between high and low scores on their circumplex and actual business performance metrics.

Like most of the firms dealing with culture assessments, Denison has taken its basic model and adapted it beyond measuring corporate culture, to include leadership development, M&A culture integration, and 360-degree feedback.

Barrett Values Centre Model

Richard Barrett is an American author, speaker and consultant on leadership, values and culture in business and society, and the "guru" behind the Barrett Values Centre models of how the values held by an individual impact the culture of an organization [68]. His primary focus is definitely on personal development and his

LEVERAGE:

culture model features the "Seven Levels of Consciousness", which Barrett has adapted from the original work of Abraham Maslow's *Hierarchy of Needs* (1943).

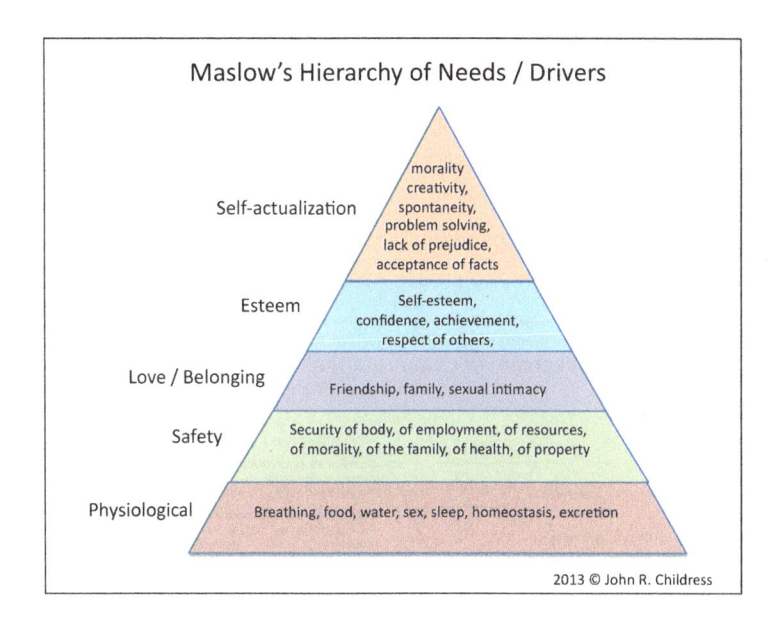

Maslow's Hierarchy of Needs / Drivers

- **Self-actualization**: morality, creativity, spontaneity, problem solving, lack of prejudice, acceptance of facts
- **Esteem**: Self-esteem, confidence, achievement, respect of others,
- **Love / Belonging**: Friendship, family, sexual intimacy
- **Safety**: Security of body, of employment, of resources, of morality, of the family, of health, of property
- **Physiological**: Breathing, food, water, sex, sleep, homeostasis, excretion

2013 © John R. Childress

As you may recall from Organizational Behavior 101, Maslow's Theory of Needs focuses on the drivers of individual motivation at various stages in an individual's development, from the lowest need, Physiological (food, water, breathing, etc.) to Safety and Security, then up to Love and Belonging, next comes Self-Esteem and the highest driver of personal development, Self-Actualization.

Basically, a starving person isn't really interested in esteem or self-actualization until his belly is full, and lower-level needs have to be fulfilled before moving to the next set of motivations.

Barrett believed that with a few '*modifications*', Maslow's levels could be used to describe and map the evolution of consciousness in individuals, and also the development and evolution of organizations (he calls this culture), communities and nations. His seven levels of individual consciousness are, from lowest to highest: Survival, Relationships, Self-Esteem, Transformation, Internal Cohesion, Making a Difference, and Service. And the corresponding levels of 'corporate culture' are, from lowest to highest: Financial Stability, Customer Satisfaction, Best Practices, Continuous Improvement, Shared Vision, Collaboration, Long-term Viability. He maps them as in the figure below. I have yet to fully understand the logic of this model and his focus on personal values coming from the human soul. [69]

He then builds a set of profile questions to assess individual values within an organization and create a map of the culture.

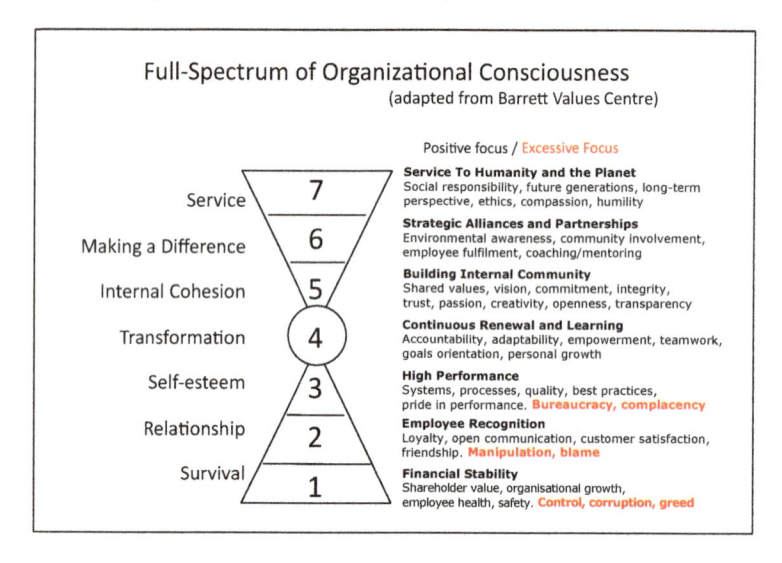

Full-Spectrum of Organizational Consciousness
(adapted from Barrett Values Centre)

Positive focus / Excessive Focus

Level	Personal	Organizational
7	Service	**Service To Humanity and the Planet** — Social responsibility, future generations, long-term perspective, ethics, compassion, humility
6	Making a Difference	**Strategic Alliances and Partnerships** — Environmental awareness, community involvement, employee fulfilment, coaching/mentoring
5	Internal Cohesion	**Building Internal Community** — Shared values, vision, commitment, integrity, trust, passion, creativity, openness, transparency
4	Transformation	**Continuous Renewal and Learning** — Accountability, adaptability, empowerment, teamwork, goals orientation, personal growth
3	Self-esteem	**High Performance** — Systems, processes, quality, best practices, pride in performance. Bureaucracy, complacency
2	Relationship	**Employee Recognition** — Loyalty, open communication, customer satisfaction, friendship. Manipulation, blame
1	Survival	**Financial Stability** — Shareholder value, organisational growth, employee health, safety. Control, corruption, greed

According to Barrett his model measures Values Alignment. *"When we ask a group of people to pick ten values that represent who they are, how their organisation/community/nation operates (current culture), and how they would like it to operate (desired culture) -- we are able to measure the level of values alignment."* [68]

Barrett seems to switch from values to behaviors and back again when talking about his culture metrics and personally, I am a little mystified by the relationship between the evolution of human consciousness and it's direct translation to business fundamentals and competitive performance. He also displays a far greater depth of focus and interest on the psychology of the individual than the basics of business and high performance cultures.

Again, this is definitely a personal Values-Fit assessment model and also asks respondents to score the current and preferred culture. The Barrett Values Centre is mostly a research and measurement organization that licenses their material to *"Barrett trained and certified"*[68] consultants for use with their clients.

Round Pegg

One of the newest on the culture assessment scene, and also one of the more innovative is Round Pegg, a Boulder, Colorado based TechStar 2010 organization founded by Dr. Natalie Baumgartner, a clinical psychologist with a specific focus on assessment and strength-based psychology, Tim Wolters , a serial software and SaaS entrepreneur, and Brent Daily, a former Yahoo executive. Round Pegg focuses its measurement technologies on Culture (measuring and managing culture), Hiring (identifying candidates that fit the desired culture), Teambuilding (improve on-boarding, coaching and conflict resolution), Employee Engagement (regularly measure and track engagement) and Mergers & Acquisitions (improving integration).

According to their website: *"Round Pegg allows you to manage your culture in the cloud. We are the future of culture management, providing web-based tools to drive business performance by measuring, managing and monitoring your unique culture. Our suite of culture alignment applications help you pull the right levers to get everyone moving in the same direction."*[69]

Round Pegg's approach and methodology is rooted in a body of research called "Person-Environment-Fit". The better an individual's personal values fit with the values of the company, the team's subculture and the manager's values, the better they will perform, longer they stay and the more they are engaged. And Round Pegg states that how well the individual's values fit the values of the company (culture) accounts for nearly 90% of their performance on the job. Poor employee engagement and lackluster company performance are a result of employee values being out of alignment with company values.[70]

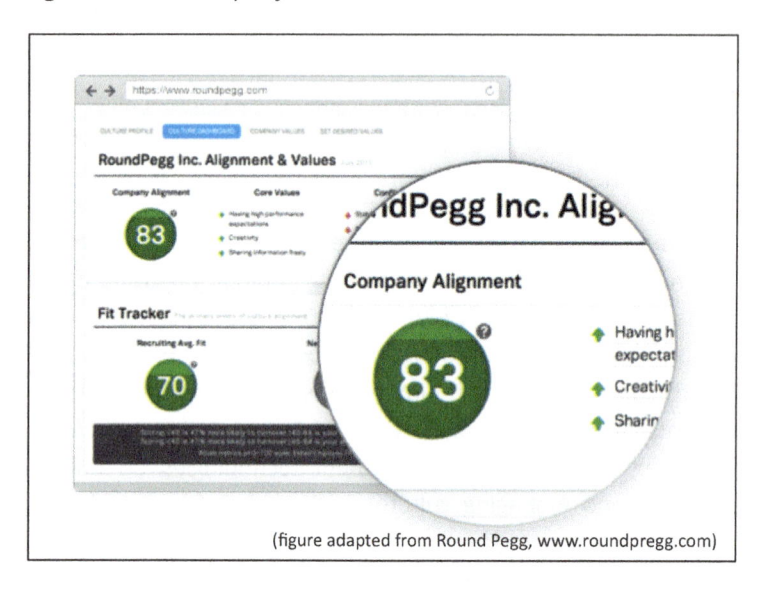

(figure adapted from Round Pegg, www.roundpregg.com)

I like an approach to measurement using software with the data and profiles being accessible via the cloud. It makes the information more accessible to leaders so they can be more engaged in managing and leading the culture. I also like the view that alignment at all levels is an important factor in business performance. Their formula for performance improvement is also different: *"Rather than attempting to influence an organization's performance by changing its culture, we propose that aligning the company around existing, or incrementally modified, shared employee values can enhance the well-being of individual employees and the organization as a whole."* [70]

What really concerns me about this start-up firm is the heavy focus on individual employee values and their person-environment-fit model (which is basically another form of the Values-Fit model). While I can easily see how their metrics and profiles can be of great use to start-up and early growth companies, I question its applicability in older, more mature organizations, unless they confine their work to the subgroup or department level. However, this firm is fairly new and time will tell how their methodologies for both assessing culture and for improving organizational performance map out.

Great Place To Work® Culture Assessment

I can't imagine anything more worthwhile than doing what I most love. And they pay me for it. ~Edgar Winter

While focusing almost solely on the *'employee experience'* at work rather than the other characteristics of traditional corporate culture measures, the Great Place to Work® Institute has amassed a wealth of information (surveying over 2 million people in 6,000 companies every year) on how the elements of Trust, Pride and Camaraderie translate into overall company performance.

In their studies, high performance cultures (what they call a *'great place to work'*) are not necessarily characterized by what the company does (perks, HR policies, benefits, work spaces, etc.), but how management and leaders treat employees. **How** is more important than **What**. In their research, performance cultures are built through developing strong healthy relationships at all levels, not on policies or practices alone. (Burchell and Robin, 2011)

Comparative Cumulative Stock Market Returns

Adapted from Great Place to Work® Institute

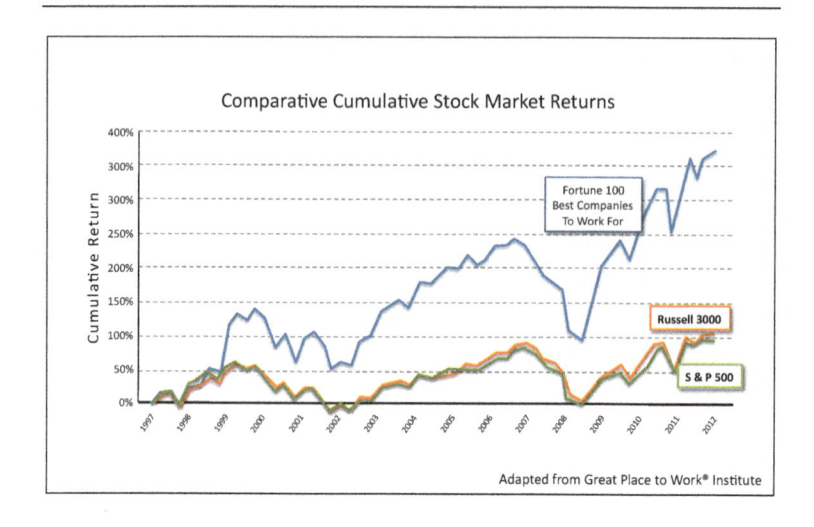

Their proprietary culture assessment is based on multiple characteristics of a Great Place to Work®, and some of the statistics they have gathered, in conjunction with the *100 Best Places to Work*, sponsored by Fortune business magazine, make a very strong case that the collective cultural elements of Trust, Pride and Camaraderie have a significant positive impact on business performance.

Dimensions of a Great Place to Work®
(adapted from Burchell and Robin,"The Great Workplace", 2011)

TRUST	**CREDIBILITY**	**Communication** – Communications are open and accessible **Competence** – Competence in coordinating human and material resources **Integrity** – Integrity in carrying out vision with consistency
	RESPECT	**Support** – Supporting professional development and showing appreciation **Collaborating** – Collaboration with employees in relevant decisions **Caring** – Caring for employees as individuals with personal lives
	FAIRNESS	**Equity** – Balances treatment for all in terms of rewards **Impartiality** – Absence of favoritism in hiring and promotions **Justice** – Lack of discrimination and process for appeals
PRIDE		**Personal Job** – in personal job, individual contributions **Team** – in work produced by one's team or work group **Company** – in the organization's products and standing in the community
CAMARADERIE		**Intimacy** – Ability to be oneself **Hospitality** – Socially friendly and welcoming atmosphere **Community** – Sense of "family" or "team"

Adapted from Great Place to Work® Institute

I believe there is great insight to be gained from the data and work of the Great Place to Work Institute® and they seem to have identified three key cultural characteristics (Trust, Pride and Camaraderie) which may account for a significant percentage of the ingredients of a high performance culture. It would be interesting to explore with them their views on the business characteristics of culture, such as strategy and leadership.

Situation-Specific Cultural Assessments

Measuring safety performance by the number of injuries you have is like measuring parenting by the number of smacks you give. ~ Dr Robert Long

A growing number of culture models and assessments have been developed and/or adapted for use in specific situations. For example, there are Nursing Culture Assessments, Hospital Culture Assessments, and numerous Safety Culture Assessments.

Probably the most widely used of the situation-specific culture assessments focus on workplace safety. Adapting one of the classical culture definitions from the work of Edgar Schein, they define a *'safety culture'* as:

> "*An organization's values and behaviors, modeled by its leaders and internalized by its members, which serve to make safe performance of work the overriding priority to protect the public, workers, and the environment*". *(EFCOG Safety Culture Task Group, 2008.)*

The major difference between a general culture assessment and, in this case a safety culture, is the overall focus on a single dimension as the key element of the culture, with all other personal and business activities impacting on overall organizational safety.

209

Proprietary Models Assessments: What Are They Hiding?

> *The very word 'secrecy' is repugnant in a free and open society; and we are as a people inherently and historically opposed to secret societies, to secret oaths, and to secrete proceedings.* ~ John F. Kennedy

There is one more category of culture assessments and tools I need to mention, and it is those that are developed and used exclusively by an individual consulting firm. Most of these are proprietary, not in the public domain, not for general use or sale, but used only in conjunction with their assignments on culture diagnosis and culture change. It seems that every culture change firm has its own model and assessment, or worse yet, have taken one of the more rigorous and tested models and modified it for their own use.

I have a big problem with these homegrown models and assessments. They haven't been subjected to the analysis, auditing, validation and scrutiny of the professional and academic community like the more mainstream models. There are numerous articles and studies about the validity and veracity of the Denison, OCAI®, OCQ and OCP models and assessments. Literally none for the proprietary ones of the consulting firms. And most of these consultant-developed models have very little, if any, normative or comparative data on companies in similar industries. What are they hiding?

I suggest a healthy degree of skepticism and questioning when approached by a consulting firm with their "own assessment model".

Corollaries of Culture

With the ability to measure corporate culture and the strong belief that culture impacts many facets of business success and employee engagement, the academics and culture consultants have extended the *'culture brand'* into adjacent areas by developing ancillary products and services such as:

- Hiring Profiles to Fit the Culture
- Assessing the 'Classroom Culture'
- School Cultures and Performance
- 360-Degree Feedback based on preferred culture characteristics
- Leadership Potential Assessment
- New CEO On-Boarding
- Customer Service Capabilities
- Leadership Development
- Employee Engagement
- Merger Integration

This brand extension is inevitable, but there is far less validation the further away from the original culture metrics you get.

Am I Any Wiser Now?

Whew! Congratulations if you made it through all the above synopses on the various culture assessment models and tools. And remember, there are over 70 different models and assessments out there.

My other big concern with most of these culture models and assessments is that a great majority of those who developed the models are academics and have never really worked in a large business at any level, and so don't fully appreciate the many issues leaders have to deal with. (My dream would be to get a group of experienced CEOs together and build a culture assessment!)

If you are considering a culture assessment to get a better understanding of your culture, then you have some key decisions to make. And my first suggestion is you make them based on your own experience about how business really works.

Here is a brief summary of the characteristics of the culture assessments reviewed:

Model	Company or Source	Structure of Model	Fundamental Belief about Culture and Performance	Culture Measurements
Wallach Culture Assessment	Wallach (1983)	3 Types	Business Characteristics	Current Culture Only
Deal and Kennedy Model	Deal&Kennedy (1982)	4-quadrant model	Business Characteristics	Current Culture Only
Organizational Culture Assessment Inventory (OCAI)	Original by Cameron & Quinn (1983), numerous variatoins	4-quadrant model	Personal Values-Fit	Current and Preferred Culture
Organizational Culture Questionnaire (OCQ)	Human Factors International	13 dimensions	Business Characteristics	Current Culture Only
Organizational Culture Inventory (OCI)	Human Synergistics	12 dimensions	Business Characteristics	Current and Preferred Culture
Denison Organization Culture Survey (DOCS)	Denison Consulting	12 dimensions	Business Characteristics	Current Culture Only
Barrett Values Model	Barrett Values Centre	7 Levels of Organization Consciousness	Heavy Focus Personal Values-Fit	Current and Preferred Culture
Round Pegg	Round Pegg Culture Management Software	(Unknown) number of dimensions	Heavy Focus Personal Values-Fit	Current and Preferred Culture
Great Place to Work Culture Audit	Great Place to Work® Institute	Measures Trust, Pride, Camaraderie	Business Characteristics to Measure Employee Experience	Current Culture Only

Basically, you have to decide between the Values-Fit approach or the Business Characteristics approach. Both have amassed some compelling evidence (mostly academic research studies) but take it all with a healthy bit of skepticism. Also, do your homework on the consulting firm, and the consultants assigned to conduct the work as well as on the culture assessment instrument. And, most culture assessments are really the first step in a *'culture change process'* and it seems that every group has their own, and different, unique culture change methodology. So before deciding to embark on a *'culture change process',* you might want to read Section Six in this

LEVERAGE:

Guide on Culture Change.

Let's Think This Through Together . . .

> *Alone we can do so little; together we can do so much*
> *~ Helen Keller*

I am frequently asked by CEOs and business leaders for my suggestions on how to decide whether or not to conduct a culture audit. Here is the list I usually bring out and together we discuss the pros and cons.

1. **Be very clear on your purpose.** What specifically about how your organization behaves do you want to know? Is there a recurring problem or issue that is behind your desire to learn more about your culture?

2. **Don't assess your company culture just for the sake of curiosity.** All assessments and surveys disrupt the '*psyche*' and normal workflow of people and often raise more questions than answers.

3. **Start with the end result.** What specifically do you want to achieve at the end of the process? What, besides information, do you need to have from a culture assessment?

4. **Match Instrument with the Purpose.** The instrument and approach chosen should be determined by your purpose.

5. Use the survey for information and ideas to **fix a specific problem, not the culture.** Employees understand fixing specific issues to improve how work gets done, but few of us at any level can get our mind around culture change.

6. **Culture or Complaints?** In most organizations employees aren't often asked to give input on the business and in many cases employees use a culture audit to air their grievances, pet issues and to complain. That's not necessarily culture but more often a sign of morale

problems, poor management or work constraints.

7. **Culture or Climate?** Be clear you are getting a culture assessment and not a 'climate' assessment.

8. **Trial Run.** You and your senior team should take the survey first and get a debrief so you can fully understand the process, the methodology, the cultural interpretations and the quality of the consultants. If it doesn't feel right (and you, the CEO, should ultimately make that call), then don't continue. If the consulting firm balks at a senior team trial, ditch the firm and find another.

And my final words on Culture Assessments:

Remember, not every business issue, or culture issue for that matter, shows up on a culture profile.

SECTION SIX: CULTURE CHANGE

One fine day, not long ago, after comparing his company's less than stellar stock price against a peer group, the Chief Executive descended from on high and gathered his trustworthy Vice Presidents around him.

"Hear ye all. I command ye to reshape our corporate culture and launch this faire company upon the seas of everlasting greatness!"

His advisors looked sheepishly at one another then stared at their shoes, none daring to speak. Finally the secretary taking notes in the corner spoke up. "Are you out of your mind?"

In the 1990's, the concept of *'Business Process Reengineering'* [71] (succinctly put forth in a best-selling business book, *Reengineering the Corporation* by Michael Hammer and James Champy, 1993), swept through executive suites like a prairie grass fire. By getting rid of layers of unproductive management staff and reducing time spent on non value-add processes, reports, meetings and other activities of waste, companies could focus their energies and resources on delivering greater customer value and improving operating performance.

The book sold over 2.5 million copies in its first year of publication and stayed atop the New York Times bestseller list for well over a year. Reengineering was adopted at an accelerating pace and by 1993, as many as 65% of the Fortune 500 companies claimed to either have initiated reengineering efforts, or had plans to do so. This trend was fueled by the fast adoption of BPR by the consulting industry eager to help dramatically improve performance.

Very quickly, however, the shine faded as the expectations for lasting and profitable change failed to materialize. One of the key criticisms was that BPR failed to look at the entire enterprise value chain, but instead focused on individual departments. Many saw it as a palliative term for headcount reductions. Some of the more savvy academics and students of change management realized that many BPR attempts were thwarted by an unresponsive and resistant corporate culture.

Culture Change

Culture change is as difficult as getting rid of dandelion weeds in your garden. Unless you get to the roots, they will just grow back.

Today there is another business prairie wildfire raging out of control. It's called '*Culture Change*'. A recent Google search using the words 'culture change' came up with 1.62 **billion** hits (compared to just 452 million for 'leadership'). Maybe we should call it a Tsunami!

Nearly every business publication, business article and best-selling business book mentions corporate culture and culture change, usually in the same paragraph. And culture change consultants are springing up like weeds, thanks mostly to the past several years of corporate layoffs and unemployed executives and HR managers reinventing themselves as culture change consultants. And everybody seems to be an expert.

But scraping away the fresh paint on these newly minted culture consultants finds the same set of PowerPoint slides taken from the few key studies of culture change by experienced practitioners such as Harvard Professor John Kotter, MIT Professor Edgar Schien, Zappos CEO Tony Hsieh, former IBM CEO Lou Gerstner, and a few others.

And each culture consultant has his or her step-by-step process for culture change. But how many of them have really designed, implemented and driven a successful culture change process? Very few. Most of their knowledge is borrowed, not their own.

And the sobering fact is, most culture change efforts fail! With or without the "culture experts".

> *Your success isn't based on your ability to simply change.*
> *It is based on your ability to change faster than your*
> *competition, customers and business. ~ Mark Sanborn*

LEVERAGE:

Chapter 13: The Inside and Out of Culture Change

The world hates change. Yet it is the only thing that has brought progress. ~ Charles Kettering

The Holy Grail - Real Culture Change

The General Motors Fremont, California plant had always been known by those in the automotive industry as a *'dysfunctional disaster'*. Opened in 1962 it closed its doors in 1982 after twenty years of strife, strikes, worker-management animosity, poor quality (the worst plant in GM global), and year after year of losses. Workers hated their jobs and hated management so much it was not uncommon to put metal Coke bottle caps inside body panels which rattled when driven, or worse yet put half a tuna sandwich inside a door panel that was then welded shut. Employees routinely drank on the job and enjoyed sex in the back seat of vehicles. Employees hated their jobs, management hated being posted there (a career *'dead-end'* assignment), and customers hated the cars.

Then in 1985 came the headline article in Car and Driver magazine: *"When Hell Freezes Over"* (the title alluding to a miracle), about the change in culture at the plant. The Freemont plant had reopened in 1984 and one year later had the highest quality of any GM automotive plant, absenteeism had fallen from above 20% to less than 2%, not one strike, with the same employees! Freemont was producing great cars by great people.

The *'miracle'* was attributed to the joint venture between GM and Toyota, so Toyota could have a manufacturing footprint in the US and GM could experience and learn. The plant was renamed NUMMI (New Union Motor Manufacturing, Inc.) and implemented the world famous *Toyota Production System*, which features extensive training, a high level of respect for people, and among other things, the ability to stop the line at any time so that poor quality could be fixed on the spot (a process known as *andon*). For the next 25 years, the NUMMI plant was a showcase of modern management and an example of a high-performance culture. Then the global economic meltdown hit in 2009 and the plant closed in 2010 due to the fall off in global automobile sales and the decline of GM into bankruptcy and bailout. The sad thing is, GM failed to effectively apply the lessons from NUMMI to its other auto manufacturing plants.

Tools and Trust

But the change miracle of 1984 was more than just the introduction of the Toyota Production System. It was a total culture change that wasn't designed as a culture change. In fact, according to Toyota manager John Shook in an MIT Sloan Management Review article, culture change was not the goal, but the natural by-product of how people were treated, and he believes, from his own experience and the early work by Professor Ed Schein, that you don't change culture by trying to change culture (Shook, 2010).

You can't be effective trying to change values or the way people think and believe (like so many culture change approaches based on values and attitudes). But you can change culture, and dramatically as in the case of NUMMI, by changing what people do, the work processes that drive behavior and the management processes that relate to how people are treated.

> *It's easier to act your way to a new way of thinking, than to think your way to a new way of acting.*

The NUMMI story is also a testament to the important role that middle managers and supervisors play in how employees feel and behave on the job. In this example, the Toyota Production System puts great emphasis on training middle managers and supervisors in the behaviors associated with respect for people, the key to employee engagement and accountability.

Ford and the Halewood Assembly Plant

> *There are no bad plants, just bad management.*
> *~ David Hudson*

The NUMMI experience matches very well with my own experience in the automotive industry with the turnaround of the old Halewood plant that made the Ford Escort models. A plant similar to Freemont, Halewood had the worst quality in all of Ford global, was seen as the *'last stop on the bus'* for failing Ford managers, and suffered numerous and sometimes violent strikes. Mattresses were hidden in the dimly lit areas so workers could sleep during their shifts, cigarette butts covered the plant floor, and the real leadership of the plant resided in the militant union whose roots went back to the socialist days of the Liverpool dockworkers.

When I first met Nicholas Scheele at an engineering awards dinner at the University of Warwick in 1996, he had just taken over as head of Jaguar Cars (then owned by Ford) and was debating what to do with the Halewood plant; close it or reinvent it as a modern Jaguar Production facility. The conventional wisdom from just about everybody in the auto industry was that Halewood was a disaster with a toxic culture that couldn't change and should be closed. The UK Government, however, wanted to keep jobs in the region and was offering an attractive investment package to save the plant and the local jobs.

Scheele decided to *'reinvent'* Halewood and produce the new Jaguar X-400 series there, but the culture had to change. My team, headed by one of the best Senior Consultants I ever worked with, John Clayton, began talking with the Halewood management team about what was possible, beginning with a new way of behaving as managers and as workers. We developed a change agenda that involved the Union heads right at the beginning, after letting go a few senior and middle managers who couldn't (or wouldn't) believe new behaviors were possible. The first task was building trust and new working relationships between management and the Union. Then we supported the installation of the Ford Production System (modeled after the Toyota Production System).

Within two years Halewood was the highest quality automotive production facility in all of Ford worldwide and a training center for lean, quality management and the Ford Production System. All with the same employees. The Halewood story is the story of a culture change that was really about implementing new work practices and new leadership behaviors, leading to new ways of thinking and working. A high-performance culture was the by-product. (Van Wagenhove et. al., 2002)

2013 Update

Since Ford sold its Jaguar and Land Rover brands to Tata Motors in 2008, the Halewood facility is now the home of the Land Rover Evoque and demand for the model has pushed the plant to 24 hour production. The Halewood culture of quality and productivity is alive and well.

> *In most organizational change efforts, it is much easier to draw on the strengths of the culture than to overcome the constraints by changing the culture. ~ Edgar Schein*

Most Culture Change Efforts Fail: The 30% Rule

> *If you want to make enemies, try to change something.*
> *~ Woodrow Wilson*

In 1996 Professor John Kotter of Harvard University published what many consider to be the first real groundbreaking work on organizational change. His book, *Leading Change*, was based on the experiences of more than 100 companies who embarked on change programs designed to make a dramatic improvement in their competitive abilities. The book reviews the many mistakes business leaders make when attempting major changes and put forth an eight-step change management process.

His change methodology has gained considerable acceptance and even spawned a bestselling business fable (based on his 8-step change process) about penguins successfully responding to climate change; *Our Iceberg is Melting* (Kotter and Rathgeber, 2006).

However, one of the most widely quoted phrases to come out of Dr. Kotter's original research is that *"only 30% of change programs succeed"*. Twelve years later, in 2008, a McKinsey &Co. global survey of 3,199 executives found that only 1/3 of transformational efforts succeeds [72].

> *Would you schedule yourself for a surgery that had a 30 percent success rate?*

Business transformation, culture change or reshaping the existing culture to dramatically improve performance is the holy grail of nearly every business leader. And with so many businesses burdened with dysfunctional or toxic cultures, culture change is seen as a desirable solution. At this very moment numerous organizations, pubic, private and governmental, are in the midst of a culture change process that has a relatively high probability of failure.

In an article titled, *Success Rates for Different Types of Organizational Change* (Smith, 2002) researcher Martin E. Smith compared 49 published reports of successful organizational change, representing over 40,000 organizations and came to some important insights:

- Published success rates vary widely depending upon the type of change, and culture change programs fail much more often than strategy implementations and organization redesign projects.

- Published success rates vary rather widely over time since the current knowledge on how to implement big changes has grown considerably.

- Success rates depend on the success criteria used. In general, financial performance metrics and shareholder value tend to show higher success rates than more behavioral measures, such as client satisfaction or management behaviors.

- Vested interests of people reporting the research may downplay actual success rates.

- Overly focusing on the low success rates is a useful tactic to sell culture change consulting services.

Whatever the statistic, the reality is, culture change is damn hard, and the CEO needs to understand why.

Success Rates of Change Programs
Summary of initiatives and success rates of 40 studies, Smith (2002).

Type of Change	No of Studies	Success Rate	Measures
Culture Change	3	19%	Changing vision, values, and culture, management style
Business Expansion	1	20%	Product introductions and sales growth
Software Development & Installation	6	26%	Failures, time, budget, features and functionalities, value creation, cost effectiveness
Reengineer and Process Redesign	7	30%	Satisfaction, side effects, business-unit costs, cycle times, productivity
Mergers & Acquisitions	9	33%	Shareholder value, return on equity and revenue growth, market penetration, problems
TQM Driven change	5	37%	Process and design quality, satisfaction, world-class standards, implementation, internal and external benefits (management control, market share)
Technology Change	5	40%	Survey perceptions, cost savings, on-time, on budget, outages
Restructuring	9	46%	Competitive value, productivity, morale, operating profits, shareholder value, customer satisfaction
Strategy Deployment	3	58%	Survey perceptions, decision success, shareholder returns

The 'Hidden' Assumptions Behind Culture Change

People don't resist change. They resist being changed!
~ Peter Senge

One of my greatest insights about culture change came early in my career from an assignment with AVCO Everett Research Labs. Basically this was a defense technology think tank filled with pure research scientists and scientists *'masquerading a managers'*. The issue to be addressed was serious infighting over research budgets, poor conversion of research funds into saleable ideas and products, plus a culture of mistrust and blaming. Seen it many times before in a dozen other companies, including other AVCO companies.

To make a long story short, the culture change was a complete failure. Dick Millman, the then CEO of the parent company, and I laugh about it now, but it was painful then. The only thing that changed was the calendar date. Basically, my assumptions about culture change, and this culture in particular, were all wrong and I limped away with a deeper understanding that culture change is not a rational or logical process and doesn't neatly follow a flow chart or programmatic, step-by-step approach.

Over the years I have rarely been tripped up by the *'hidden assumptions'* behind culture change. Once bitten, twice smart?

The following are some of the assumptions that nearly everyone makes as they begin planning a culture change process. And we all know what happens when you ASSUME: *"You make an ass out of u and me."*

And many of these assumptions are just plain wrong.

- **There is a clear relationship between culture and performance.** While this is often assumed to be the case, and we all intuitively believe that culture impacts performance, most of the academic studies are based on correlations, not direct cause and effect. A lot more work needs to be done here.

- **Culture is the problem to be fixed.** The problem may not be one of the cultural characteristics measured, but an entirely different or related issue.

- **Culture can be changed.** There is a large body of evidence that says culture change is extremely difficult, risky and more often than not doesn't really work. You should think about smaller and focused changes that might have a higher probability of success.

- **The benefits outweigh the cost.** Very few (almost none) of the culture change consulting firms are willing to work on a *'no gain, no fee'* basis. Identifying and measuring the actual financial and organizational benefits expected must be done early on and takes considerable skill and attention. There are very few examples of tangible ROI gains from culture change programs.

- **Culture change does more good than harm**. All change efforts, but especially culture change programs, produce collateral damage of one kind or another that is often not anticipated and may create additional problems.

- **Culture change is a logical decision**. The big assumption here is that employees will change their working habits if it makes logical sense. Human change is emotionally driven and you are messing with social dynamics, not reprogramming machines.

- **Culture change is another business project**. If anything, culture change is a major leadership activity, not a management project and the CEO and senior team must be prepared to spend 40-60% of their time on leading, imbedding and sustaining the new culture.

- **Culture change is about values**. All experience points to the fact that internal policies and procedures drive culture as much, or more, than employee values and leadership styles. Be ready to rethink, lean and streamline everything you do so that your internal processes drive the desired behaviors.

Those who reach senior management positions in most organizations (certainly in the US, UK and Western Europe) are skewed from the natural population distribution of behavioral types described on the Myers Briggs Type Indicator (MBTI) and other behavioral profiles. Typically very few are people-centric or perceiving types; the majority being extroverted, logical and judgment types. This skews how management teams think and work and when making decisions around change they are more likely to put emphasis on the business case for change, and less likely to consider or worry about the effect on people.

> *What does NOT work in changing a culture? Some group decides what the new culture should be. It turns a list of values over to the communications or HR departments with the order that they tell people what the new culture is. They cascade the message down the hierarchy, and little to nothing changes. ~ Professor John P. Kotter*

Tomatoes and Culture Change: Unintended Consequences

Several years ago, plant scientists discovered a genetic mutation that caused the tomato to ripen evenly, instead of leaving a greenish-yellow top on an otherwise ripe tomato. Since consumers in supermarkets preferred a fully red tomato to one with a yellowish top, the mutated plants were propagated and even though the tomatoes were picked somewhat green, they ripened evenly, producing a lovely fully red tomato.

However, there was a slight problem with this otherwise brilliant solution. They weren't as sweet as yellow-topped (non-mutated) tomatoes. In fact, they were pretty bland. Beautiful, but bland. Seems that the gene that controlled the yellowish tops also had something to do with sweetness and flavor.

This is an excellent example of what I will call a *'brilliant solution with unintended consequences'.* Military drones (UAVs) are another excellent example where the solution, a precision strike, often has the unintended consequences of civilian collateral damage. And culture change programs are a third example!

Ignoring Strong Subcultures

Another of the *'hidden'* reasons why culture change efforts often fail is the lack of understanding of the power of subcultures within an organization. Most leaders at the top, who usually decide on the need for a culture change and agree to the methodology to be used, don't have a clue about what the subcultures are, where they are, or how strong and influential they are. If you recall the *'We Be'* experience of a strong subculture at Bell Helicopter, you can see how difficult culture change can be.

The Backbone of Most Culture Change Methodologies

"The individual activity of one man with backbone will do more than a thousand men with a mere wishbone.
~William J. Boetcker

One of the earliest, and still one of the most widely used organization change approaches was developed by Kurt Lewin, an early 20th-century German-American psychologist, MIT professor and one of the modern pioneers of applied psychology and organization dynamics. The Lewin Change Model is commonly described as "*Unfreezing – Realigning – Refreezing*" (Lewin, 1935) and in relation to culture change pertains to both tangible elements of a business (structure, policies, processes, plans) and intangible elements (work habits, mental models, behaviors at all levels).

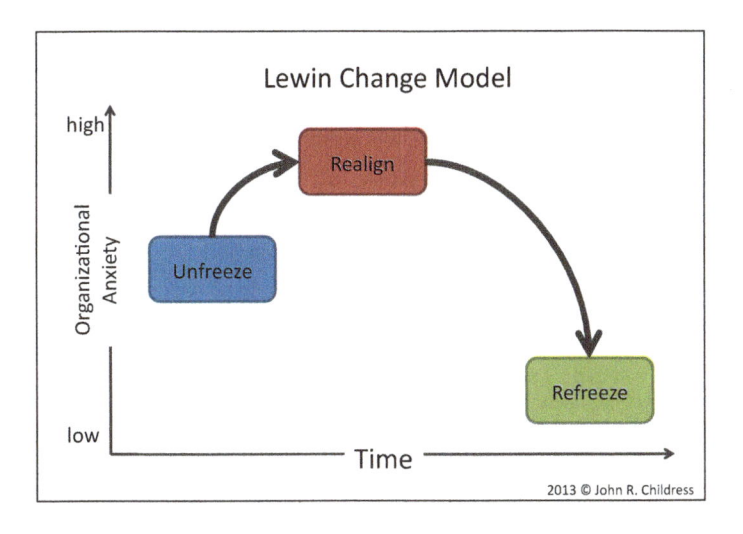

I would say this model, in one form or another, is the backbone of most change management and culture change methodologies used today.

The problem is, many organizations attempting culture change focus mostly on step two (Realigning). They reorganize. They adopt a new set of objectives. They may even develop a change management map and step-by-step action plans. And then they wonder why they can't get traction.

The critical first step (Unfreezing), which creates and imbeds the logic and motivation behind *'why we must change'*, is too often given casual attention by senior management and as a result employees don't fully understand the need for change nor the rationale behind the change decisions. In addition, passing lightly through step one ignores the most important change that must first happen before the culture can shift: a change in the behavior of the senior leadership team. And every culture change academic and consultant will tell you that unless leadership understands that a new set of behaviors is critical for successful culture change, not much will shift in the organization.

Step three (Refreezing) also gets superficial attention. In most cases, cascading rollouts of culture change seminars, workshops, PowerPoint briefings, or special multimedia communications are substituted for the hard work of changing processes and procedures to reinforce (refreeze) the new cultural behaviors. They are routinely light on the real elements of imbedding change (new work practices, *'real-time'* feedback, coaching, rewards, recognition and consequences).

The other issue with most culture change methodologies is that they are usually *'one size fits all'* with the belief that people are the same and respond in the same manner to change efforts. Where this really breaks down is when culture change methodologies developed in the US are exported to multinationals and global organizations where national cultures are very different. The difference in thinking patterns and reasoning between different cultures is a major source of difficulty with US-centric change methodologies.

The six dimensions of national cultural differences studied by Geert Hofstede show quite clearly that different national cultures respond differently to change initiatives and what might work well with the *'Just Do It'* culture of North America is less than effective with the *'shared interests'* cultures of Scandinavia, and even less effective in other cultures, like China (Hofstede, 2004).

Understanding People Is A Big Key

I always find it amazing to listen to workers complain about early morning meetings and having to get up early to get to work on time. This is not an uncommon complaint. Yet many of these same individuals cheerfully get up at *'zero-dark-thirty'* on a weekend and drive long distances to play golf, go duck hunting or fishing. Not one complaint! So it's not the early hour that depresses them, but something about their work environment is not very motivating. Obviously the corporate culture is not giving them all they need from work.

A great number of culture change methodologies are long on processes and short on understanding peoples' motivations and the key to any real and sustainable change is individual motivation. And in the case of human social motivations and what employees need from work, it's pretty much the same the world over, at all levels.

Dr. Jack Wiley is the creator of *WorkTrends™*, an annual survey of employee engagement launched over 25 years ago and now with data from 28 countries and over 200,000 employees. His findings, summarized in the book *RESPECT: Delivering Results by Giving Employees What They Really Want* (Wiley And Kowske, 2011), fits well with the many other employee motivation and engagement studies, which is a growing industry.

What's useful about this data, and other employee engagement surveys, is that 75% of what people want from work is NOT pay related! And as you can see, much has to do with the corporate culture.

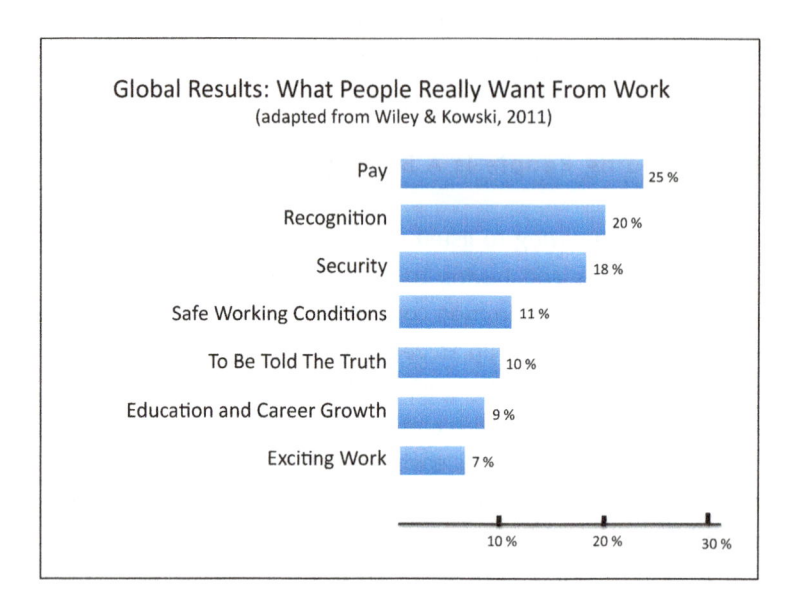

Global Results: What People Really Want From Work
(adapted from Wiley & Kowski, 2011)

Category	Percentage
Pay	25%
Recognition	20%
Security	18%
Safe Working Conditions	11%
To Be Told The Truth	10%
Education and Career Growth	9%
Exciting Work	7%

Ignoring this information during the planning and execution of a culture change program is definitely a design to fail.

Doctor: "I have good news and bad news. The good news is the surgery was flawlessly executed. The bad news is the patient died!"

Chapter 14: The Human Brain and Culture Change

When the rate of change on the outside exceeds the rate of change on the inside, the end is near. ~ Jack Welch

To better understand the process of culture change and what makes it successful or not, we need to pause a moment and learn something about the human brain, neurophysiology, and the experience of being human.

Cognitive Dissonance

Logic and reason, unfortunately, have little to do with making change actually happen.

Cognitive Dissonance is a term invented by psychologist Leon Festinger to describe the conflict an individual feels when confronted with change and the choice between what a person currently knows and believes to be true, and new contradictory information (Festinger, 1957). Cognitive dissonance is that discomfort we feel when we hold two conflicting thoughts in the mind at the same time. For example, if you see yourself as an inherently good person, then when you do something bad, you feel dissonance. Also you can feel uncomfortable (dissonant) when someone you know well acts differently from your normal experience of them.

Cognitive dissonance also impacts how people behave during culture change when they are presented with a new culture that is different from their habits and conventional ways of working. And strong cultures experience strong dissonance during a culture change process because in a strong culture a large number of people believe the same way and have similar working habits. In weak cultures the dissonance and change difficulties are mostly with individuals, not groups or subcultures.

Cognitive dissonance is such a powerful part of the human behavioral makeup that it can lead individuals and groups (subcultures) to react in dramatic ways. To release the tension (dissonance) during culture change, individuals and subcultures often take one of several classical responses:

- Play dumb, ignore the process and wait it out (remember the *'We Be's'*).
- Attack the new processes with multiple reasons and excuses why it won't work.
- Give up and become disenfranchised.
- Malicious obedience (e.g. pretend to accept and go along, but only fake it; no real commitment).
- Begrudgingly adopt the new changes and behaviors.

A classic example of these responses is the various tactics smokers use to justify their unhealthy habit when presented with the overwhelming logical facts.

However, it is important to remember:

Without cognitive dissonance, there can be no change!

Culture change is not about avoiding dissonance, but working through it together so that fear of loss is lessened and the attraction of new ideas and different ways of working can be embraced.

The *Hold-On/Let Go* Dilemma

The human race is a marvelous creation, especially when you take into account the amazing amount of progress made from the early days of the nomads and cave dwellers to the modern city builders and space travelers, all in just a short 80,000 years! How have we made such progress? Obviously the size of the human brain, the opposable thumb, large eyes and upright posture are important factors, as is our inherently social nature and ability to communicate ideas. But we are also creatures of comfort and all progress requires a certain level of risk and discomfort.

Enter the *Hold-On/Let-Go* dilemma. Basically, every human being is wired with a strong urge for safety, security and comfort. However, at the same time we are also genetically predisposed to seek adventure, new opportunities and certain levels of risk. Thus we constantly live with two opposing forces at all times: the force of change and the force of resistance.

And now we come to culture change and the classic resistance to change. It's not that employees and executives don't want change, we are just conflicted with these two opposing forces. And of course the initial reaction is resistance, especially against fear of the unknown (and leadership promises of a brighter future are not always credible or trusted).

"Hold-On / Let Go" Dilemma During Culture Change

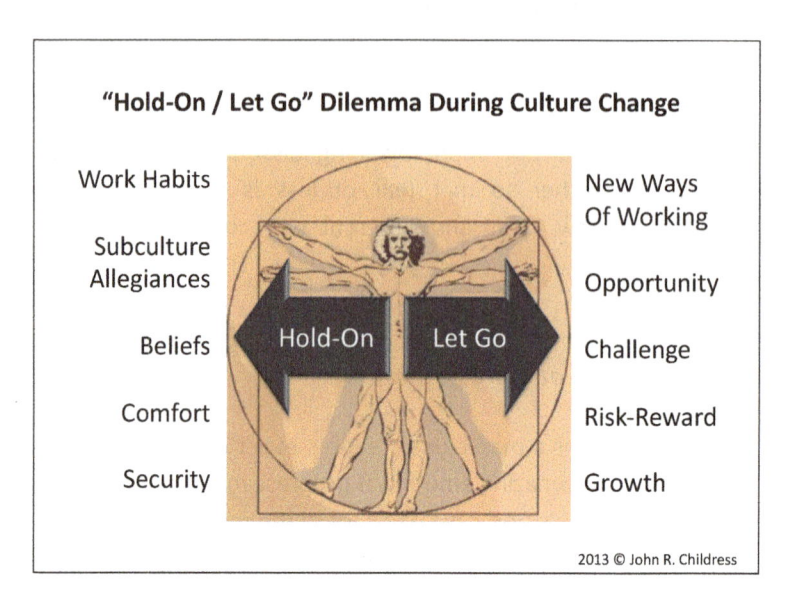

Hold-On:
- Work Habits
- Subculture Allegiances
- Beliefs
- Comfort
- Security

Let Go:
- New Ways Of Working
- Opportunity
- Challenge
- Risk-Reward
- Growth

2013 © John R. Childress

When designing and implementing a culture change process it is critical to understand the *Hold-On/Let-Go* dilemma everyone faces. Irrefutable logic and small steps works far better than "trust me". Listening to people's concerns (really listening) works even better.

Hear with your ears, listen with your heart.

The Brain Is A Wonderful Organ

The brain is a wonderful organ; it starts working the moment you get up in the morning and does not stop until you get into the office. ~ Robert Frost

Most programmatic and top-down culture change efforts fail. Essentially senior management decides what needs to be changed, tells everyone how to get it done, even hires top flight consultants who utilize the *'best in class'* change methodology, and everyone else is supposed to implement according to the plan. We all know about the best laid plans!

One of the reasons this structured, programmatic approach tends to fail has to do with how the human brain is wired. It turns out there is a scientific reason why employees are less effective when tasks are dictated to them.

Amy Arnsten, a neuroscience professor at Yale University, studies the human need for feeling in control and reports some interesting insights (Arnsten, 2009). Specifically, parts of the brain such as the basal ganglia (the brain's habit center), the amygdala, (an area related to emotions such as fear and anger), and the hypothalamus, (which manages instinctive drives such as hunger and security), all come into play when an individual begins to feel out of control. Research indicates that people who feel out of control revert to the basal ganglia's processing (habit center) because it is physically comforting and rewarding to do so. Put another way, *'entrenched'* (literally hardwired in the basal ganglia) behavior is satisfying to enact and with the very act of falling back on the entrenched behavior, the pattern is further engrained in the neural center. Hence, resistance to change by reverting to old ways of working is actually mentally and physically rewarding.

It takes a habit to break a habit. ~ Stephen Covey

Therefore to bring about culture change (changes in habitual behaviors) we would need to build a new set of habits into the basal ganglia, and that is accomplished through repetition. I believe that most culture change efforts fail because the consultants and business leaders underestimate the amount of repetition of new behavior(s) required in order to successfully *'rewire'* the basal ganglia and other neural pathways. A culture change workshop or a few skill-training sessions won't do the job! The new behaviors need to be *'grooved'*, which requires time, investment and coaching at all levels. Everyone in the organization needs to become accountable to coach and develop each other on a *'real time'* basis for these new work habits to become ingrained.

> *Successful people are simply those with successful habits.*
> *~Brian Tracy*

Loss of Initiative and Creativity

When people lose their sense of control, such as when tasks or changes are dictated to them, the brain's cognitive centers, the prefrontal cortex, actually experience a decrease in cognitive functioning (Arnsten, 2009; Turturici, 2013; Garms, 2013).

This perception of not being in control, whether real or imagined, can lead to a drop in creativity, accountability and productivity. However, if tasks are explained as the *'outcomes required'* but not how to get it done, the feeling of being in control is enhanced and cognitive functioning increases. Potential result? Creativity, greater motivation and task commitment, and most importantly, personal accountability.

When individuals feel *'out of control'* they tend to manufacture reasons and excuses for their resistance and failure, even before it happens. Classic unaccountable statements such as *"There was nothing I could do. It's not my department. I tried but they wouldn't listen. I'm too busy already. Why bother, they won't understand anyway"* are rampant in cultures where people don't feel in control of their work or objectives. People who believe they can make a difference and see evidence of this in the corporate culture tend to find creative ways to solve problems and make things happen.

For those interested in the topic of accountability, being in control and leadership, I suggest you read an excellent Harvard Business Press book by Justin Menkes, *Better Under Pressure: How Great Leaders Bring Out the Best in Themselves and Others (2011).*

The P&L of Neuroscience?

If we use these principles of neuroscience to rethink the steps in Lewin's Change model, some of the suggestions for improving the odds on culture change might be:

- Status (and therefore security) is important to our brains, and not knowing the new organization structure and reporting relationships can be anxiety-producing. Make organizational decisions quick and early and publish them to everyone. The longer you wait to publish the new organization chart the more resistance there is.

- Lack of information triggers insecurity and threat in our brains. Share information and then share it again and again, even if the only thing you can say is more information is coming. Then be specific as to the time frame and keep to the deadline. Trust based on timely follow through increases security and reduces anxiety.

- Feeling out of control is often the case during change. Feelings of helplessness cause emotional responses such as depression and apathy. Get people engaged at all levels. Ask for ideas. Create ways for people to feel in control of their part of the change process.

- Don't automatically disband tight-knit groups and subcultures, which can cause a feeling of isolation. Reinforce existing group relationships where possible and actively encourage the building of new relationships when things change.

Ideas not coupled with action never become bigger than the brain cells they occupy. ~ Arnold H. Glasow

Chapter 15: Instant, Sheep-dip or Viral?

When we are no longer able to change a situation - we are challenged to change ourselves. ~ Viktor E. Frankl

There are numerous culture change methodologies, too numerous to mention here (we'd both fall asleep). However, it is important to take a look at some of the basic underlying principles of several key change methodologies and to assess their pros and cons. In the UK we have a saying; *'Horses for courses'* which in our case roughly means that one size doesn't fit all and different methods might be appropriate for different cultures and business challenges.

Instant Culture Change

Nothing exciting or significant ever happens in a refrigerator. You have to turn up the heat!
~ Thomas D. Willhite

Many years ago my consulting team and I were about to implement a performance improvement process for a company in Florida. The CEO was fully engaged and ready to lead the process. The need was definitely evident: information was not flowing between departments; turf wars and resource battles were rampant. The business result was a decline in sales and falling customer satisfaction. The most common word used to describe other parts of the company was *'THEM'*. Definitely a *'them vs us'* culture which was sapping productivity and draining everyone's energy, as well as negatively impacting business performance. A classic candidate for a business transformation.

A week before we were to begin, there was a fire at night and their office building burned to the ground. Needless to say, our consulting engagement was cancelled as the CEO and the management team scrambled to find new office space to get up and running again.

I met the CEO about 6 months later and heard a story that significantly shifted my thinking about culture change.

Here's how he put it:

> *"The only space we could find quickly that fit our needs was a large, open plan arrangement, all on one floor in an industrial complex. I looked at this big empty space and suddenly had a thought. What if I use this catastrophe to make some changes in how we work?*
>
> *I set up the space so that people had to interact with each other, departments that were previously at war I located together, and I put all the executives in the middle of the warehouse, in open cubicles. We built a few closed meeting rooms for external client meetings, but all internal meetings were held in our open conference rooms in the middle of the warehouse.*
>
> *If this had been a planned change the bitching would have been non-stop. But since it was an emergency and everyone was focused on keeping the company working*

> *and servicing clients, there was no time to complain! They just got on with it. And, they got on with each other! These past six months have been the most enjoyable and productive I can remember. People are more relaxed, there is more laughter, friendship circles have expanded, and ideas are bubbling up. It's a real culture change!"*

He then added:

> *"I wouldn't recommend burning down your company to shift the culture, but what we really did was change the way people work together. It was our work processes and the subcultures that formed around them that were causing us to behave so badly."*

"Big Change": Rapid Culture Change

Conventional wisdom is not always wisdom.

Salesforce.com provides on-demand services for customer-relationship management and every day processes over 100 million transactions from its 2,100,000+ subscribers. Inside the company the services technology group is responsible for all product development. Salesforce.com has grown into a global powerhouse and like all fast growth organizations, at some point bureaucracy sets in and things begin to slow down.

Salesforce.com was no exception to this phenomenon. In its early years, the group was delivering an average of four major new releases each year. By 2006, the pace had slowed to one major release a year. Salesforce.com was losing its edge.

Conventional wisdom suggests embarking on a measured transformation process to shift the culture of bureaucratic hierarchy, the aim being to develop more agility and speed. But the CEO, Marc Benioff, is never one for conventional wisdom. Instead, he decided to shift the core management process of the company, how they develop software and innovations, from traditional waterfall methods to the rapid-iteration processes of Agile and Scrum. And he wanted it all done at once! So he decided to go all out with change right across the whole organization, simultaneously!

Developer Mike Cohn detailed the Salesforce.com rapid culture change in his book *Succeeding with Agile* (Cohen, 2009) :

> During the first year of making the switch, Salesforce.com released 94% more features, delivered 38% more features per developer, and delivered over 500% more value to their customers compared to the previous year. Fifteen months after adopting Scrum, Salesforce.com surveyed its employees and found that 86% were having a *'good time'* or the *'best time'* working at the company. Prior to adopting Scrum, only 40% said the same thing.

While conventional culture change *'wisdom'* is all about changing values and adopting new leadership behaviors, sustainable culture change also requires changes in business processes and policies.

Fast Break Culture Change

And if you find room for improvement, don't buy into the commonly held view that culture change takes years and tons of management time and effort, plus endless workshops and all-hands communication meetings. It can happen relatively quickly if you take the right actions and are truly committed.

Take a page from the playbook of the New York Police Department's *'Broken Windows'* policy on reducing violent crime [73]. The theory is simple (and easier to enact inside a company than it is in a sprawling metropolis like New York City):

> **Broken Windows Policy**: *untended disorder and minor offenses give rise to serious crime; therefore dealing with minor offenses now is a significant deterrent to serious crime later.*

This is how the banking industry got itself in trouble, by ignoring its *'broken windows'* with an eventual build up of tolerance for outside the norm behavior and risky deals, finally leading up to the excessive risk taking and blatant disregard for governance and self-regulation. The result being the recent global financial meltdown, the disappearance of once venerated institutions and the colossal bailout using public funding.

Once you have decided on the culture you want and have defined the leadership activities and business processes you need to run the business and build a high-performance culture, take a *'high visibility'* approach to holding people accountable.

The first time you terminate a senior executive for flagrantly acting against the desired culture, you will have fired the *'shot heard round the cubicles'*. Everyone will know that this company is serious about its values and building a high-performance culture.

And it won't be long before employees start holding each other, and themselves, more accountable, just as community anti-crime groups began to spring up all around New York after the police began to take a high visibility approach to minor crimes. Deal with your broken windows before they become serious crimes.

Adapting the Lewin Model for Culture Change

Professor John Kotter's 8-Step model [74], one of the most highly regarded culture change processes, closely follows the Lewin *'Unfreezing-Realignment-Refreezing'* approach.

While this is a very comprehensive culture change approach, and several other models follow a similar process, the sad fact is that many times the entire process is not carried through to completion, for a variety of reasons:

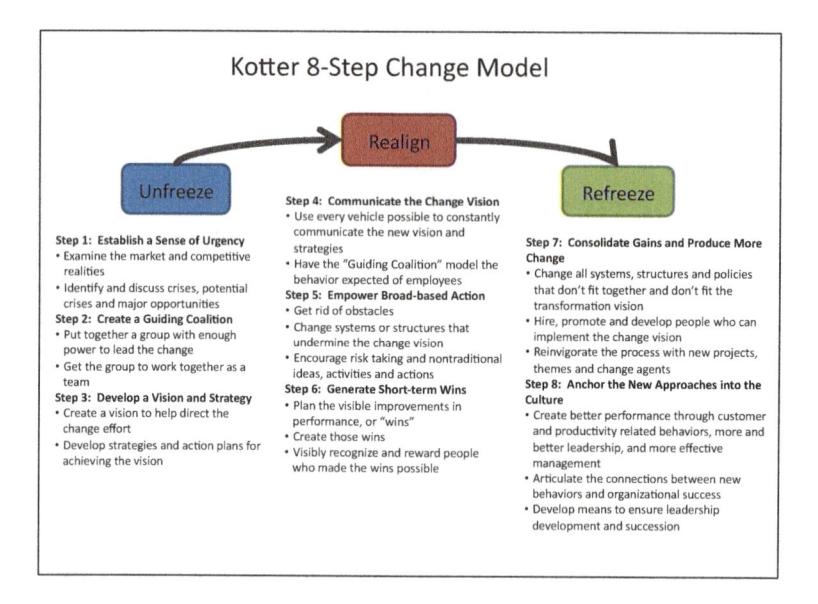

Kotter 8-Step Change Model

Unfreeze → Realign → Refreeze

Step 1: Establish a Sense of Urgency
- Examine the market and competitive realities
- Identify and discuss crises, potential crises and major opportunities

Step 2: Create a Guiding Coalition
- Put together a group with enough power to lead the change
- Get the group to work together as a team

Step 3: Develop a Vision and Strategy
- Create a vision to help direct the change effort
- Develop strategies and action plans for achieving the vision

Step 4: Communicate the Change Vision
- Use every vehicle possible to constantly communicate the new vision and strategies
- Have the "Guiding Coalition" model the behavior expected of employees

Step 5: Empower Broad-based Action
- Get rid of obstacles
- Change systems or structures that undermine the change vision
- Encourage risk taking and nontraditional ideas, activities and actions

Step 6: Generate Short-term Wins
- Plan the visible improvements in performance, or "wins"
- Create those wins
- Visibly recognize and reward people who made the wins possible

Step 7: Consolidate Gains and Produce More Change
- Change all systems, structures and policies that don't fit together and don't fit the transformation vision
- Hire, promote and develop people who can implement the change vision
- Reinvigorate the process with new projects, themes and change agents

Step 8: Anchor the New Approaches into the Culture
- Create better performance through customer and productivity related behaviors, more and better leadership, and more effective management
- Articulate the connections between new behaviors and organizational success
- Develop means to ensure leadership development and succession

- First, it takes a significant commitment of time, money and resources. The day-to-day business can't stop functioning and such an all-encompassing change agenda adds additional resource pressure.

- Second, very few consulting firms have the breadth of business knowledge, training skills, organization design background and facilitation skills to support all three phases, which usually means the consulting firm focuses most heavily on their area of expertise and the other steps get minimal attention.

- Third, the senior team gets distracted with new business issues, like growing competition, market shifts or demands from corporate for greater cost reductions.

- Fourth, it is difficult to evaluate whether or not real change is happening and the metrics used are often weak and anecdotal.

LEVERAGE:

Everybody Needs The Sheep-dip

WE plan, WE decide. YOU implement.

The Sheep-dip, or *'Roll Out'* is perhaps the most widely used approach for business change initiatives and often contains many of the elements of the Lewin and Kotter Models. Senior leadership discusses changes that would improve performance, make business and strategic decisions, then pass their plans down to the operational levels for execution, with the basic belief that, besides new role modeling from the senior leadership, a *'critical mass'* of employees need to embrace the new cultural vision and change their behavior. This critical mass then creates a *'tipping point'* scenario where the rest of the organization is swept along.

In principle I agree with this concept. What's not to like about creating a tipping point process by having a large number of employees understanding the new changes required and shifting their behavior accordingly? But the devil is in the details and in particular the approach used.

Many culture change consultants base their approach on a workshop or seminar model, and many of these firms have their roots in the human potential movement of the 1970's, founded by personal change gurus such as Werner Erhardt, Thomas D. Willhite and John Hanley. Their approach to change is based on the strong belief that *'experiential training'* (using structured group activities to produce personal insights and change readiness) will move people to *'want to change'* and adopt the new culture.

Experiential training is a powerful group technology and often produces deep insights into personal behaviors and attitudes that an individual was previously unawares. But insight (the "Ah-Ha!" or Eureka! Moment) alone does not change habits. As we have said before, **it takes a habit to change a habit**. Insight is the necessary first step, but that's a long way from culture change.

The Sheep-dip approach usually has several parts and is quite compelling in many ways. First, it usually starts with a culture assessment to show the gap between current and desired culture. Second, and here is the seductive part, is a senior leadership team off-site specially *'customized'* for the organization by the consultants and usually of a 3-4 day duration. Enough time to really get away from it all, have some meaningful discussions and start the leadership behavior changes required. These are very engaging and often insightful processes and most senior teams come back to work recharged and ready to change the culture.

Next each member of the senior team holds a similar off-site retreat for their direct reports and key management staff, in order to give them the same great set of insights and experience in the new cultural behaviors. Now we have a huge release of energy. Some individuals even have life-changing positive insights about themselves.

Now comes the Sheep-dip! How do we get all employees to have this change and insight opportunity, without breaking the budget? The usual solution is to have internal facilitators trained by the consultants to conduct a *'modified'* 1-day version of the culture change workshop, and also to get one or more senior executives to attend the opening and give a talk (with PowerPoint) about the need for a new culture and the behaviors everyone needs to adopt. Everyone attends the workshops, takes away the new Company Values and Behaviors on a printed card, and goes back to work. All in all a great personal experience, but rarely a cultural game changer.

Because the cost is now climbing up into the million plus range (with rental of meeting rooms, AV equipment, time off work, plus the consultant's fees), the CFO starts to question the ROI, of which there are as yet no metrics.

All this and we have only gotten to the *'unfreezing'* phase of the Lewin model! Since most training oriented culture change firms are strong on facilitation skills and very weak on Business Process Improvement, Lean, Organization Design, Spans of Control, HR and other skills needed for the realignment phase, it is usually left to an ad hoc internal culture change team, who also have important day jobs.

I think you can begin to see the decline of the effectiveness of this process, and we haven't even thought about the Refreezing phase yet!

I have, however, seen this training-based Sheep-dip approach work well in several organizations which completely reshaped their culture in less than a year. But as I examined each and every one of these culture change successes, a common pattern began to emerge. It wasn't the training or the Sheep-dip that created the real culture change; it was the fanatical belief, hard work and determination of the CEO!

A great example is the turnaround of Navistar International in the late 1990s under the leadership of CEO John Horne. Or the spectacular growth and dominance of Yum! Brands (Pizza Hut, KFC, Taco Bell) under the charismatic leadership of David C. Novak, who was named CEO of the Year in 2012. The case for strong, committed leadership in order for culture change is seen in these two examples, and in several others. In cases where the leader or CEO was less than fanatical about building a high-performance culture and less committed to the time it takes, the Sheep-dip approach produced a good personal development experience and very little culture change.

Unleashing 'Viral' Change

There is no change unless there is behavioral change.
~ Leandro Herrero

John R. Childress

I entered the University of California as a freshman in 1966 and a social revolution was underway on the majority of college campuses across the United States. This was the time of the Hippie movement of alternative life styles, protest songs and outlandish dress combined with the anti-war demonstrations, all fueled by the sudden explosion of drugs and acid-rock music. Where did all that come from? Was it a top down mandated social movement? Did someone in authority proclaim 1966 National Anti-Establishment Year? (Maybe they did and I was too wasted to notice!) It was a movement, a social contagion that swept the nation. How did it grow?

I remember very vividly my senior year in High School when a couple of the really cool and respected kids started growing their hair and wearing loose fitting bell bottom jeans instead of tight legged jeans and loafers. And they were listening to English rock music instead of the Beach Boys! At first it was weird, but these were the cool kids and before long, more and more kids in my class were beginning to experiment with alternative dress and alternative thinking. Social networks and the desire to belong are powerful change agents and motivators.

Coming from a background of psychiatry and then senior management in the pharmaceutical industry is an unlikely pedigree for one of the newest, and I must say, extremely effective methodologies for large organizational change, and culture change in particular. This change methodology, championed by Dr. Leandro Hererro, is based on a few simple facts of organizational life when dealing with change that those at the top are, for the most part, out of touch with:

- an organization is actually a network of relationships and not a hierarchy of authority.
- the powerful role played by *'respected'* influencers and informal leaders.
- the power of groups or subcultures.

Basically, changes and new ways of working are either promulgated or resisted through a social network of influencers and relationships.

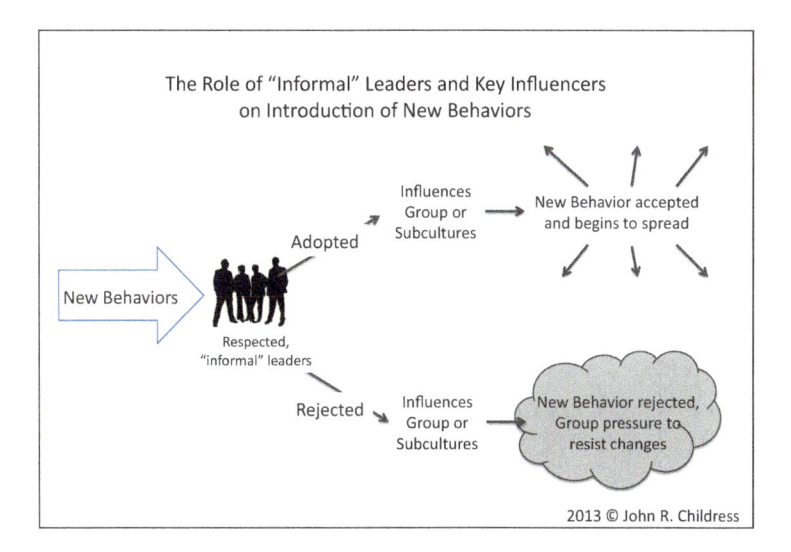

The Role of "Informal" Leaders and Key Influencers on Introduction of New Behaviors

2013 © John R. Childress

Dr. Leandro Herrero, thanks to his psychiatric background and executive business experiences, had the unique insight that social networks, in conjunction with peer pressure, have a great impact on the development of corporate culture. And therefore one particular group of individuals in an organization holds the key to rapid and sustainable culture change.

They are the individuals, from all levels (hourly to executive) that are the most respected by their peers and others in the company. People listen when they speak. People follow and imitate their behaviors, attitudes and points of view about work, management, customer service and culture. They are the trendsetters and the *'informal leaders'* with great power to sway opinion and behavior. And most senior executives don't even know they exist!

In reference to the Sheep-dip and Roll-Out approaches, Herrero believes that triggering change is easy, but spreading, sustaining and maintaining is the hard part. And the hard parts are the behavioral changes that are adopted, not because of top down proclamations of senior management about new corporate values, but of the acceptance (or rejection) by key-influence individuals and small groups. Instead of the top-down push process of the Sheep-dip and other forms of the classic roll-out, real culture change is a pull effect, a social contagion, a social movement, with senior leadership as the back-up support.

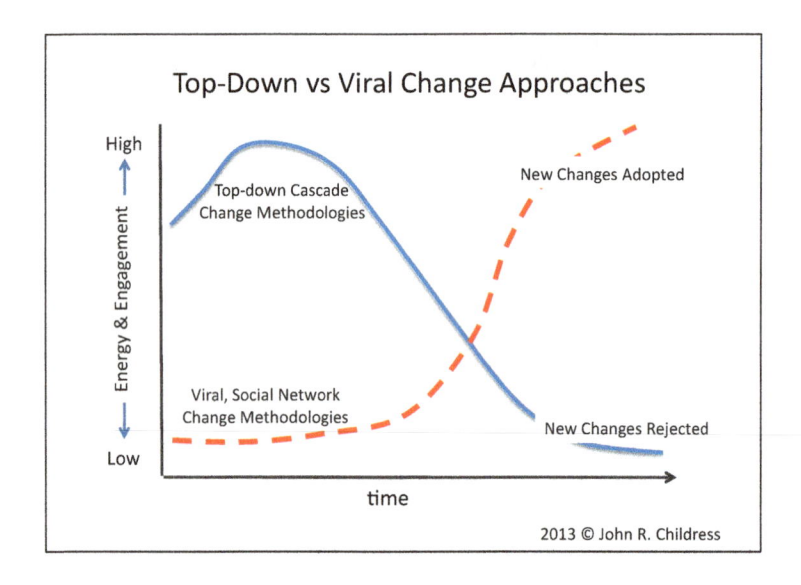

Top-Down vs Viral Change Approaches

Chart showing Energy & Engagement over time: Top-down Cascade Change Methodologies (blue curve) rises high then declines to New Changes Rejected. Viral, Social Network Change Methodologies (orange dashed curve) starts low then rises to New Changes Adopted.

2013 © John R. Childress

Real culture change is about new behaviors. For example, a true safety culture is not about training and safety values, but about the everyday use of safe behaviors. And PowerPoint slides or training sessions don't produce new behaviors, at best they introduce and reinforce new information.

Sheep-dips and rollouts spread information. Social Networks spread beliefs and behaviors.

In his two key books on how social networks drive change *Viral Change™* (Herrero, 2006) and *Homo Imitans* (Herrero, 2010-2011), Dr. Leandro Herrero shows that a viral change process is the opposite of the traditional change management processes and is fueled by the power of internal social networks, peer pressure and the human need to belong to something that has positive energy and excitement.

According to Herrero:

> *"Viral Change™ uses the power of a small set of well-defined non-negotiable behaviors, spread by small groups of highly connected individuals within the organization. Their peer-to-peer influence creates new norms, new ways of doing, new cultures. When groups start doing things the new way, other groups follow. Stories of success spread. Stories are memorable, behaviors are contagious. PowerPoints are not."*

As a methodology, Viral Change™ seems to have all the elements of the Lewin model in it, although *'Unfreezing'*, *'Realigning'* and *'Refreezing'* seems to be happening continually across social networks as social influencers display new behaviors that are then taken up by others in their sphere of influence. Behavior change spreads across the organization like an infection, not in the linear top-down passing of information used in most change methodologies.

The Viral Change™ process is roughly divided into five phases and is based on the age-old truth that peer-to-peer influence is greater than hierarchical influence:

Phase 1. Discovery:
- creating or revisiting a vision.
- uncovering and articulating non negotiable behaviors.
- mapping the networks of change.
- uncovering the real influencers within the organization.

Phase 2. Development:
- identifying peer groups and visualizing peer-to-peer influence.
- aligning management.
- recruiting selected people to participate.

Phase 3. Engagement:
- creation of a community of change agents
- helping them with their role.
- aligning further leaders and managers.

Phase 4. Diffusion:
- behaviors spread, support the community of champions
- peer to peer influence is orchestrated and supported.
- progress is tracked and evaluated; stories of success are spread.

Phase 5. Sustain:
- key behaviors are now embedded.
- new directions are evaluated.
- refocus and restart.

Major social movements eventually fade into the landscape not because they have diminished but because they have become a permanent part of our perceptions and experience.
~Freda Adler

LEVERAGE:

Chapter 16: Rethinking Culture Change

Change Management seems to result in lots of management and little change. What I'm really looking for is Change Leadership!~ a very frustrated CEO

From Toxic To High Performance:

Success has no autopilot switch! ~ Gordon Bethune

Successful business turnarounds often provide a unique glimpse into culture change. Funny thing is, turnaround specialists don't call it a culture change, they see it as a business recovery, but for the turnaround to be sustainable, the culture must shift as well. While a turnaround is different from most *'elected'* culture change programs (in a turnaround it's fix or die) in that the sense of urgency is real and the loss of jobs and/or company identity immanent, the principles of successful culture change can be clearly seen in a successful and sustainable turnaround.

One of my favorite examples of the turnaround of a failing

John R. Childress

organization and highly toxic culture into a high-performance company (and culture) is the story of Continental Airlines (*Bethune and Huler, 1998*). If you haven't read the book, *From Worst to First* by Gordon Bethune, I consider it mandatory reading for all CEOs. You will definitely see your organization somewhere in the story, sometimes painfully so.

I'll give you a brief overview (but you really should read the book). Here's the situation at Continental Airlines in 1994:

- Company facing it's third bankruptcy in a decade.
- $2.5 billion in default; not debt, default.
- 10 years of consecutive losses.
- Amalgamation of 7 airlines (and very different cultures) with 40,000 employees.
- Worst customer service record among the 10 major US airlines.
- Highest number of baggage complaints.
- Worst record for on-time departures and arrivals.
- Most involuntary denied boarding (overbooked and you get bumped).
- 10 CEOs in 10 years.

Want to sign up for that job? Gordon Bethune, an executive from Boeing and a former mechanic and pilot, thought the Board was nuts when they offered him the job. But Gordon knew that the issue wasn't lack of money, they had raised money before and their performance hadn't improved. The issue for Gordon was lack of pride and teamwork, poor management skills, no real behavior standards, too much focus on costs and not enough on the customer, weak leadership, too many plans and initiatives and no clear strategy.

Anytime you are in a company that is broken, often what's

LEVERAGE:

been ignored are three things: the people, the training of those people, and the systems. ~ Lawrence Kellner, CFO Continental Airlines

Here's the situation in 1996, just two years later:

- Continental Airlines returned to profitability in 1995.
- 1996: Voted airline of the year, against 300 global competitors.
- Ranked in the top 5 of all global airlines ever since 1996.
- Among the top 4 in all Department of Transportation airline customer service statistics since 1996 .
- 16 straight quarters of record profits.
- Share price from $3.30 to $50 in 4 years.
- Employee turnover reduced 45%.

Gordon and the senior team at Continental delivered a sustainable turnaround, and along the way built a high-performance culture, without culture change consultants! In my evaluation of what took place at Continental, some key elements relevant to culture change stand out.

- Gordon fired those senior and middle managers who no longer believed in the company and hired executives and managers who understood the business and who deeply cared about employees and customers.
- He built a simple and clear strategy based on what's good for the customer and the company, and used simple, straightforward language to communicate.
- He told the truth to employees (face to face, no memos or emails) and made the hard business and cost decisions understandable.
- He established a few non-negotiable behaviors about how to treat customers and each other.
- He understood the subcultures and looked for key influencers to help him in the turnaround.
- He gave control for how to serve the customer and do their

- jobs back to the employees (eliminated micro-management and onerous rule books).
- He gave all employees a monthly bonus on certain customer-centric targets, like on-time and complaints.
- And lastly, he loved the company, its people and its customers. People respect and follow those who believe and show it.

A bankruptcy judge can fix your balance sheet, but he cannot fix your company. ~Gordon Bethune

Culture Change, Leadership and the Non-Negotiables

Only the wisest and stupidest of men never change.
~ Confucius

After being in the business of culture change for over 35 years and making all the mistakes, and having some incredibly huge successes, I can now tell you, emphatically, what it takes to successfully change culture. All these elements are required. Skip any one and the culture won't change. And by the way, it's going to take a lot more leadership time than you originally planned. How much? How about 40% of the time of senior executives devoted to reshaping the culture! If you can't commit, don't start.

- **Change the Leaders or Change the Leaders.** The CEO and senior team must be willing to change their individual and collective ways of working and their personal behaviors to match the new cultural behaviors required inside the company. The key principle here is that: "organizations are shadows of their leaders, and that's the good news and the bad news!"

- **An aligned senior team that accepts the accountability and responsibility to lead the culture change.** If any one individual, say the CFO, believes that he has real work to do and the rest of you can deal with the 'soft stuff', and chooses not to accept the mantle for either personal change or actively leading the culture change effort, the change won't take hold. It's all in or all out!

- **Behaviors, Behaviors, Behaviors**. Frame the new culture and your new requirements for work around observable behaviors, not Values.

> *It's easier to act your way to a new way of thinking, than to think your way to a new way of acting.*

- **Overcome the critical mass of inertia.** Unless you get the critical mass of *'undecided or cautious'* to change, the inertia of the old culture will bring the entire change process to a grinding halt. One way is to enroll those key influential employees in the organization who are most respected and enthusiastic about the culture change and train them to be internal facilitators, mentors, coaches and guides. Another way is to ask those most negative and caustic about change to go somewhere else! Then develop tangible business processes, like Continental's monthly employee bonuses, to enroll the large group of *'undecided'*. They are looking for leadership and a reason to change, so show them the way.

- **Redesign the daily business processes so that they promote the behaviors required of the new culture** (recall the NUMMI GM-Toyota example). And place a special emphasis on redesigning the HR processes to better match the new culture desired. If you want a new culture of more innovation and accountability, reduce the amount of meetings where people are scrutinized for every little detail by senior management. Give awards for new ideas and even *'almost good ideas'*. Reevaluate your hiring profile and redesign your new employee induction process to stress the new cultural requirements. Reevaluate your promotion and development policies; do they match the new culture desired? Evaluate middle managers on how well they develop people as well as how well they meet budgets.

- **Measure, Readjust, and Measure Again**. While measuring the overall impact of culture change is not an easy task, it is absolutely necessary to find those elements of the culture that can be measured and tracked on a relatively frequent basis. If your changes are taking hold, these indictors should move. Waiting a year or two to have another culture survey is like driving your car blindfolded and only peeking every once in a while! My suggestion is to find or create two kinds of metrics: behaviors that are key to the new culture, and business performance metrics that should be impacted by the new culture forming.

There is no short-cut to reshaping culture. Miss any one of these elements, or try to cut back on them, and you will definitely fail.

Which Methodology?

As I advise CEOs and senior leadership teams on culture, strategy execution and performance improvement I am continually asked: *"Which culture change methodology do you think we should use?"*

My first reply is a question: *"Tell me what you want to accomplish."* All change is disruptive and how to go about it and the amount of disruption you can deal with often depends on the magnitude of the change you need to deliver.

My second question is: *"Tell me the kind of culture (use behavioral terms not value statements or broad platitudes) you need and why."* To me this is the killer question and most senior executives are very unclear about the exact behaviors they need in a new culture.

Here's the list I usually get:
- Better teamwork
- More Collaboration
- Innovation
- Sense of Urgency

- Customer Focused
- Risk Taking
- Respect for People
- Openness

By now you and I are both yawning, and an employee would probably be rolling her eyes at these useless platitudes. These are not behaviors, they are ... attributes or dreams or wishes! Go back to the lessons learned from the NUMMI story and the Toyota Production System, which have specific behaviors required of managers and supervisors when a specific issue arises, like a worker has pulled the red chord to stop the assembly line for a perceived quality issue. Whether or not workers will actually take that risk (do that behavior) all depends on the behavior of the supervisor who comes over. Their behavior will either show respect for the individual and move the solution process forward or not. Behaviors either support other behaviors or kill them. Platitudes do nothing for anyone.

After this, I am either shown the door or we get down to the business of building a high-performance organization. I do, however, have a few *'rules of thumb'* on culture change methodologies that get us all thinking productively.

Small or Early-stage company:

- Develop a hiring profile that will bring in people who best fit the behaviors and attitudes the culture requires, and use it on everyone, even senior executives.

- Have a robust new employee *'Welcome Orientation'* program. Not a handout and a handshake. Think Disney or Nordstom or Starbucks. Days or weeks of learning about the culture and the behaviors required to thrive and survive.

- Quickly get rid of those existing employees and executives who don't fit.

- Make certain everyone in the company understands that keeping the culture and living the behaviors is everyone's accountability, and so is coaching others who make mistakes or aren't behaving appropriately. It's your culture, don't let it drift away.

- Establish rituals, rewards and recognition that are directly tied to the culture and the customer.

Large entrenched company:

- Think very long and hard on whether you really have the courage and commitment to embark on a culture change. It's either all in or all out.

- Discover the subcultures and the 'informal leaders'; understand how they see their jobs, the customer and the company.

- Conduct a culture audit if you want, but I suggest you use a Business Characteristics culture profile.

- Establish a realistic vision, a clear strategy, and match both with a set of non-negotiable behaviors that will define the new culture. It should be clear and easy to understand how we have to work and behave in order to deliver the vision and execute the strategy. No platitudes, describe real work behaviors!

- Decide the type of *'change methodology'* you most believe will fit the challenges faced by the company. And don't rush into this decision. Do your research and your homework.

- Fully fund the process (not just the consultants) and dedicate at least 40% of senior leadership's time. *'Culture is Job One'* to paraphrase an old Ford slogan on quality. Think NUMMI and Continental; it can be done!

My Other Advice?

Don't call it culture change! The word *'culture'* creates confusion and concern and the word *'change'* just creates more resistance, especially at a subconscious level, than you need. Find a slogan or phrase that people in the company will believe. For Continental it was: *"Becoming profitable in 1995 and running an airline we can all be proud of."* No mention of culture. Let culture change be the *'intended'* byproduct.

> *Company cultures are like country cultures. Never try to change one. Try, instead, to work with what you've got.*
> *~ Peter F. Drucker*

LEVERAGE:

SECTION SEVEN: CULTURE CLASH

I've reviewed your vital statistics and checked your bank balance, let's get married!

On 6 May 1998, the largest corporate merger ever was announced between two automotive companies, Daimler-Benz and Chrysler [75]. With combined revenues of $130 billion and a market capitalization of $92 billion, the new company, DaimlerChrysler (DCX) instantly became the 5th largest automaker in the world.

Hailed by the two CEOs as a *'merger of equals',* the opportunities for both sides looked perfect. Daimler had a high quality brand in Mercedes but wanted to broaden its product line and gain greater access into the huge North American market. Chrysler, on the other hand, wanted access to the famous German technology and supply chain. And both companies felt that by merging they could successfully enter and gain significant share in the growing Asian and South American markets. And also by combining their two operations there was an estimated $1.41 billion in cost savings the first year alone.

Easy to fall in love with those numbers and future opportunities. The CEO of Daimler-Benz was subsequently named Business Manager of the Year for pulling off such a *'perfect marriage'*. And all for only $38 billion!

By 2000, just two years later, the share price of DaimlerChrysler (DCX) had fallen from its 1998 high of $97 to $41 and after a myriad of losses and falling car sales, Daimler sold off Chrysler several years later to a private equity group, Cerberus Capital for just $7.4 billion. From heaven to hell in a few short years.

The post-mortem analysis of the DaimlerChrysler merger shows a story of greed on one hand and lack of trust on the other, but mostly the sad story of the clash between two very different cultures. Daimler was a German company described as *"conservative, efficient and technology driven"*, while Chrysler was an American company known as *"daring, flamboyant and marketing driven."* The Daimler culture was methodical, with centralized decision-making and a high regard for tradition and hierarchy. The Chrysler culture valued efficiency, equality and empowerment in order to produce cost-efficient, mass-market vehicles. Not exactly equals! [75]

A similar story of hype and then failure was repeated several years later, to great fanfare as a *'merger of equals',* between AOL and Times Warner [76]. And earlier, in 1968, two longtime railway rivals, New York Central Railroad and Pennsylvania Railroad merged to become Penn Central, the sixth largest corporation in America. What Penn Central did not expect was that years of fierce competition made it impossible for the two cultures to work cooperatively together. The company filed for bankruptcy after only two years [77].

Then of course there was the disastrous Sprint-Nextel merger. In 2005, in a bid to keep pace with industry giants like Verizon & AT&T, Sprint acquired rival Nextel for $35 billion. By 2008, the company had written down 80% of the value of the Nextel, confirming the widely held belief that the merger had been a failure. That failure is widely attributed to a culture clash between the entrepreneurial, khaki culture of Nextel and the buttoned-down formality of bureaucratic Sprint. [78]

And the beat goes on . . .

Basing an acquisition or merger on business data (balance sheet, PE ratio, profitability, product lifecycles, complimentary product lines, etc.) is like two people getting married based on compatible height, weight and bank accounts and forgetting about personalities and love. Everyone knows the poor statistics on marriages these days (the divorce rate in the US is around 46-50%) [79], and the success of M&A is equally poor. Different corporate cultures and the resulting culture clash has a lot to do with this high failure rate, as does greed and a poor understanding by senior executives of human behavior.

I think I'd rather date from now on than ever get married again.~ a two-time divorcee

Chapter 17: Corporate Culture and M&A

Every single time you make a merger, somebody is losing his identity. And saying something different is just rubbish. ~ Carlos Ghosn

A lot of articles have been written about the role of corporate culture and culture clash in mergers and acquisitions and I have made a list of a few of the better articles at the end of this chapter. What I believe will be of most value to the CEO and business leaders is a discussion of how best to understand the potential for culture clash before it happens and how to make culture an ally in the M&A process.

Seeing the 'Cultural Landmines' Before It's Too Late

Textron Systems Companies (TSC) make, among other things, smart munitions and military Armored Security Vehicles (ASVs) that have a greater survivability probability than the traditional military version Hummer vehicles. Specially designed hull angles and blast resistant plating, along with heavy duty axles, have saved hundreds of lives of coalition forces against landmines and Improvised Explosive Devices (IEDs).

To expand its portfolio of products, Textron Systems ($1.4B) acquired $600M AAI (a division of United Industrial Corporation) in late 2007, a maker of reconnaissance drones (UAVs) for battlefield surveillance and target acquisition. AAI's products and engineering expertise fit perfectly into Textron's Intelligent Battlefield strategy. Plus, both were New England based companies. The financials worked, the product portfolios worked, they were not far apart geographically, and the price was right for both parties. Due diligence was conducted with the assistance of McKinsey & Co., and on paper everything seemed to fit together perfectly.

But Textron Systems CEO Frank Tempesta wanted to make certain there were no *'hidden landmines'* in the deal, especially since this was a major acquisition and TSC previously had a relatively few number of acquisitions. Once the deal was agreed, along with the normal integration planning activities, Tempesta decided to commission a custom-developed culture assessment of both organizations, filled out by senior and middle managers, the ones who really had the job of *'in the trenches'* integration. In addition, face-to-face and telephone interviews were conducted to gain a broader perspective of the culture than could be obtained from just a questionnaire.

> *While the numbers added up and AAI was by all accounts a perfect fit for our long term business strategy, I was concerned about how we were going to integrate such a large number of AAI employees into the Textron family and what that influx would do to our own culture.*
> ~ Frank Tempesta, CEO Textron Systems Companies

In partnership with Frank and his senior team, I was asked to quickly developed a customized *'culture due-diligence'* survey to illuminate the behavior norms around how each organization went about planning, goal setting, communicating, leading, training, measuring and motivating.

What emerged, in as little as two weeks from start to finish, was a graphical snapshot of the differences and similarities of the two company cultures, which showed visually some key culture integration issues that had previously been unrecognized. They posed potential risks for the success of the integration.

During a presentation to the senior teams of both TSC and AAI, the information from the Culture Due-Diligence Assessment sparked a lively debate that resulted in a number of key actions that had not previously been in the plans from the traditional business due diligence assessment, including reviewing and adopting some key best practices of AAI across the entire Textron Systems family of companies, a revised senior team configuration, as well as dramatically expanding the acquisition communication process.

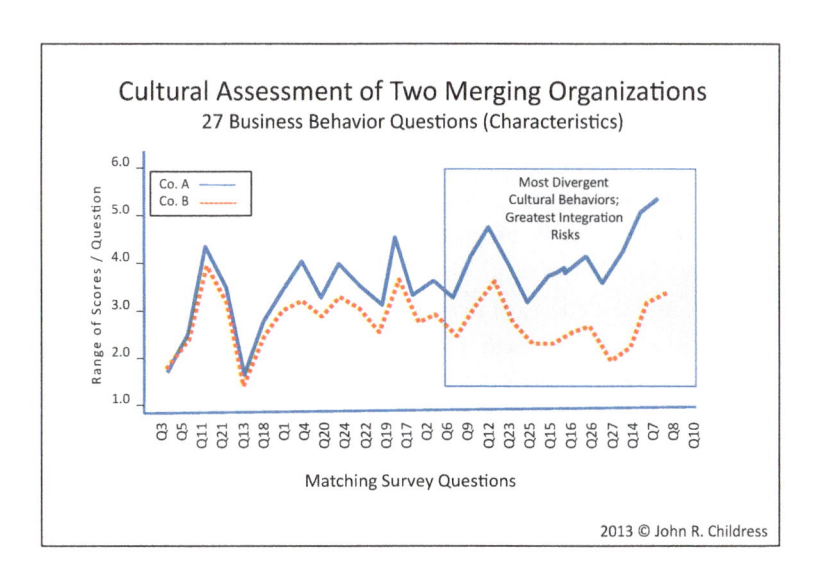

Cultural Assessment of Two Merging Organizations
27 Business Behavior Questions (Characteristics)

2013 © John R. Childress

> The results from the culture due-diligence assessment took me by surprise. It pointed out, in a very visual way, the areas that we had overlooked in our traditional integration assessment. But it didn't take us long to plug this new information into our plans. ~Ellen Lord, Integration Manager (now CEO of Textron Systems Companies)

AAI is now fully integrated into the TSC family of companies and the acquisition, in the first year, generated new business opportunities where the two organizations were able to combine their strengths to win significant new US Defense contracts.

Culture Influences Integration Approach

What's the best approach to acquisition integration? Depending on whom you ask you will get very different replies, and some of the best advice comes from those who have bought and integrated dozens of organizations in their careers. A group of experienced CEOs with a long pedigree of acquisitions got together in 2000 for a roundtable discussion in Scottsdale, Arizona [80].

While everyone agrees that acquisitions and integration pose considerable challenges, the real driver behind M&A is that it presents a much faster route to business growth than organic growth, and speed is of great value in this fast moving global economy. But if the acquisition gets bogged down in internal issues, mass defections of talent, and too much focus on positions and politics, then growth can suffer and the benefits of the acquisition are difficult to deliver.

One of the best ways to ensure the acquisition delivers on its growth opportunities is to use an in depth understanding of the cultures of both companies as a guide on how to approach the integration. When the internal ways of working (cultures) are similar, it can make sense to use an assimilation strategy for the integration.

When the cultures are very different, yet there is a good business rationale for joining forces, there is the option of allowing it to maintain its identity as you slowly begin to build trust and understanding of the people and their capabilities and learn how to best leverage this new acquisition for the benefit of everyone. The Disney acquisition of Pixar is a great example.

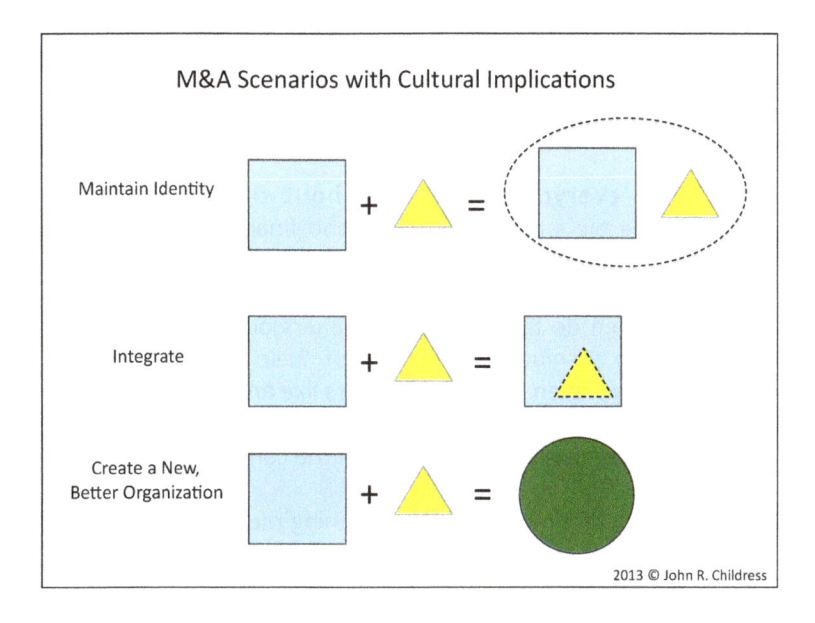

M&A Scenarios with Cultural Implications

Maintain Identity

Integrate

Create a New, Better Organization

2013 © John R. Childress

And every once in a while, an acquisition comes along where 1+1 = 3 and there is the ability to take the best elements from both organizations to create a new entity whose combined power becomes a significant competitive force. The successful merger and integration of Exxon and Mobil, to form ExxonMobil, the largest corporation in the world, is a good example.

For years I have used this chart when a CEO and I are in discussions about a potential merger or acquisition. It adds the cultural dimension to the discussion and often leads to fruitful and otherwise overlooked insights.

Cultural Hints For Successful Acquisitions

Not too long ago I was on a panel of speakers at a NatWest Bank conference with Alastair Mills, the former CEO of SpiriTel Plc, and now CEO of Six Degrees, an Internet and cloud computing company. In just two years Six Degrees has made over 13 acquisitions and Alastair considers culture to be a critical factor in the success or failure of an acquisition. Based on his extensive and mostly successful M&A track record, his key cultural hints are important to consider [81]:

1. **Learn everything you can about the company**, not just the big stuff like products and financials. What is the dress code, and why? Where do they tend to recruit from? How much information do they have about their customers? How often do they contact customers outside of problems or issue resolution? Take one of their customers out to lunch and listen. What do suppliers like and dislike about the company? These are valuable cultural insights to help ensure a clearer understanding of the company.

2. **Retire the Founders**. Your opening merger or acquisition discussions should be that you will not be keeping the founders. Most entrepreneurs don't want to work for someone else anyway. If they stay they often just keep running their company the same old way and can easily sour key employees.

3. **Integrate all your systems**. Having multiple systems for information and financials makes extra work and cost and is an easy way to miss (or hide) important information about the health of the businesses. Integrating information and other systems is painful, but has proven to be critical in integration success.

Culture Shock: M&A and the Lawyers

As in almost every area of business these days, lawyers and lawsuits are fast becoming one of the key issues a CEO has to face. And the law has even begun to recognize culture as a key element of M&A deals. Recently a Delaware court recognized culture as a valid criterion for deciding a deal's merit and ignoring corporate culture could bring shareholder law suits.

The Last Word on M&A

There is no such thing as a merger of equals!

Going back to the earlier DaimlerChrysler example and the bold announcement of a *'merger of equals'*, during 1998-2001, Chrysler was neither integrated or granted equal status, and top executives from Daimler moved in to run Chrysler, prompting an exodus of key Chrysler top management.

And in the autumn of 2000, DaimlerChrysler CEO Jurgen Schrempp stated publicly in the German newspaper *Handelsblatt*, that he had always intended Chrysler to be a subsidiary of Daimler. "The merger of equals statement was necessary in order to earn the support of Chrysler's workers and the American public, but it was never reality. [77] "

When you hear the words *'merger of equals'*, grab your wallet and run!

Some Good M&A References

Christensen, Clayton, Richard Alton, Curtis Rising and Andrew Waldeck. *The New M&A Playbook.* Harvard: Harvard Business Review, March, 2011.

Sherman, Andrew. *Mergers and Acquisitions from A to Z.* Third Edtion.. New York: Amacom, 2010.

275

Stieglitz, Richard G. and Stuart H. Sorkin. *Expensive Mistakes When Buying and Selling Companies.* Potomac, MD: Acuity Publishing, 2009.

Tualli, Tom. *The Complete M&A Handbook: The Ultimate Guide to Buying, Selling, Merging, or Valuing a Business for Maximum Return.* Vinemont, AL Prima Lifestyles, 2002.

LEVERAGE:

SECTION EIGHT: CORPORATE CULTURE MYTHS

The great enemy of the truth is very often not the lie, deliberate, contrived and dishonest, but the myth, persistent, persuasive and unrealistic. ~ John F. Kennedy

Corporate culture is one of those business issues that, as we have seen, is difficult to define and certainly more difficult to manage than a supply chain or even the business brand. And yet corporate culture is one of the most talked about topics. I recently spoke with a senior investment manager who had just returned from an investor conference in Brazil and he was floored by the number of times corporate culture came up during investment presentations!

Anything popular is also subject to exaggeration, misinformation and just plain myths. Corporate culture is no exception. Below are some of what I believe to be the most pervasive myths relating to corporate culture.

Myth 1. Culture is built from the top-down

While the rules, processes, business model and behaviors laid down by the founders are the fundamental building blocks of a corporate culture in early stage companies, quickly a second, and I believe even more powerful determinant of culture comes into play. And that is group socialization, peer pressure and the human need to fit in and belong. Often subcultures are far stronger than the original beliefs and ways of working set down at the beginning by the founders. And if culture is not continuously managed by the leaders, then the influx of new employees make peer pressure a powerful force in shaping the culture.

Myth 2. There is an overall corporate culture

While everyone knows there are subcultures, and some culture assessments can slice their data by employee or management level or by department, most culture metrics look at the overall average scores, plot them on their culture map and *voila*, there's your culture. There is no single, overriding central corporate culture, but instead most organizations are a collection of subcultures of various strengths and characteristics. In the case of high-performance and cult-like cultures (where culture is actively led and managed), subcultures have more or less the same characteristics, giving a great deal of alignment and strength to the overall culture.

Myth 3. Culture can be measured

Yes and No! Predetermined characteristics that probably are a part of the cultural makeup can be assessed on a scale (say 0–5) and when combined with the scores for other characteristics can present a picture or description of the existing culture. The question that all culture assessment begs is: Do these characteristics accurately describe the culture? I would say that the well researched *'business and behavioral characteristics'* provide a closer estimate to the culture than the assessment of individual values.

One of the ways that we can get a good understanding of culture is when the same assessment is conducted in the same company at two or three different time periods, say one year apart and the resulting culture descriptions compared against actual business changes and pressures the company has faced over that period of time.

Another key point here is to be able to distinguish between a culture assessment and a climate survey. The climate survey really looks at current employee feelings and morale more than the actual business characteristics and habitual behaviors that drive the way we do business.

Myth 4. A high performance corporate culture cannot be defined.

One aspect of this myth is absolutely true. It is next to impossible to define a high performance culture by asking employees to choose the elements of the 'desired' culture! Culture is more than just how well employees feel they fit with the company and how well the company matches their personal values. There are business processes and other characteristics that go into the make up of corporate culture which I believe carry a great deal of weight in determining a high-performance culture.

That said, every industry has different success drivers and by looking at the success drivers of your industry in a balanced format (employees, customers, financials, products, operations, etc.) a management team who understands their business can craft a good list of the behaviors required by all employees, and the ways of working, that will best ensure competitive advantage and effective internal functioning.

Myth 5. Developing a high-performance corporate culture is too expensive.

The Deepwater Horizon oil spill and the poor handling of the situation by the leadership of British Petroleum ultimately cost its shareholders upwards of $40 billion and cut the share price in half. The failed merger between Daimler and Chrysler cost a minimum of $38 billion and loss of market share. Culture has a ROI as well as a cost.

Because most companies already have training budgets and spend time and money on developing internal business processes, integrating the elements of culture into these and other normal business activities is not really an extra cost. Developing a high performance culture is not a special program or extra activity, but a more effective way of running your business. According to the research of Eric Flamholtz on the 18 Divisions of one company, corporate culture can account for as much as 46% of EBIT. [82]

Myth 6. Culture is more important in retail companies than in engineering or technology centric organizations.

If you define culture as being nice to customers then you may understand where this common myth comes from. Culture not only has a customer dimension (or should), but also many internal dimensions about how we treat each other and the habitual ways people react to business challenges and change requirements. While retail is mainly about product appeal and customer service, engineering and technology firms are greatly impacted by the degree of open information sharing, new ideas and innovation, as well as project disciplines. All of these are highly impacted by the corporate culture.

Myth 7. Large or multi-national companies cannot manage culture effectively

Managing a large or multi-national company is hard, period. The diversity of people and national cultures, combined with the time zone distances and language differences make the role of senior management extremely complex. In that situation, we see culture as a *'force-multiplier'* in that a high-performance culture creates alignment among people and helps keep things aligned.

Consider Wal-Mart, with 8,970 global locations, revenues of $470 billion and 2.2 million employees, which has a very strong and high performance culture that was built by the founder, Sam Walton, and kept alive by successive leaders. In his book, *The Walmart Way*, Don Soderquist, former Senior Vice-Chairman states:

> *"The Walmart Way is not about stores, clubs, distribution centers, trucks or computers. These tangible assets are all crucial ingredients in the company's business plan, but the real story of success is about people; how Walmart treats its employees and its customers."*

Myth 8. Culture is all about having a happy workforce

This is connected to the myth of *'culture is about soft stuff.'* There is great logic and considerable evidence that employees who feel respected, trusted and have fulfilling work are more productive and creative. But even respected and trusted employees get the blues!

Happiness is akin to weather, while a culture of respect and trust are everyday experiences in high-performance work cultures. The sad fact is, there are numerous employees with unhappy home lives who come to work to either cheer up or get away from the pain of home. A high-performance culture is about consistent work practices and behaviors that promote the overall business agenda while also treating people with respect and trust.

Myth 9. A Charismatic CEO is necessary to build a high-performance culture

The myth of a cult-like or high-performance culture being the result of a charismatic CEO or founder has been amply fueled in the press and even certain academic circles on the shoulders of such CEOs as Steve Jobs, Jack Welch, Tony Hsieh, Richard Branson, Lee Iacocca, Oprah Winfrey. There are even a dozen business books about charismatic leadership.

The leader with special charisma has a great deal of personal power and influence, especially among those in the inner circle, who then can spread the message. But not all charismatic leaders build high-performance cultures. James Dimon has considerable power and charisma, yet the culture within JP Morgan Chase is not considered high-performance, but trends more towards dysfunctional or even toxic in some subcultures of the bank. Richard Fuld was charismatic and forceful, and turned Lehmans Brothers into a highly toxic organization that eventually imploded. Lloyd Blankenfield has definitely changed the original culture of Goldman Sachs for the worse.

A bad leader can ruin a good culture faster than a good leader can turnaround a bad culture.

Force of character and charisma among founders sets in place strong behaviors and approaches to business that often have great staying power, especially if the founder stays on for a long time. A good example is the Virgin empire of Richard Branson, whose personal beliefs about being different and offering a fun and positive customer experience is mirrored in his many company brands.

However, I don't believe anyone thought of Sam Walton as charismatic in the public relations sense, at least not in the extroverted manner of behavior. He was definitely not a *'CEO Rock Star'*! But he was highly focused and strong in his beliefs about how a good business should be run and how people should be treated. Perhaps more than charisma, we should be looking at the relationship between the leader's commitment to beliefs about how to treat employees and customers and the development of a high-performance culture.

Myth 10. Culture can be managed like any other complex business program or process

Culture can and should be managed, and more than managed, it must be led by a senior team dedicated to living, role modeling and promoting the behaviors of the corporate culture. But building a high performance culture takes more than just good project management skills and definitely more finesse, since milestones and metrics are not nearly as concrete and measurable for culture as they are for a business program. In the case of culture, leadership is required far more than management skills, and not just from the leadership team. Every employee needs to feel accountable for promoting the culture, modeling the behaviors, and coaching others who *'forget'* or need some reminding. Culture is the *'uber-program'* and everyone is a project leader.

Myth 11. A company serious about its culture needs a CCO (Chief Culture Officer)

Wrong! One of the key lessons learned from most strategy execution failures is the fact that most functions or departments tend to stick to their own expertise and focus on their own goals and objectives. They live and work in silos. Culture, like strategy, is a horizontal value stream, connecting every single department or function and every single employee no matter at what level. If anyone is the CCO it is the Chief Executive, who has the ultimate responsibility for the strength and alignment of the culture to the business strategy. But it's better to create an entire army of CCO's. Mainly, your employees.

Myth 12. Culture is fundamentally about values and beliefs

Companies don't have values, people have values, and no two people have the same values and therefore there will always be misalignment between people's values and the organization. So to say that culture is about values is actually saying that culture is about people. Okay, but so what? I think what is really important here is to understand that we can't easily, if ever, change human values, but behaviors in the workplace can be modified or realigned to produce better outcomes. New hires coming into an organization don't change their basic values, but they quickly tend to shift their behavior to fit in with the subculture, mostly in response to strong peer pressure and to fit in with their immediate boss. Culture is about the visible and habitual behaviors used to deal with each other, customers and business issues.

Myth 13. Culture is the biggest reason for resistance to change and failed business initiatives or mergers

Culture is indeed a factor in resistance to change, even in the most cult-like cultures, because resistance to change seems to be hard wired into our DNA for survival reasons. The classic response of *'flight or fight'* is connected to our human resistance to change. And the organization is a collection of people, so resistance to change is to be expected, no matter how sound the change logic. And I think this is the real important point, all change is first looked at with resistance, period. *"Let's go down to the bank, they are giving away free $100 bills! Oh, I don't know, that's a big change!"* (Okay, I'm exaggerating, but you get the point).

Most resistance to change is not about the culture, or the change itself, but how it is presented! Few managers and executives stop to consider how to minimize the human resistance to change when introducing something different. It seems as if they actually believe that because the boss said it, people will automatically fall in line and change. At best they get *'malicious obedience'* with zero commitment or creativity.

Myth 14. Culture Change takes 3-5 years

In some cases, particularly with the traditional top-down or sheep-dip approaches, culture change can and does take years, if ever. And at times, a slow but steady change is perfect for the business situation required. At other times, speed is the requirement. In that case, the *'broken windows'* approach, new leadership, some clear non-negotiable behaviors (with consequences), serious focus on better training for middle managers and supervisors, and rewards and incentives tied to the new culture, can accelerate the process. The whole point about culture change is, it takes a new habit to replace an old habit, and new behaviors take time to introduce and require constant reinforcement to become habits.

Myth 15. Culture can be changed

What do you think?

Section Nine: The Culture of Banking is Broken

It is well enough that people of the nation do not understand our banking and money system, for if they did, I believe there would be a revolution before tomorrow morning. ~ Henry Ford

Not long ago, Bob Diamond, Barclays' former chief executive, spent nearly three hours answering questions from a UK House of Commons committee about the bank's role in the industry-wide Libor scandal and the rigging of benchmark interest rates. Committee members and Mr. Diamond himself kept coming back to one issue, referred to fifty times during the hearing: **corporate culture.** [83]

Today there are numerous discussions in newspapers, business journals and government corridors chanting the mantra that the culture of banking is broken. They cite examples such as the mad rush into derivatives and other risky investment vehicles, obscene bonuses paid to young traders, the endless search for acquisition targets in order to expand scope and scale, the lack of focus on customer service, the retreat from lending, and the obsessive focus on internal profits as opposed to providing a public service.

I happen to believe that Banking, in all forms (retail, commercial, investment, private, etc.) is one of the key elements of a strong and robust economy and the only way to effectively support the growth and development of businesses and individuals. The banking and financial services industry is vital to the world economy as well as to families. And for the most part, it works well, with proper checks and balances to mitigate risk and guard against criminal and negligent behavior. But I am not alone in my deep concern that the culture of banking is broken and the fixes are multiple, and not just regulatory. Leadership is critical if the financial services industry is to recover from its currently damaged brand image.

I am both a fan and a critic of today's global banking sector and in the following chapters I hope to add some insights into how we can begin to return this important service to leadership and respectability.

> *"The most remarkable finding is that risk professionals – on the whole a highly analytical, data rational group – believe the banking crisis was caused not so much by technical failures as by failures in organizational culture and ethics."*
> ~ UK Institute of Risk Management

LEVERAGE:

Chapter 18: Why Banks Should Focus on Culture, Now More Than Ever

I saw a sign that said '24 Hour Banking,' but I don't have that much time. ~Steven Wright

Ever since the global economic meltdown beginning in 2008, government agencies and business leaders have been engaged in an intense and very public debate about how to prevent another financial disaster, and another bailout, now that the global economy seems to be headed for recovery. The big issue concerning regulators is that unless real change is implemented in how banks conduct their business and how they are managed, the world could easily find itself in the same situation as before; the combination of excessive risk taking, lax regulation and weak leadership leading to another global financial crisis.

While everyone seems to be focusing on regulation as the key strategy for bringing the situation under control, other avenues should be both understood and explored if a sustainable solution is to be created. One of these important avenues is **corporate culture**.

An insightful comment on the banking situation comes from Paul Moore, former head of risk for HBOS, now part of Lloyds TSB:

> *There is no doubt that you can have the best governance processes in the world, but if they are carried out in conditions of greed, unethical behavior and an indisposition to challenge they will fail.*[84]

Paul Moore got fired for his comments at the time; a testament to the openness of the previous banking culture to criticism about its internal culture and ways of working.

I strongly believe that reshaping corporate culture, in conjunction with prudent regulatory changes, courageous leadership and revised internal policies and procedures, can work together to help build a stronger, more responsive and responsible banking industry. One of the challenges of banking reform, however, is that corporate culture is not well understood. To many bank executives and regulators, corporate culture is *'soft stuff'* with little relevance to the analytical and highly technical world of global finance.

Big Banking is Broken

It's no secret that the recent global economic meltdown and resultant bailouts caused more than just financial damage. The brand image of banking, and bankers in general, has taken a major hit for the worse. Where banks were once respected institutions of integrity and financial prudence, and bankers admired for their business acumen and community service, today the reputation of banking is at an all time low.

The poor image of banking is not solely in the eyes of the public.

Sadly the stain is internal as well. Inside many major banking organizations morale is at rock bottom and feelings of professional pride are a distant memory. And the rush to rebuild their image and business standing through the implementation of new business models, restructuring, advertising campaigns, social media, and *'transformation'* programs may actually be making things worse.

Long-term employees feel insecure about their future, new employees are wondering how to get ahead amidst all the changes, and corporate, commercial and retail customers are wondering whom to trust. To make matters worse, several of the large banking institutions are losing top talent in droves as individual performers search for a *'better fit'* at other banks or even in private financial institutions such as hedge funds and private equity firms.

I believe this time of upheaval and transition provides a perfect opportunity for leaders of courage and wisdom to remake the image and brand of banking and grow shareholder value by building healthy, high performance corporate cultures.

While it may be tempting to believe that culture is an internal issue, how we work together inside the firm, it should also be understood that culture directly impacts how we deal with clients and customers. Expecting alignment and collaboration on a new client pitch from a dysfunctional culture of silos and fiefdoms is both naive and costly. The fact is, a culture will cause staff to treat its customers in exactly the same way they treat each other and other departments. No wonder several big banks are looking for that magic training course to improve the teaming abilities of various bank departments during a major new client pitch.

"We simply do not know if we have the tools to change the banking culture." ~Lord Turner, FSA Chairman

The Real Drivers of Banking Cultures

So, if culture impacts financial performance and our ability to implement business strategies and change, then why isn't corporate culture more valued in the executive suite at banks and financial services institutions?

One of the key reasons stems from the so-called culture gurus who have for the past three decades (ever since the publishing of *In Search of Excellence*) been focusing entirely too much on teambuilding and communication and not enough on what really creates and drives the culture of banking in the first place. The majority of those involved in consulting and writing about corporate culture and culture change have been far too interested in pushing executive coaching or team training as their solutions and have missed the three most powerful shapers of corporate culture in big banking: **repetitive business processes, the behavior of the CEO and senior executives**, and **the human need to fit in.**

While these forces are also present in all other organizations, there is one significant difference within the world of banking (and big banks in general) that explains why these three elements are such powerful shapers of corporate culture. That difference is **money,** and is reflected in the enormous amounts of compensation available. Enough money for young investment bankers to retire at an early age and live a life of luxury. Bonuses running into the millions are not uncommon. Getting out of the toxic trading room culture and stress filled world of banking with millions in hand is the goal, the dream, and for many worth doing *'whatever it takes'*.

As a result, these three key cultural drivers cause employees to behave in very predictable ways, which creates the culture.

Business Processes

The corporate culture of banking is heavily influenced by the internal business processes the company adopts. People can give lip service to a set of values on the wall or a fancy mission statement, but can't escape complying with internal business processes. And those who don't adhere to the internal business process are few and usually gone before too long.

Poorly designed business processes not only dictate certain *'ways of working'* and foster specific work behaviors, but also do double damage by fostering *'malicious obedience'* and cynicism, while at the same time prompting time consuming workarounds that hinder productivity and reduce performance.

The *'Annual Bonus Process'* within most banks is an excellent example. Not only is the process based on a false assumption (that the only way to keep high performers is to pay them big bonuses) but an inordinate amount of valuable senior management time is taken up every year in seemingly endless meetings with *'high performance'* employees in a negotiation process to find a compromise between individual expectations (and often demands) and the size of the overall bonus pie handed down from corporate. In this case, the unwritten process (individual bonus negotiations, along with threats of jumping ship) has definitely shaped a key part of the culture of banking. It's not about the customer, it's all about the size of my bonus!

It makes good sense for senior executives to look closely at the business processes they are using internally. What they will find is that many of them are **legacy processes**, developed some time ago when business conditions were different, or at another bank and acquired during a merger, and may not be fully appropriate for the current banking strategy or the requirements of business today.

A Process Example: The 'Sub-Texting' of Conference Calls

Now, let's look at just one of the many big bank processes, this one unwritten yet still very powerful, that contributes to the toxic culture within big banks today. **It's the conference call**.

Most non-business people would be amazed at the number of conference calls that take place inside of big banks in one day. A conference between bank executives on three different continents, bringing together dozens of people, is not uncommon. Besides the time zone differences, there are national and language difficulties to contend with. One would imagine that people would need to concentrate hard in order to understand the various discussions and to accomplish the agenda.

Wrong! Here's how a typical big bank conference call goes. First of all, most of the time the conference callers stay in their offices to take the call, even if they are in the same building or on the same floor. (One of the values of a meeting should be to get people together physically so that they can build strong communication pathways, better understand where each other are coming from and read the clues of body language and facial expressions so important in human to human understanding – I call it getting *'eyeball to eyeball'*) So those who easily could get together in one room, don't. Why? Because they consider these calls boring and a waste of time.

And it gets better (worse, actually). While they are in their offices on the speakerphone, they are simultaneously texting, messaging and emailing **the other participants on the conference call**, as well as keeping an eye on their trading screen or the bank's electronic financial dashboards. But it's more than just multitasking. They are texting and messaging their friends who are also on the same conference call. And the texts go something like this:

- *"Can you believe what this d*!%head is saying?"*
- *"Those guys in Hong Kong haven't got a clue about this issue."*
- *"I'm so bored. What did you do last night?"*
- *"What a wa@%ker my boss is, he's always going on about headcount."*
- *"Why don't they outsource the senior team as well?"*

Get the picture? Very few people are fully paying attention, yet there are serious issues to deal with and difficult multi-national issues as well. Instead of really listening and talking out issues of disagreement, they send rude and insulting texts to their friends about their colleagues. Let me ask you this, if all these people were in a room where they could be seen and all these texts and messages were made visible, what would you do as the leader of the meeting? How long do you think this type of behavior would continue?

So, you might ask, why does this type of behavior go on at the management and executive level? Simple. Because leadership allows it to continue. If you allow bad behavior to continue, it becomes the norm, which soon becomes ossified as the culture! By not having clear ground rules and non-negotiable behaviors, and by not enforcing them, leadership is creating a culture that is not only highly inefficient and wasteful, but fosters lack of respect and distrust as well. The perfect ingredients for reckless risk taking and in some cases corporate criminal activity.

Leadership Shadows

The second key driver of corporate culture in banking is leadership, and specifically I am referring to the senior executive team. High performance leadership teams understand that their collective work processes (e.g., meetings, performance management, quarterly reviews, new project investment requirements, etc.) and their collective behavior (teamwork, turf-battles, blaming, respect for others ideas, etc.) cast a positive or negative shadow across the entire organization. And since employees tend to take their cues on what is important and how to behave from their leaders, negative activities and toxic behaviors at the top foster negative behaviors far down into the organization, adversely impacting performance and productivity.

If you want teamwork and collaboration on major client pitches as a core value and business driver, it better happen at the top or you won't achieve it anywhere else, even with the best consultative selling training or cross-functional collaboration workshops. If two senior executives won't support each other and openly bad-mouth each other, as is the case with many co-head arrangements currently in fashion, you can forget about any meaningful support and cooperation, let alone intelligent collaboration on major client deals.

The cultural impact of the position of CEO carries even more weight in the financial world, since many see themselves (and are seen by others) as *'business rock stars'* with the power to influence not only bonuses and products, but the course of global business as well. Speaking at Davos or playing Pro-Am celebrity golf at Pebble Beach brings an added level of influence, along with mega-salaries. Standing up against the CEO in a meeting and pushing a different point of view is often seen as business suicide, not to mention *'bonus suicide'*. The toxic behavior of Dick Fuld, former CEO of now defunct Lehman Brothers, is legendary and still has a hold-over effect on up and coming young bankers.

Cultural Assimilation: The Human Need to Fit In

Perhaps only in the military is the requirement to fit in and conform greater than it is in banking and financial services. Some of this is positive, especially when fiduciary behavior and ethics in dealing with customers and investor money is concerned. But much of the pressure to fit in and conform is a major driver of the current toxic culture of banking. The Libor rate fixing scandal went on for years and many people knew what was happening, yet none spoke up.

Where bonuses are big, peer pressure and conformity often trumps personal values and ethics. Besides, so far not one senior banking executive has gone to jail, so the consequences of having to pay a fine (with the bank's money, excuse me, customer's money) while keeping your job, or getting a very generous severance bonus, makes fitting in and going along very attractive.

The Culture they Created

> *Physicians the world over follow the Hippocratic Oath, which basically says: "Do no harm". Many bank employees believe their executives follow the 'Hippocritical Oath.'*

The culture of banking has changed significantly over the past 40 years, and based on the state of the global economy, not for the better. The banking world now has the culture it created. Whether by design or default, the current toxic culture of banking was created by choices made concerning business processes and leadership styles!

Over the past 40 years many of the internal business processes in banks and financial institutions have changed dramatically. Processes focused on credit risk assessment and processes steeped in the ethos of '*stewardship of other people's money*' have given way to new processes focusing on deal making, profit maximization, product development, advisory services and asset securitization.

A major cultural shift took place with the migration away from the skills and processes of portfolio lending to the more lucrative generation of new products and services to create additional revenue streams. This was to prove to be perhaps the single most significant change in the culture of banking, and brought with it a fundamental shift in priorities, values, systems, rewards, and behaviors.

The process of originating debt was no longer just to serve the needs of the borrower, but was now perhaps more to serve the needs of the investor. *'Originate-and-hold'* had become *'originate-and-sell'*, which eventually became *'originate-to-sell.'* Critically, banks had also learned that the faster they could originate and distribute their paper, the better the return on capital employed. A new element thus entered the commercial banking culture and lexicon - speed, to the overshadowing of responsibility or accountability.

Hiring processes also shifted dramatically. Rather than hiring experienced individuals to develop and manage departments, banks began to aggressively poach whole teams from rival institutions. When a whole team migrates to a new bank, they bring their culture with them! And many times they negotiate hard with their new bosses to be left alone to do their jobs (make money for the bank), making it clear from the outset that they don't want to be part of the new bank culture.

Another large set of processes that shifted during this time was training. The fundamentals of credit and risk, as well as management training all but disappeared in the big global banks, being replaced instead with sales training, negotiation skills and profit maximization training.

New Leadership

During this time period the profile of those in leadership positions changed dramatically as well. Rather than a diverse representation of all the various banking functions and disciplines, top teams became more and more populated with investment bankers and rainmakers. The management and leadership qualities of the David Rockefeller era were replaced with the brashness of the likes of Richard Fuld, the greed focus of RBS CEO Fred Goodwin, the overall incompetency of James Crosby at HBOS, and others. What was valued in leadership style switched from one extreme to the other. This trend followed the *'cult of the charismatic leader'* syndrome so prevalent in big business during the hectic growth years of the 1980's and 1990's. Thoughtful and inclusive was replaced with loud and aggressive.

In addition, the notion of a leadership team aligned around a vision of public service and sharing a set of common values was replaced with a view that *'this is a jungle and the biggest and meanest will survive'*. Stress and internal politics were the environment senior managers had to live with, or get replaced. And it became a 24/7 global business where speed was the forcing function and profit the only yardstick.

And big deals were happening at all hours day and night. Many believed the large amounts of money paid out in salary and bonuses compensated for the stress and long hours, but the children who rarely saw their banker parent didn't always agree.

With a new set of internal processes and a reconfigured leadership ethos we wound up with a banking culture radically different. This whole process of banking culture change was further accelerated (some say caused) by the systematic dismantling during the 1980's and 1990's of the Glass-Steagall legislation and the wholesale lack of accountability on the part of the regulators.

As a result, like it or not, we have the toxic banking culture we created. The good news, however, is that it's possible to reshape it again, this time by careful attention to the requirements of modern business. After all, unless banks take the accountability to create more workable and ethical cultures, the regulators may try to mandate a banking culture. The worst of both worlds!

The Beginning

So where's the silver lining in the dark cloud of bank regulation and reform? I believe this is the perfect time to ask two fundamental business questions:

- *What kind of culture do today's global banking institutions need to win in the marketplace with their clients and to win employee hearts and minds?*

- *What is the enduring purpose of global banking and why do we really exist as an organization? (And remember, profit is a by-product, not a purpose!).*

I believe the current crisis and aftermath represents one of the most important opportunities in decades for ambitious and courageous CEOs to strengthen and deepen their franchises. It is also the perfect time to begin to shift the culture of banking internally, before drastic and costly regulatory measures are imposed out of public frustration and anger. The sensible and I believe workable solution is for regulation and self-regulation (internal culture change) to work hand in hand to bring about both opportunity and stability.

Reshaping culture is the role of the CEO and the senior team. It is not an HR or OD exercise as much as it is a leadership responsibility. What is the best culture for the bank? One that is aligned and fully supports the strategy and structure of the organization and allows for positive impact on the global communities it serves. With a little help from outside experts, the

CEO and senior team can quickly come to grips with what processes, actions and behaviors most fit and support the strategic interests of the business and the culture required.

If a bank decides to shift its internal culture, we suggest they DON'T begin by issuing lofty mission statements or long lists of core values. Begin instead by taking a hard look at the current culture, particularly its strengths and weaknesses, and also the existing business processes and the work attitudes and behaviors they foster.

Then the CEO should take a hard look at the senior leadership team. What shadows are they casting over the organization? What is the culture they allow and foster as a result of the way they work and behave? It's also a good idea for the CEO to take a hard look in the mirror: assess your own leadership style, the processes used to run the business and how you deal with issues and people. An important question is: *What 'shadow' am I casting?*

A Culture of Clarity

Clarity of purpose is critical in helping to define the culture most appropriate for your business strategy. If you are clear on *'why we exist as an organization'* then your non-negotiable behaviors will easily follow, as will your culture. We have seen too many sets of values and mission statements that have no connection to the actual running of the bank other than they are a *'nice to have'* and look good on the lobby wall.

Today in most organizations the message inside is clear – corporate values statements are nice words, but actually are totally meaningless in connection to the everyday running of the bank. We can remember the dates of our kids' birthdays and our wedding anniversary because they are important to us, but most banking executives can't write down their company values!

So spend some time getting very clear on your purpose as a business and then build your non-negotiable behaviors based on that. If it's what you are really passionate about and what you really believe in, then you will easily be able to rattle off what you and your bank stand for, and you will even have personal stories and examples ready to share. Then build other examples of day-to-day situations within your bank that show how the new behaviors are meant to be applied.

Make a list of executive behaviors that are in-bounds (that are consistent with the purpose and values of your bank) and those behaviors that are out of bounds. Talk about the culture and behaviors at every staff meeting. Talk about how the new culture supports every part of your business: sales, new client development, client satisfaction, revenue generation, productivity, and of course profitability. If you make the connection, so will your people.

Why is this critical? Remember that it is impossible to treat clients any better than we treat each other so instilling the new culture into everyone will actually show up in radically improved service to clients. And after all, they pay the bills (and the bonuses).

Bringing culture into alignment with strategy and structure is the role of leadership.

Chapter 19: Banking Leadership?

You can avoid reality, but you cannot avoid the consequences of avoiding reality. ~ Ayn Rand

There is another growing trend that defies the logic of leadership accountability and contributes to the toxic culture in many big banks. It's the trend of appointing Co-Heads to run functions or lines of business. Let me translate. It simply means that instead of one person being the Head of Capital Markets, there are two leaders. They are called Co-Heads, as in both are leaders of the same business. And it's quite popular, especially when there is a merger or integration and there are two very qualified leaders for one position. It has recently happened in spades now that there is a new CEO at Deutsche Bank who has made multiple Co-Head appointments. The Co-Head phenomenon is also rampant in another broken financial institution, Citibank.

Did you hear about the banker who named his two sons Ed? Why? Because two 'Eds' are better than one.

Now having two highly qualified people overseeing and running a large function or department seems like a good idea. Two points of view to help find the best solution; two sets of experiences to make certain nothing is overlooked; two leaders to travel the globe meeting with customers and rallying employees around a common message.

Maybe this is the motivation for the popularity of Co-Heads, but I honestly doubt it. Mainly because the overwhelming evidence is that Co-Heads don't work! Ask any bank employee and especially the executives who report to Co-Heads and you will hear the same thing (maybe not in the same words):

> *It's a joke! They don't work together at all nor do they strive for a common view. One is there to make the other look bad so he (she) can get the top job for themselves. And they constantly bad-mouth each other to anyone who will listen.*

So if it has been proven time and again not to work, why continue appointing Co-Heads? There is a simple reason: the CEO is unwilling to make that hard decision!

CEOs who routinely appoint Co-Heads are abdicating their leadership responsibility to choose the best team, align them around a common direction and set of behaviors, and go forth to serve the needs of the customer. Instead, they take the easy route, appoint two people and let them slug it out. Survival of the fittest (or the most devious) is alive and well inside of big banks. Great for the CEO who can abdicate his responsibility of leadership so easily but not so great for employee morale and team alignment. Employees wind up not respecting the two combatants and definitely not respecting cowardly leadership at the top. Another reason why morale and productivity is so poor in our *'too-big-to-fail'* institutions.

Leadership is about making the difficult decisions that are in the best interests of the organization for which they have been appointed to lead. Leadership is an obligation, not a position!

> *The ultimate measure of a man is not where he stands in moments of comfort, but where he stands at times of challenge and controversy. ~ Martin Luther King Jr.*

What's Really Important at your Bank?

Unless the senior leaders of the big banks take a good honest look at their culture, assess its strengths and weaknesses, and focus on shifting the current toxic banking culture, their ability to rebuild the image of banking and help grow the global economy will be significantly jeopardized.

I recently read an article about J.P. Morgan Chase Bank and its CEO, Jamie Dimon, that gives me a giant clue about the current banking culture.[85] Basically the article stated that executives were so obsessed with getting close to the CEO (who has *'business rock star'* status) that they have an internal chart showing how close or far away they are to the CEO, and that executives will take a lower profile position if it means reporting directly to Dimon. Is this what you want from your bank? Is this the group you want advising you on your next investment or acquisition? Are these the people we want guiding our global financial markets?

In my mind when leadership is more focused on getting close to the CEO than getting close to the customer, the end is near!

Governance and 'governance'

> *It is clear that good corporate governance makes good sense. The name of the game for a company in the 21st Century will be conform while it performs. ~Mervyn King, former Governor of the Bank of England*

As a result of the banking crisis and current global economic recession we hear a lot of talk about *'governance'*. Was the banking crisis a failure of governance? Where was the governance process around the Madoff financial scam? What about the governance process at BP leading to the Deepwater Horizon explosion and the resultant oil spill in the Gulf of Mexico? Was there any governance around the Libor rate fixing scandal?

It is obvious that the term governance has a much broader and deeper usefulness inside of modern organizations than just the traditional focus on compliance to regulatory and legal requirements.

In my experience consulting on turnarounds, culture change and strategy execution, governance is a useful term if properly understood and exercised with good leadership. I see governance as having, like an onion, several important layers.

The first layer of this particular onion is the most obvious; I call it **Governance** with a capital 'G.' This is the compliance and conformity to legal and regulatory requirements. Timely and accurate business reporting is an example of Governance. As are accurate minutes of Board of Director meetings, regular filing of various legal and tax forms, and reporting of bank and insurance company reserves. "Big G" governance is usually the responsibility of a few key individuals in the organization, notably the CEO, CFO, Chief Legal Counsel, Head of Risk and Head of the Tax Department, among others.

If good governance were really that simple, we wouldn't have all the scandals, bankruptcies and lawsuits that abound in today's business world. But there is more to good governance, much more. This is what I call little 'g' governance, which has several additional layers; the effective governance of various organizational responsibilities and the governance of self.

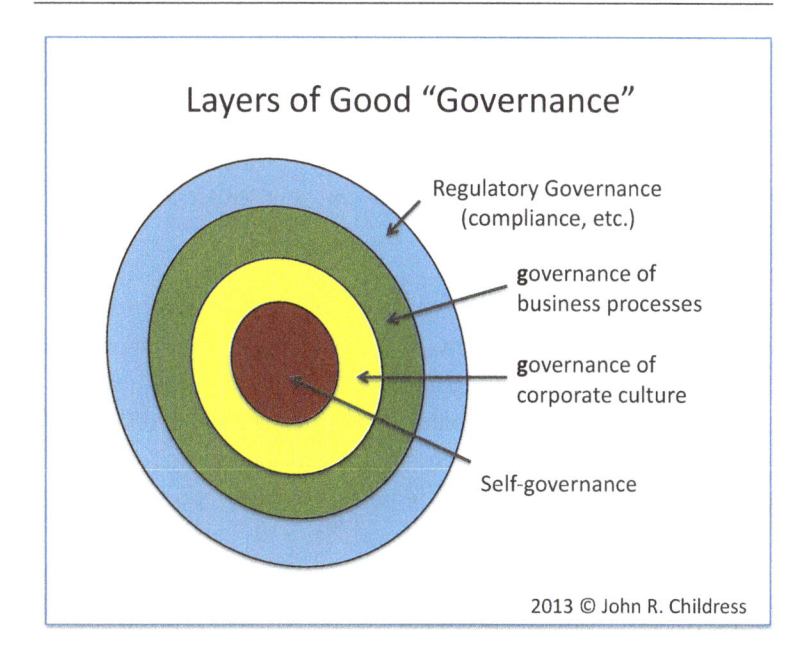

Layers of Good "Governance"

- Regulatory Governance (compliance, etc.)
- governance of business processes
- governance of corporate culture
- Self-governance

2013 © John R. Childress

The second layer deals with the effective oversight and governance of processes (business and management) that are critical to the performance of the organization. Such processes as staff meetings, strategy reviews, performance reviews, operational reviews, project and program reviews are critical to effective business performance and unless carried out with good leadership and governance, can waste time, energy and resources.

The third inner layer of leadership governance deals with the culture. Do leaders understand, respect and care for the corporate culture? Do they role model the stated behaviors or do they say one thing and yet behave as if they are exempt? Do they coach or criticize? Do they accept accountability or point fingers and pass the blame? The effective governance of leadership behaviors has proven to be instrumental in either superior performance or corporate demise.

That brings me to the inner core of the governance principles. **The**

governance of self. The governance of self is perhaps the most important and in many ways the core of all good governance. Those who fail to exercise self-governance will have a very difficult time adhering to other governance requirements. After all, governance in any situation requires discipline.

The discipline of self-governance applies to each of us in the ways we set our own personal goals, how well we keep agreements and commitments, and the degree to which we actually live our personal lives. Without disciplined self-governance it is difficult to face the challenges and pressures of organizational and business governance. Good governance requires discipline and leadership, not just in name, but in day to day practice.

> *Without diligent leadership and governance, culture drifts towards the lowest common denominator.*

LEVERAGE:

SECTION TEN: Q&A ABOUT CORPORATE CULTURE

Over the past several years of helping CEOs and senior teams think through, plan and execute on issues of corporate culture, there have naturally been some common concerns and questions. In this section I have highlighted some of the most frequent questions and my attempts to respond appropriately.

Q1. Why aren't more CEOs and Senior Executives passionate about corporate culture?

If you've ever witnessed a day or week in the life of the average CEO or senior executive, then you will understand the enormous number of demands placed on their time. Stakeholders from all corners want airtime, and then there are legal and regulatory issues to contend with, besides trying to out think and maneuver a growing pack of hungry competitors. It's a 24/7 life! So time is at a premium and culture doesn't seem to yell as loud as an angry customer or supplier.

But besides the time constraints, most MBA and Executive

Advanced Education courses don't really stress culture as a tool to leverage performance. They give modules, provide one or two case studies, but very few actual tried and true *'how tos'* on culture. In addition, there are very few CEOs who really are passionate about culture and therefore not many mentors to learn from. Hopefully that will change.

Q2. **Why can't the experts agree on a definition of culture and its components?**

Culture, like leadership, is a metaphor, not a P&L line item and thus is not easy to define. And academics find it difficult to collaborate anyway, their reputation being made on their own research, interpretations and models. I do, however, believe that there needs to be more collaboration between academics themselves, and with the business community, to develop a deeper understanding of culture and its impact on performance. I am amazed at the major advances the cancer research community has been able to accomplish with collaboration and shared data from around the world. And learning how to run better businesses and organizations is a worthwhile objective for everyone.

Q3. **Why aren't more Board Directors concerned about corporate culture if it has such a great impact on strategy execution and business performance?**

Don't get me started on the behavior and motivations of Board Directors. First of all, at least in the UK, non-executive board positions are traditionally filled by a very small group. And the same group of people, usually retired senior executives, just exchange companies every few years. And many hold multiple board memberships, sometimes as many as 8-10. And to say that the average non-executive board member reads all the relevant documents, does his/her homework prior to the meeting, visits the company and its executives regularly, and cares passionately about the employees is just not reality. Many are there to feel relevant at the end of their careers, to get some extra income, and for the bragging rights, and of course the business class airline tickets.

And in general, most executives, retired or not, don't really believe in the importance of corporate culture anyway, or they believe in it but don't have the understanding or skills to add value or assist. I believe as time moves on, the next generation of board members will be more knowledgeable and passionate about seeing culture as something the board must pay attention to.

Q4. If we are going to conduct a culture survey, how long should we wait before doing it again?

My first response is to decide if you want to do a **culture assessment** or a **climate survey**.

A **climate survey** measures the current state of staff morale, feelings, etc. at a specific period in time, while a **culture assessment** digs deeper into the habitual behaviors that determine characteristic ways of working. Either way, one of the indicators of how frequently to resurvey is how fast your industry and company is changing and the challenges you are facing.

If your business is relatively stable, then a longer period, say two years between culture surveys is sufficient. On the other hand if your business or industry is in a high rate of change or facing a significant emotional event, such as impending bankruptcy or a significant slowdown in your sector, and you need to transform your business, then having much more frequent feedback on the culture and the new behaviors you are trying to imbed, is critical.

On the other hand, there is a growing trend in many companies to conduct frequent *'pulse surveys'* concerning employee and staff engagement, which is one element of culture. Using online measures and easy to use survey apps, it is not uncommon to conduct monthly assessments to spot any unusual or growing influences.

Q5. **What is the best type of culture?**

Now that is a very difficult question. The easy answer is that all cultures are different and therefore there is no single best culture. That's not very helpful, however. If you recall the study of four different departments in the South African insurance company, Liberty Life conducted by Ellen Wallach [64], it clearly shows that the two departments described as Innovative delivered better performance against the SLA targets than those departments with cultures described as Bureaucratic or Supportive.

I tend to agree with both Dr. John Kotter and Dr. Clayton Christensen, as well as Jim Collins, that those cultures that are most flexible and adaptable, as well as having a high degree of innovation and risk taking, seem to be better suited for today's global, fast moving and highly competitive business landscape.

Q6. **Can a subculture be high-performance but the overall company culture dysfunctional?**

I think we have all seen at one time sparks of brilliance in otherwise lackluster organizations. In those cases where a subculture seems to exhibit repeated high-performance but the overall company turns in mediocre or miserable results, look no further than the leader of that department, function or region, as the driving force for the culture. And this is especially true if that leader has the autonomy to hire their own people, in which case you can be assured they have developed a hiring profile, as well as a weeding out process, that fits the high performance requirements.

But don't expect that brilliant culture to spread and change your organization. Chances are just the opposite, the good leaders and managers in that subculture will get tired of working for a lackluster company and leave.

Q7. **I'm a new CEO, what is the best and fastest way to begin to understand the corporate culture I have parachuted into?**

This is a really great question, and to those of you who have been asked to take over a function, region or division, the same responses should apply.

One of the first places to learn candidly about your new company culture is to talk with suppliers and customers. If it is a retail company, become a mystery shopper for a day. Call the help line or customer service hotline with a question or issue. Search out and speak with some former executives who have moved on. Have someone make a list of all the standing meetings and their frequency. How many meetings do the members of your senior team attend in a week? Wander around the office and look into cubicles. What kinds of cartoons and sayings do you find pinned up? Read the graffiti on the bathroom stalls. Come in on 3rd shift and watch the activity and how people behave. When does the parking lot fill up and when does it empty? What are the rituals about the culture, if any? Is there signage up in the halls promoting the company, or just random pictures? Do executives eat lunch in their offices or head to the cafeteria and interact with employees? Check the personnel records and see why people were terminated in the past 3 years.

As you can see, if you really want to know the culture, it's all around you.

Q8. How do we know if we need a culture change?

Not every business problem signals a dysfunctional culture, and culture change is not the solution for every business failing. In fact, my advice would be initiate a major *'culture change'* program only if everything is falling apart and you need to massively restructure the company.

But if you believe, or have evidence that the current culture is a barrier to sustainable performance and growth, then decide on the one or two non-negotiable behaviors that would make a significant positive impact on the business and relentlessly drive them into, first the senior team, then recruit key influencers to help begin a viral spread of the new behaviors.

For example, the culture at the Three Mile Island Nuclear Power Stations was shifted by a relentless focus on one concept, Safety, and all the various behaviors that a safety culture required. When Alan Mulally came in as the new CEO of Ford Motor Company, he realized there was little synergy or cross regional support when problems arose in one business area, and since the previous culture was punitive for subpar performance, there was very little honest discussion of bad news or problems. He created a weekly forum of all senior executives from around the world who had only a few slides to present their current business issues and problems. Open and honest flow of real-time information was one of the new behaviors, and asking: *"How can we help you move forward?"* was the other behavior. He relentlessly drove these two key behaviors into habit patterns among the senior team, and then it began to spread throughout the Ford empire. The result, a turnaround and a culture change.

LEVERAGE:

SECTION ELEVEN: THE FUTURE OF CORPORATE CULTURE

The future ain't what it used to be!
~ Yogi Berra

HSBC (Hong Kong Shanghai Bank Corporation), "*your local global bank*", has for the past several years been running an advertising campaign about how the world of business is changing. They have teamed up with researchers and futurists to explore how business might change. I normally see the ads in airports and along the jetway while boarding or disembarking my flights. They always cause me to think differently and challenge my traditional points of view.

- *In the future, even the smallest business will be multinational.*
- *In the future, age will be no barrier to ambition.*
- *In the future, there will be no difference between waste and energy.*
- *In the future, education will be your wisest investment.*
- *In the future, South-South trade will be the norm, not a novelty.*

When studies of corporate culture first began and as the books and research on culture blossomed, the companies studied were mostly large and in traditional industries, like Johnson & Johnson, Frito-Lay, Procter & Gamble, Walt Disney Co, Walmart, Southwest Airlines, Hewlett Packard and IBM. Mostly brick and mortar companies. The original concepts of corporate culture were developed and refined using these types of organizations as the models.

But times have changed, and continue to change at a faster and faster pace. Some of the most influential companies in the world are just 20 years old, or less (Amazon.com, Facebook, Google, eBay, Twitter, Vodafone, YouTube, Netfix, Zappos.com), and the next generation of global powerhouses is already emerging. And they are anything but brick and mortar businesses. The traditional concept of corporate culture based on large numbers of employees located in factories or office cubicles is rapidly giving way to small groups of distributed networkers linked to the company and each other via the Internet. The number of new start up companies increases each year and entrepreneurs are everywhere, and every age. Barriers to entry for starting a business keep being lowered.

All these changes will have a profound impact on the relationships between company, employee, customers and stakeholders. And the determinants and characteristics of corporate culture will change as well.

The empires of the future are the empires of the mind.
~Winston Churchill

LEVERAGE:

Chapter 20: Corporate Culture Ain't What it Used to Be!

*Change your opinions, keep to your principles;
change your leaves, keep intact your roots.*
~ Victor Hugo

My Office Is Anywhere and Everywhere

One of the most significant shifts in how work is done involves teleworking or telecommuting (working from home or on-the-road through the Internet and phone). Research from the World at Work Institute (WorldatWork, 2011) estimated the number of teleworkers at 26.2 million in 2010 or about 19% of the US working adult population. The Global Workplace Analytics and the Telework Research Network estimate upwards of 30% annual growth in telework among industrialized nations (Global Workplace Analytics, 2013). And telecommuting could have significant economic benefits.

If those with compatible jobs and a desire to work from home did so just half the time, the US national savings would total over $700 billion a year including:

- A typical business would save $11,000 per person per year.
- The telecommuters would save between $2,000 and $7,000 a year.
- The oil savings would equate to over 37% of our Persian Gulf imports.
- The greenhouse gas reduction would be the equivalent of taking the entire New York State workforce permanently off the road.

At least one culture research and consulting firm, Denison Consulting, is beginning to look into the cultural impact of teleworking and some of their research is showing some interesting insights, especially involving the importance of high levels of consistency in systems, procedures, policies and communications (Nieminen et. al,, 2013). It is also easy to understand that those cultures that encourage high levels of personal responsibility and autonomy are more conducive to successful teleworking.

Those cultures with weak communications and performance evaluation systems tend to create unnecessary frustration among teleworkers and reduce overall productivity. Because teleworkers are removed from supervision and face-to-face interaction with coworkers, the culture must support increased coordination, communication and feedback in order for the productivity benefits of teleworking to be realized.

With virtual work arrangements comes a change in communication patterns, a key component of culture. The loss of the daily face-to-face interaction changes the relationship between manger and employee, and the culture. And this creates two major concerns for the teleworking employee: professional and social isolation.

Professional isolation occurs when telecommuters fear that they will be bypassed for promotions or other organizational rewards. Social isolation occurs because of the lack of interaction with people and the ability to build interpersonal bonds of trust and understanding. The most important perceived disadvantage of telecommuting seems to be missing out on the peer and boss interactions critical for professional development and advancement (Kurland and Bailey, 1999)

The trend towards more and more telecommuting poses a challenge because those who telecommute are no longer be exposed to the traditional company culture. They have a harder time becoming acculturated and understanding the informal organization and how to get things done easily. They miss the company jokes, the inside gossip, the stories that tend to define the culture and what is accepted behavior or not. While they may save time by not physically commuting, they may actually have reduced productivity due to *'cultural alienation'.*

Globalization and Diversity

If we cannot end now our differences, at least we can help make the world safe for diversity. ~ John F. Kennedy

I live in London, one of the most cosmopolitan cities on the globe. It is estimated that within London over 200 different languages are spoken. Like London, companies around the world are becoming more and more diverse with people of different nationalities and ethnic groups all working together. Today, businesses are becoming global not just in their business reach, but also in the make up of their employee base. And this trend is impacting our understanding of corporate culture and our ability to build high-performance organizations.

For me, this is where the recent trend in defining corporate culture based on individual values and beliefs becomes less useful. Developing a corporate culture based on the individual Values-Fit concept for companies with many different nationalities and ethnic groups would wind up looking and feeling like the United Nations, one of the least effective organizations on the planet at getting things done with speed and efficiency! Core values like respect for the individual, trust and honesty, open communications take on very different meanings depending upon your national culture or religious background.

To build a high-performance culture within such diversity is not something taught in most MBA courses and most executives and CEOs are currently poorly equipped to deal with such diversity of beliefs and values. As the trend of multinational and multiethnic work forces increase, hiring profiles and new employee orientation training will need to become more robust and better designed. Bosses and managers must better understand how to motivate and develop people with beliefs and values quite different from their own. Building a shared identity and allegiance to the organization will become more complex.

Goodbye Baby Boomers, Hello Generation Y

I recently attended a conference sponsored by Telefonica, the Spanish global telecoms company, having to do with how Generation Y is beginning to impact, and change, the traditional world of business and work. Generation Y, also called the *'Millennial Generation'* is a reference to those individuals born between 1975 and 1995 who have grown up with the Internet as their key tool for interacting with and understanding the world. They are the Apple, Facebook, YouTube, iTunes, Google, Twitter and blog generation and they have very different ideas about life and work (due to the technological and economic impact of the

Internet) than the Baby Boomer generation (those born between 1946-1964).

Baby Boomers today occupy many of the senior positions in traditional businesses and government and their values and beliefs have influenced the development of many corporate cultures. Generation Y, in contrast, are building and leading many of the new organizations founded on social networks, technology and shared social values. The theme for Generation Y in business has been described as *'doing well while doing good'*, in recognition of their focus on the environment and social issues, as well as the P&L and their own high income expectations.

Generation Y sees the world of work very differently from how traditional businesses have been organized. Long hours at the office to impress the boss are less important than getting the job done with creativity and efficiency. Work ethic is replaced with *'worth ethic'*. Building businesses that have a positive social and environmental impact are important to them. And many prowl websites to learn about the culture of the organizations they are thinking of joining. Corporate culture is as important as salary. Working with jerks is not tolerated. In fact, one organization even has, as one of their core behaviors, *'don't be a jerk'*. Being able to work on interesting problems with interesting people is one of the key elements of the values of Generation Y.

Traditional companies are only just learning to adapt to Generation Y employees. The Culture Decks, which describe in detail the type of culture desired and behavior required for success in Generation Y companies such as Netflix, Zappos and Hubspot are designed to build a connection between the values of a new generation and the needs and realities of running a for-profit business.

Recently a consumer goods company asked a group of Generation Y staff to rethink and redesign its new employee on-boarding and induction training program. What emerged has become a highly popular course using touch screens for questionnaires and cartoon figures as program guides. Another Internet company devised an HR administration system that works like a video game rather than a series of forms to be filled out.

Job Hopping

The new generation of workers see *'job hopping'* as the way to get ahead, stay current with new technologies and work on interesting projects. Eighty-one percent of Millennials expect to be in the job only 3 years before they move on [86]. This will have a major impact on the development and sustainability of high-performance cultures.

Job hopping can also lead to greater job fulfillment, which is more important to Generation Y workers than it is been for previous generations. A 2012 survey by Net Impact[87] found that 88% of workers considered a *'positive culture'* important or essential to their dream job, and 86% said the same for work they found interesting. Job-hopping helps workers reach both of these goals, because it means trying out a variety of roles and workplaces while learning new skills along the way.

The philosophy of the schoolroom in one generation,
will become the philosophy of government in the next.
~ Abraham Lincoln

Big Data and Culture Analytics

One of the new technology developments reshaping today's business world is the concept of *'big data'*. Big data can be described as *"high volume, high velocity, and/or high variety information that requires new forms of processing"* [88] and is being used more and more to facilitate decision making, discovering insights and trends, and for business and technical process optimization. Scientists are using big data analysis techniques to discover new ways of diagnosing, understanding and treating various forms of cancers, while marketers are using its capabilities to spot developing consumer trends and niche markets.

The continual increase in computing power, processing speeds and information storage is making real time information available like never before. And many organizations are beginning to see the application of real time information for tracking trends and changes in employee attitudes and other elements of corporate culture.

For example, a young software company based in Melbourne, Australia called *Culture Amp* [89] is applying the same modern, data-driven customer intelligence gathering techniques used by major marketing organizations to develop real time metric driven surveys and tools to better understand employee engagement and other elements of corporate culture. Using easily customizable surveys and dynamic reporting, executives can get continuous feedback from their employees, surface critical insights about engagement, morale, the impact of changes, and elements of corporate culture on a daily basis, allowing them to make data-driven decisions about people issues that impact productivity and performance.

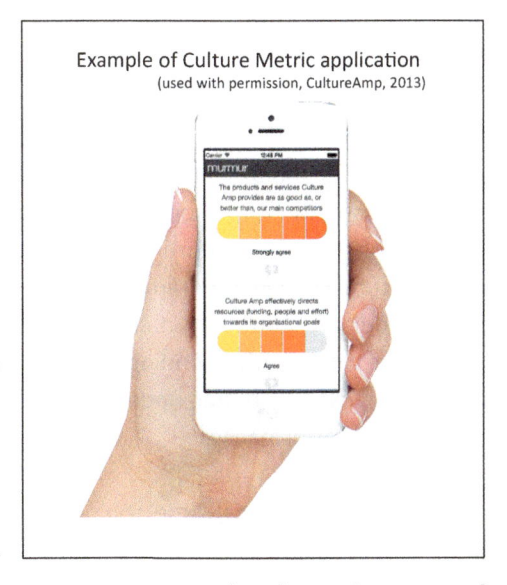

Example of Culture Metric application
(used with permission, CultureAmp, 2013)

One of the key uses of the new tools of *'culture analytics'* is to gain a better understanding of cultural drivers of employee engagement and productivity in different company locations and even between various subcultures within the same company. This has the potential to allow business leaders to spot concerns quickly and with adequate data and information begin to understand root causes and plan appropriates responses.

There is even a recent iPhone app, *CultureGPS*,[90] which uses the work of Gert Hofsteder on the differences between national cultures to help managers better understand the challenges of communicating and managing those from other national cultures.

Coming Attractions

It is my belief that more and more *'pulse'* survey tools, enabled by user friendly technologies and easy visual reporting of data will be used to continuously monitor the employee and customer elements of corporate culture and that massive sheep-dip and top down culture change programs will become a technique of the past. In addition, with quick data gathering and assessment tools, more focus will be put on finding and assessing subcultures within an organization and better understanding their impact on overall organization performance.

As these and other real time tools for gathering and assessing culture information become more available, I foresee a greater level of understanding of the importance of corporate culture and more and more senior executives will begin to use cultural analytics to improve business performance. The study of culture will migrate from highly anecdotal to more data driven assessments used to diagnose poor performance, much like six sigma analytics are used to determine process breakdowns.

I also believe the recent stampede towards assessing culture using personal values and values match will give way to a focus on additional important drivers of productivity and culture, such as work space design, updated and flexible work policies and work practices that can support greater employee diversity and lifestyle choices while at the same time providing for creativity, innovation and performance effectiveness. In addition, hiring profiles that match the cultural behaviors will become more sophisticated and tailored to fit the work behaviors and attitudes required for both in office and home working lifestyles.

This new level of understanding of the importance of corporate culture will demand changes in the way we think about work, management and leadership.

The culture is in the details!

LEVERAGE:

So, Just What the Heck is Corporate Culture?

Culture is a business metaphor and a leadership opportunity

Okay, you have finished reading this guidebook and hopefully have gained greater insight into the concept of corporate culture, its impact on performance, and how to manage and lead culture to become a strategic asset. Also, it is my hope that this book has prompted you to do some personal reflection on your own leadership skills and, perhaps more importantly, your purpose as a business leader and executive.

Culture is like the water in a fish tank, let it get dirty or contaminated and everything inside suffers. And the smell is horrible!

Some Guiding Principles About Corporate Culture

As I speak about corporate culture to audiences large and small, and in my advisory work with CEOs and senior leadership teams, I often use the following Guiding Principles as we chart a course together for sustainable competitive advantage and a well-run business.

- Every organization, large or small, start-up or mature, has a culture.

- Culture impacts performance, but figuring out exactly how is often extremely difficult.

- Culture is either designed, or left to develop by default. Either way, you will have a culture.

- If the overall corporate culture is ignored, it tends to fractionate into strong subcultures.

- Not all elements of culture have the same impact on performance. Don't believe in averages.

- Leadership behavior is most impactful in determining culture in the early start-up years. Over time, peer pressure and subcultures becomes increasingly more important.

- Most senior executives have no clue about the subcultures in their company or their influence on performance.

- You get the culture you ignore.

- Every day is filled with *'coachable moments'* to help build a strong and aligned culture.

- People don't change their values when they enter your company, but they can change their ways of thinking and workplace behaviors to match the existing culture.

- Culture is most easily recognized through habitual behaviors, rituals and policies.

- Culture assessments can never measure the *'real'* culture, only an approximation. Choose the assessment that best fits the business challenge you are trying to solve.

- Policies and work processes are extremely strong determinants of corporate culture, because they ingrain repetitive behaviors.

- A strong culture is one which best matches the strategy.

- Weak cultures usually are a collection of strong subcultures but with no alignment or common purpose.

- Don't confuse a culture audit with a climate survey. You might go charging off in the wrong direction.

- A strong culture won't make up for a poor strategy, and a great strategy can't be delivered by a weak culture.

- A bad leader can ruin a good culture faster than a good leader can turnaround a bad culture.

- Consultants don't change cultures, leaders and employees do.

- Avoid using the term culture change, it just adds resistance you don't need.

- There is no perfect corporate culture.

- Find the one or two non-negotiable work behaviors that will most dramatically improve the business. There lies your leverage to reshape the culture.

- Most culture value statements are useless. Less than 50% of executives can name all their cultural values.

- Selective hiring is more effective than culture training.

The Final Exam

All the vice-presidents hate the new CEO, as do most of the executives. He demands unthinkable hours, he's verbally tough and abusive on his direct reports, and will not tolerate poor performance. He was once so unhappy with the response to a question about missed goals from a female VP that he cleared off her desk by picking it up and tipping it over. He is rude to subordinates, foul-mouthed in meetings and humiliates staff in public.

However, this particular bank had been a loser for several years prior to the new CEO coming on board. For the past six straight quarters since he arrived there have been record profits, record growth and record high share price. The Board and shareholders gave him a standing ovation at the last AGM after he presented the prior year results and projections for the upcoming year. Performance is up and the senior team and other executives are threatening to quit!

If culture is so important and impacts performance; if organizations are shadows of their leaders; if the way we treat each other trickles down to how we treat customers; and if a big part of culture is behavior, what would you do as the Chairman of the Board?

PS: this is NOT at trick question!

Acknowledgements

All I have done is put words on paper. The real authors are the many clients and colleagues I have had the good fortune of getting to know through hundreds of consulting assignments. There are too many to mention them all, but I want to single out a few, since from them I learned more about corporate culture than from all the books and articles I have ever read, or written.

Dr. Larry E. Senn and I were partners and co-founders between 1978 and 2000 as we built the Senn-Delaney Leadership Consulting Group, the first international consulting firm dedicated to culture change and leadership team alignment. I learned many business principles and life lessons from Larry, for which I will be forever grateful. And during those explosive growth years the team at Senn-Delaney built, nurtured and enjoyed a high-performance corporate culture. It was a people-centric, performance-based culture built by design from the beginning.

Philip Clark, CEO, General Public Utilities Corp., and Dr. Robert L. Long, Head of Nuclear Technology took over the leadership of the Three Mile Island Nuclear plants following the accident and led a transformation to build a culture of safety from an old culture focused too much on technical expertise and not enough on open communication and the transparent sharing of information between departments. They both taught me about the ingredients for a culture of accountability and professionalism, lessons learned from Admiral Hyman Rickover and the US Nuclear Navy. It was at TMI that I learned first hand the power of corporate culture and how a dysfunctional culture can lead to a business disaster, and then how a high-performance culture can put the company back on the right track.

Sir Nicholas Scheele, former COO of Ford Motor Company understood the importance of corporate culture when he decided to change the old Ford Halewood Escort automobile manufacturing plant, then one of the worst performing facilities in Ford worldwide, into a modern and high quality Jaguar Assembly Facility.

Ronald Burns taught me about courage and making the right decisions for the right reasons. Ron took over as President of Enron Pipeline Operations and realized that integrating four different pipeline operations required a culture change, and he became the 'Chief Culture Officer' of the process. Ron made many positive contributions to the P&L of Enron as the performance of the pipeline group pumped life back into a heavily leveraged organization. Ron resigned as President of Enron Pipeline Operations when Jeffrey Skilling took over the company and the *'energy trading silliness'* started.

Lewis Booth, recently retired CFO of Ford Motor Company was a client twice, first as CEO of SAMCOR in South Africa and then as CEO of Ford of Europe. Lewis is a car man through and through, but above all he was deeply concerned about leadership team dynamics. He let us experiment on him, twice, and we refined our process under his guidance. Also our client mentors at Ford, John P. Fleming (now Global Head of Manufacturing) and David Schoch (now CEO of Ford of China) were both supportive and challenging as we helped with a massive cultural transformation.

Ian Walsh, former VP/GM of Lycoming Engines (now SVP/GM of Textron Defense Systems) showed me the importance of enthusiasm and an unwavering belief in people during a massive culture change and business transformation. Ian was one of the first to understand that corporate culture is largely influenced by internal business processes, which he improved with the tools of lean and six sigma, thereby kick-starting a massive culture shift.

Finally, John Mahoney, Hank McCard, Dick Millman and Frank Tempesta, all former CEOs of Textron Systems Company (formerly Avco Systems Division) for their continuing 30 year commitment to building a high performance culture through boom and bust times in the aerospace and defense industry.

There are also numerous consultants, staff and business partners who have contributed to my ever deeper understanding of corporate culture; Blackburne Costin, Rena Jordan, Delia Horowitz, Paul Walker, Michael Mooney, Mike Birtwistle, Paul Nakai, Robert Kausen, George Pransky, Michael McNally and dozens of others too numerous to cite here. Thank you all for helping to uncover the hidden truths of corporate culture.

And to my wife and partner, Christiane Wuillamie, who not only improves my understanding of business realities, but also tolerates and even supports my travel and the long nights of proposal writing. A double "thank you!"

To You . . .

My last acknowledgement is to those of you who read this guidebook and look with a critical eye at your own organization with a desire to make things better, to build a high performance culture. And to the CEO and those in leadership roles: after a long hard look in the mirror, if you do decide to tackle the challenge of leading and/or reshaping corporate culture, I hope these thoughts and ideas are of use.

> *Knowledge is, in the end, based on acknowledgement.*
> *~ Ludwig Wittgenstein*

About The Author

John R. Childress is a pioneer in the field of strategy execution, culture change, executive leadership and organization effectiveness, author of several books and numerous articles on leadership, an effective public speaker and workshop facilitator for boards and senior executive teams.

Career

Between 1974 and 1978 John was Vice President for Education and a senior workshop leader with PSI World, Inc. a public educational organization. In 1978 John co-founded The Senn-Delaney Leadership Consulting Group, the first international consulting firm to focus exclusively on culture change, leadership development and senior team alignment.

Between 1978 and 2000 he served as its President and CEO. His work with senior leadership teams has included companies in crisis (GPU Nuclear – owner of the Three Mile Island Nuclear Plants following the accident), deregulated industries (natural gas pipelines, telecommunications and the breakup of The Bell Telephone Companies), mergers and acquisitions, and classic business turnaround scenarios with global organizations from the Fortune 500 and FTSE 250 ranks. He has designed and conducted leadership workshops in the US, UK, Europe, Middle East, Africa,

China and Asia.

After retiring to France in 2001 John turned his hand to writing thriller novels. In 2004, he began to work again on consulting and coaching assignments where he subsequently developed much of the material and leadership processes used by The Principia Group in its work with senior executive teams on strategy execution.

Education/Interests

John was born in the Cascade Mountains of Oregon and eventually moved to Carmel Highlands, California during most of his business career. John is a Phi Beta Kappa scholar with a BA degree (Magna cum Laude) from the University of California, a Masters Degree from Harvard University and was a PhD candidate at the University of Hawaii before deciding on a career as a business entrepreneur in the mid-70s. In 1968-69, he attended the American University of Beirut and it was there that his interest in cultures, leadership and group dynamics began to take shape.

John currently resides in London and the South of France with his family and is an avid fly fisherman, with recent trips to the Amazon River, Tierra del Fuego, and Kamchatka in the far east of Russia. He is a trustee for Young Virtuosi, a foundation to support talented young musicians.

You can reach John at: john@johnrchildress.com

About The Principia Group

The Partners, Consultants and Staff at The Principia Group are dedicated to supporting CEOs and executive teams with robust business processes, management tools and consulting to deliver effective strategy execution, without an army of consultants.

> *You don't need an army of junior consultants running all over your company... but there is value in a senior 'business thinking' partner providing honest input, challenging your ideas, bringing new tools and approaches, assessing your team, working with you to build a better business.*
> *~ John R Childress, Founding Partner*

The Principia Group is a global consulting practice that believes no one knows more about a business than the people who run it. We are a global team of senior business executives with expertise in strategy deployment, organization design, leadership development, merger integration, culture change and performance improvement using an integrated methodology. We work closely with your senior team to build and implement business results, without an army of consultants. We like to think of ourselves as the consultancy that arrives without consultants.

The strength of The Principia Group is built on a commitment to rethinking the traditional, costly and invasive style of consulting so common today. Instead of armies of junior consultants descending on your company with the inevitable disenfranchisement of staff, we bring just two or three senior advisors with robust problem-solving methodologies who work alongside a selected group of your key people in building and implementing approaches that deliver targeted outcomes.

As a result, our consulting engagements are cost effective and deliver sustainable business results. Because we systematically transfer our skills, tools and methodologies to your own designated people during the process your company becomes stronger and more agile – which in the end, is the only good reason for hiring consultants.

To learn more about The Principia Group, visit our website at www.theprincipiagroup.com or email info@theprincipiagroup.com.

CITATIONS

1. Webb, Tim. BP Boss Admits Job on the Line over Gulf oil spill. *The Guardian*, 13 May 2010.
2. Mouawad, Jad; Krauss, Clifford. Another Torrent BP Works to Stem: Its C.E.O. *The New York Times*, 3 June 2010.
3. Goldenberg, Suzanne. BP Oil Spill Blamed on Management and Communications Failures. *Theguardian.com,* 2 December 2010.
4. Jnj.com
5. Estes, Adam Clark. Meet Apple's Original Genius, Now JC Penney's Anointed Savior. *The Atlantic Wire*, 15 June 2011.
6. Online MBA. Let-Go Lessons: Learning From Fired CEOs. *Online MBA,* 06 May 2013.
7. Nisen, Max. Michael Woodford: My Firing Was An Eight-Minute Corporate Execution. *BusinessInsider.com*, 26 November 2012.
8. Ackman, Dan. Excellence Sought – And Found. *Forbes.com*, 04 October 2002.
9. Sellers, Patricia. Warren Buffett, Corporate Culture Guru. *CNN Money.com*, 17 March 2011.
10. humansynergistics.com
11. Schein, E. M. *Organizational Culture and Leadership*. Third Edition. San Francisco: Jossey-Bass, 2004.
12. Hofstede, Gert and Gert Jan Hofstede. *Cultures and Organizations: Software for the Mind*. Second Edition. New York: McGraw-Hill, 2004.
13. Entrepreneur.com – 14
14. Human Synergistics. How Culture Works. *Human Synergistics.com*
15. John, Schulz. Culture, a Definition, *TorbenRick*, 22 June 2013.
16. Kotter, John. The Key to Changing Organizational Culture. *Forbes.com*, 27 September 2012.
17. BBCNewsToday. Barclays Chief Executive Bob Diamond has Delivered the Inaugural Today Business Lecture. *BBCNewsOnline*.2011.
18. Financial Times Lexicon. Corporate Culture Definition. *Financial Times Lexicon.*
19. Wikipedia. Organizational Culture.*Wiipedia.com.*
20. Business Dictionary. Organizational Culture Definition. *Business Dictionary Online.*
21. Christiansen, Clayton M. What is an Organization's Culture? *Harvard Business Review*, 2 August 2006.

22. Enron Corporation Annual Report, 2000.
23. Litchman, Jim. Integrity Matters. *It's Ethics Stupid*, 03 October 2012.
24. Mintzberg, Henry. *The Rise and Fall of Strategic Planning*. New York: Prentice-Hall, 1994.
25. Dishboards.com
26. Robert W. Baird. Treating Company Culture as a Profit Centre, *GreatPlacetoWork.co.uk*
27. Atkins, Derek and Anthony Fitzsimmons, Chris Parsons, Alan Punter. Roads to Ruin, a Study of Major Risk Events: their Origins, Impact and Implications. *Report by Cass Business School on behalf of Airmic.* London, 2011.
28. *US Government. Oversight of the Nuclear Regulatory Commission: Hearing before the Subcommittee on Clean Air, Climate Change and Nuclear Safety of the Committee on Environment and Public Works, United States Senate, 108th Congress, 20 May 2004.* Washington: US Government Printing Office, 2006.
29. Institute for Global Environmental Leadership. *Special Report: Disasters, Leadership and Rebuilding – Tough Lessons from Japan and the US.* Wharton: University of Pennsylvania, 2013.
30. Peterson, Joel. *Corporate Culture.* Stanford Graduate School of Business Seminar. March 2010.
31. US Department of Labor, Mine Safety and Health Administration. US Labor Department's MSHA Cites Corporate Culture as Root Cause of Upper Big Branch Mine Disaster. Massey issued 369 citations and Orders with $10.8 million in Civil Penalties. *MSHA News Release*, 06 December 2011.
32. Birch, L.L. Effects of Peer Models' Food Choices and Eating Behaviors on Preschoolers' Food Preferences. *Child Development*, 51,1980, pp.489–496.
33. Kell, Thomas and Gergory T. Carrott. *Culture Matters Most.* Harvard: Harvard Business Review, May 2005.
34. Epsonline. Ritz Carlton's Gold Standard Service. *Epmsonline.com.*
35. Schwartz, Tony. The Twelve Attributes of a Truly Great Place to Work. *Harvard Business Review Blog*, 19 September 2011.
36. Mottioli, Dana. Lululemon's Secret Sauce. *Wall Street Journal Business.* 22 March 2012.
37. Lululemon Athlietica. *Annual Report.* 2012.
38. Kickbully. Identifying a Toxic Workplace. *Kickbully.com.*
39. Smith, Greg. Why I am Leaving Goldman Sachs. *The New York Times*, 14 March 2012.
40. ABC News. Review slams 'toxic' culture in Olympic Swim Team. *ABC News.* 20 February 2013.

41. Blitz, Amy. John Whitehead, Goldman Sachs. *Harvard Business Review Interviews*, 2002.
42. Maanen, J. V. and S. R. Barley. Cultural Organization: Fragments of a Theory, in P. J. Frost, L. F. Moore, M. R. Louis, C. C. Lundberg and J. Martin. *Organizational Culture*. Beverly Hills: Sage, 1985, pp. 31-53.
43. Williams, Richard, Wallace Higgins and Harvey Greenberg. The Impact of Leader Behavior on Employee Health: Lessons for Leadership Development. *Northeast Human Resources Association*, 11 February 2011.
44. DuBois, Shelly. Merrill Lynch Settles Discrimination Lawsuit. *USA Today*, 29 August 2013.
45. Groeger, Martin. The HP Way - an Example of Corporate Culture for a Whole Industry. *Silicon-valley-story.de*
46. Deloitte Consulting Research. *Core Beliefs and Culture Survey. Culture of Purpose: A Business Imperative*. Deloitte.com, 2003.
47. Gollom, Mark. Does BlackBerry have a Future? *CBC News*. 20 September 2013.
48. Musil, Steven. Executive Infighting Reportedly led to BlackBerry's downfall. *NewsCnet.com,* 29 September 2013.
49. Nadler, Mark. Hard Part: Strategy Execution: Bridging the Gap Between Vision and Action. *Oliver Wyman Journal*, 2009.
50. Jamrog, Jay, et. al. *The Keys to Strategy Execution*. New York: American Management Association, 2007.
51. Merchant, Kenneth. A. and Wim A. Van der Stede. *Management Control Systems: Performance Measurement, Evaluation and Incentives*. London: Pearson Education Ltd., 2007.
52. Lepsinger Richard. *Closing the Execution Gap: How Great Leaders and Their Companies Get Results*. San Francisco: Jossey-Bass, 2010.
53. Lovallo, Dan and Olivier Sibony. 'The Case for Behavioural Strategy.' *McKinsey Quarterly*, March 2010.
54. McKinsey. *Improving Strategic Planning: A McKinsey Survey*. McKinsey Quarterly, September 2006.
55. Charan, Ram. Why CEOs Fail. *Fortune*, June 1999.
56. Smither, James and Manuel London (eds). *Performance Management: Putting Research into Action*. San Francisco: Jossey-Bass, 2009.
57. Mankins, Michael C. Stop Wasting Valuable Time. *Harvard Business Review*, September 2004.
58. Nucor.com
59. Miller, Chris. *Ryanair and Easyjet: The History of the Peanut Airlines*. BBC News, 20 June 2013.

60. Whitelegg, Drew. Flying for Peanuts: the Rise of Low-Cost Carriers in the Airline Industry. *Journal of Transportation History* 26: 2, September 2005.
61. Ryanair.com and Easyjet.com
62. Which? Brand Survey. *Which? Reveals Best and Worst Brands for Customer Satisfaction: UK's Biggest Brands Rated on Service*. 19 September 2013.
63. Lewin, K. *A Dynamic Theory of Personality*. New York: McGraw-Hill, 1935.
64. Cunningham, Lillian. New Data Show only 30% of American Workers Engaged in their Jobs. *Washington Post*, 30 April 2013.
65. Wallach, Ellen J. Individuals and Organizations: the Cultural Match. *Training & Development Journal*, 37:2, 1983.
66. Cameron, Kim and Robert Quinn. *Diagnosing and Changing Organizational Culture: Based on the Competing Values Framework*. San Francisco: Jossey-Bass, 2005.
67. Denisonconsulting.com
68. Barrettvaluescentre.com
69. Roundpegg.com
70. Roundpegg.com. Culture Alignment Research. *Roundpeg.com*.
71. United States General Accounting office. *Business Process Re-engineering Assessment Guide*. May 1997.
72. Aiken, Carolyn and Scott Keller. The Irrational Side of Change Management. *McKinsey Quarterly*, April 2009.
73. Kelling, George and Catherine Coles. *Fixing Broken Windows: Restoring Order and Reducing Crime in Our Communities*. London: Simon & Schuster, 1998.
74. Kotter International. The 8-Step Process for Leading Change. *Kotterinternational.com*.
75. Finkelstein, Sydney. The DaimlerChrysler Merger: A Business Case Study. *Tuck School of Business at Dartmouth*. 1-0071, 2002.
76. Barkham, Patrick. The AOL Time Warner Deal. *The Guardian*, 11 January 2000.
77. Daughen, Joseph and Peter Binzen. The Wreck of the Penn Central. Hopkins, MN: Beard Books, 1999.
78. Moore, Heidi. *Sprint – Nextel: Officially a 'Deal from Hell.'* Wall Street Journal Blog, February 28, 2008
79. Wikipedia. Divorces in the United States. *Wikipedia.com*.
80. Carey, Dennis. Lessons from Master Acquirers: A CEO Roundtable on Making Mergers Succeed. *Harvard Business Review*, May 2000.
81. Anderson, Elizabeth. How To Make A Successful Acquisition. *Management Today*, 31 May 2013.
82. Flamholtz, Eric and Yvonne Randle. *Corporate Culture: The Ultimate Strategic Asset*. Stanford: Stanford Business Books, 2011.

83. Hill, Andrew. Corporate Culture: Lofty Aspirations. *Financial Times,* August 18, 2013.
84. Moore, Paul. *Risk Management and Compliance: a Way to Achieve Business Excellence or a Bureaucratic and Expensive Nightmare.* Institute of Risk Management, Risk Lenders Conference, November 2010.
85. Borchardt, Debra. J P Morgan Execs Are So Obsessed With Getting Close to Dimon, They Even Have a Chart. *Business Insider,* 14 July 2011.
86. Meister, Jeannie. Job Hopping is the New Normal for Millennials: Three Ways to Prevent a Human Resource Nightmare. *Forbes.com,* 14 August 2012.
87. Net Impact. Talent Report: What Workers Want 2012. *NetImpact.com.*
88. Laney, Douglas. The Importance of 'Big Data': a Definition. *Gartner,* 21 June 2012.
89. Cultureamp.com
90. Culturegps.com

References

Anderson, Elizabeth. How To Make A Successful Acquisition with Alastair Mills. *Management Today*, 31 May 2013.

Aon Hewitt Report. *Engagement 2.0: Focus on the Right People. Build the Excitement. Preserve the Passion.* Aon plc., 2010.

Arnsten, Amy. Stress Signalling Pathways that Impair Prefrontal Cortex Structure and Function. *Nature Reviews Neuroscience 10*, June 2009, pp. 410-422.

Atkins, Derek and Anthony Fitzsimmons, Chris Parsons, Alan Punter. Roads to Ruin, a Study of Major Risk Events: their Origins, Impact and Implications. *Report by Cass Business School on behalf of Airmic.* London, 2011.

Bethune, Gordon and Scott Huler. *From Worst to First: Behind the Scenes of Continental's Remarkable Comeback.* London: John Wiley & Sons, 1998.

Barrett, Richard. *The Values-Driven Organization: Unleashing Human Potential for Performance and Profit.* London: Routledge, 2012.

Bratton, William and Peter Knobler. *The Turnaround: How America's Top Cop Reversed the Crime Epidemic.* New York: Random House, 1998.

Buckingham, Marcus and Curt Coffman. *First, Break All the Rules: What the World's Greatest Managers Do Differently.* London: Simon & Schuster Business Books, 1999.

Burchell, Michael and Jennifer Robin. *The Great Workplace: How to Build It, How to Keep It, and Why it Matters.* San Francisco: Jossey-Bass, 2011.

Cameron, Kim. S. and Robert E. Quinn. *Diagnosing and Changing Organizational Culture.* Third Edition. San Francisco: Jossey-Bass, 2011.

Carey, Dennis. Lessons from Master Acquirers: A CEO Roundtable on Making Mergers Succeed. *Harvard Business Review,* May 2000.

Childress, John R. *Fastbreak: The CEO's Guide to Strategy Execution.* London: Principia Associates, 2012.

Christensen, Clayton. *The Innovator's Dilemma: When New Technologies Cause Great Firms to Fail.* Harvard: Harvard Business School Press, 1997.

Christensen, Clayton and Michael Raynor. *The Innovator's Solution: Creating and Sustaining Successful Growth.* Boston, MA: Harvard Business School Press, 2003.

Christensen, Clayton, Scott Anthony and Eric Roth. *Seeing What's Next: Using the Theories of Innovation to Predict Industry Change.* Boston, MA: Harvard Business School Press, 2004.

Christensen, Clayton, Jerome Grossman and Jason Hwang. *The Innovator's Prescription: A Disruptive Solution for Health Care.* New York: McGraw-Hill, 2008.

Christensen, Clayton, Richard Alton, Curtis Rising and Andrew Waldeck. The New M&A Playbook. *Harvard Business Review*, March, 2011.

Cohen, Mike. *Succeeding with Agile: Software Development Using Scrum.* New York: Addison-Wesley Professional, 2009.

Collins, Jim. *Good To Great: Why Some Companies Make the Leap... and Others Don't.* New York: Random House Business, 2001.

Collins, Jim and Jerry Porras. *Built To Last: Successful Habits of Visionary Companies.* New York: Random House Business, 2005.

Cooke, R. A., and J. L. Szumal. Using the Organizational Culture Inventory to Understand the Operating Cultures of Organizations, in Ashkanasy, N. M., Wilderom, C. P. M., & Peterson, M. F. (Eds.), *Handbook of organizational Culture and Climate.* Thousand Oaks, CA: Sage. 2000.

Corporate Leadership Council. *Building the High-Performance Workforce: a Quantitative Analysis of the Effectiveness of Performance Management Strategies.* Arlington,VA: Corporate Executive Board, 2002.

Deal, Terrance E. and Alan A. Kennedy. *Corporate Cultures: The Rules and Rituals of a Corporate Life.* New York: Perseus Books, 1982.

Deal, Terrance E. and Alan A. Kennedy. *The New Corporate Cultures: Revitalizing the Workplace After Downsizing, Mergers, and Reengineering.* New York: Basic Books, 2000.

Denison, Daniel. R. Bringing Corporate Culture to the Bottom Line. *Organizational Dynamics* 13:2, 1984, pp. 5-22.

Denison, Daniel. R. *Corporate Culture and Organizational Effectiveness.* London: John Wiley & Sons, 1990.

Denison, Daniel, Levi Nieminen and Lindsey Kotrba. Diagnosing Organizational Cultures: a Conceptual and Empirical Review of Culture Effectiveness Surveys.' *European Journal of Work and Organizational Psychology*, 2012.

De Smet, Aaron, Mark Loch and Bill Schaninger. The Link Between Profits and Organizational Performance. *The McKinsey Quarterly* 3, 2007.

Drucker, Peter F. *The Essential Drucker*. Second Edition. A Butterworth-Heinemann Title, 2007.

Dyer, Jeff, Hal Gregersen and Christensen, Clayton *The Innovator's DNA; Mastering the Five Skills of Disruptive Innovators*. Harvard: Harvard Business School Press, 2011.

Edersheim, Elizabeth Hass. The BP Culture's Role in the Gulf Oil Crisis. *Harvard Business Review Blog Network*, 8 June 2010.

EFCOG Safety Culture Task Group, 2008.

Effective Crisis Management. The Tylenol Scandal. *Effective Crisis Management Blog*, 1982.

Finkelstein, Sydney. The DaimlerChrysler Merger: A Business Case Study. *Tuck School of Business at Dartmouth*. 1-0071, 2002.

Festinger, L. *A Theory of Cognitive Dissonance*. Stanford, CA: Stanford University Press, 1957.

Flamholtz, Eric G. and Yvonne Randle. *Corporate Culture: the Ultimate Strategic Asset*. Stanford, CA: Stanford Business Books, 2011.

Gallop,Inc. *State of the American Workplace: Employee Engagement Insights for U.S. Business Leaders*. PDF Report, 2013.

Gaberman, Ira, Ingrid Devoi, Kevin Crump and Marieke Witjes. *Demystifying Corporate Culture: Why People do what they do*. A.T. Kearney, 2011.

Garms, Erika. How Could Neuroscience Change the Way We Manage Change. *Blog post from ASTD.org*. 06 February 2013.

Geldenhuys, Tania. *Organizational Culture as a Predictor of Performance: a Case Study in Liberty Life*. University of Pretoria, MBA Dissertation, November 2006.

Global Workplace Analytics. *The State of Telework in the US*. 2013 Survey Updates.

Hammer, Michael and James Champy. *Reengineering the Corporation*. New York: Harper Business, 1993.

Handy, Charles. *Gods of Management: The Changing Work of Organisations*. London: Souvenir Press Ltd, 2009.

Handy, Charles. *Understanding Organizations*. Fourth Edition. London: Penguin Books, 1993.

Hastings, Reed. The Nexflix Culture. *Netflix.com*.

HCA Magazine. The Reason Female Execs Leave Is Not Glass Ceiling. *www.hcamag.com*, 18 June 2012.

Heath, Chip and Dan Heath. *Make to Stick: Why Some Ideas Take Hold and Others Come Unstuck*. New York: Random House, 2007.

Hererro, Leandro. *Viral Change: The Alternative to Slow, Painful and Unsuccessful Management of Change in Organizations*. Meeting Minds, 2006.

Hererro, Leandro. *Homo Imitans: The Art of Social Infection: Viral Change™ in Action*. Meeting Minds, 2011.

Hill, Vernon and Bob Andelman. *Fans, not Customers: How to create Growth Companies in a no Growth World*. London: Profile Books, 2012.

Hofstede, Gert and Gert Jan Hofstede. *Cultures and Organizations: Software for the Mind*. Second Edition. New York: McGraw-Hill, 2004.

Hseih, Tony. *Delivering Happiness: A Path to Profits, Passion and Purpose*. New York: Round Table Press, 2012.

Hughes, Mark. Do 70 Percent of All Organizational Change Initiatives Really Fail? *Journal of Change Management* 11:4, 2011.

Johnson, G. and Scholes, K. *Exploring Corporate Strategy*. Third Edition, New York: Prentice Hall, 1993.

Keller, Scott and Colin Price. *Beyond Performance: How Great Organizations Build Ultimate Competitive Advantage*. London: John Wiley & Sons, 2011.

Kelling, George L. and Catherine M. Coles. *Fixing Broken Windows: Restoring Order and Reducing Crime in Our Communities.* London: Simon & Schuster, 1998.

Kelly, Chris, Paul Kocourek, Nancy McGaw and Judith Samuelson. Deriving Value from Corporate Values. *The Aspen Institute and Booz Allen Hamilton Inc*, 2005.

Kotter, John. P. *Leading Change.* Harvard: Harvard Business School Press, 1996.

Kotter, John. P. and Dan S. Cohen. *Heart of Change: Real-Life Stories of How People Change Their Organizations.* Harvard: Harvard Business Review Press, 2012.

Kotter, John. P. and Holger Rathgeber, *Our Iceberg is Melting.* London: Macmillan, 2006.

Kotter, John. P. and James L. Heskitt. *Corporate Culture and Performance.* Cambridge, The Free Press, 2011.

Korte, Russell F. A Case Study of the Socialization of Newly Hired Engineers: How New Engineers Learn the Social Norms of an Organization, in *Academy of Human Resource Development International Research Conference in the Americas Panama City, FL.* Feb. 20-24, 2008.

Kurland, Nancy and Diane Bailey. Telework: The Advantages and Challenges of Working Here, There, Anywhere, and Anytime. *Organizational Dynamics*, Autumn 1999.

Lencioni, Patrick.*The Advantage: Why Organizational Health Trumps Everything Else in Business.* San Francisco: Jossey-Bass, 2012.

Levering, Robert. *Great Place to Work: What Makes Some Employers So Good—and Most So Bad?* New York: Great Place to Work®, Institute, Inc. 2000.

Levering, Robert. *Transforming Workplace Cultures: Insights from Great Place to Work® Institute's first 25 years.* New York: Great Place to Work® Institute, 2010.

Leslie, Keith, Mark Loch and William Schaninger. Managing your Organization by the Evidence. *McKinsey Quarterly* 3, 2006.

Lewin, Kurt. *Resolving Social Conflicts: Field Theory in Social Science.* Chicago: American Psychology Association, 1997.

Maanen, J. V. and S. R. Barley. Cultural Organization: Fragments of a Theory, in P. J. Frost, L. F. Moore, M. R. Louis, C. C. Lundberg and J. Martin. *Organizational Culture*. Beverly Hills: Sage, 1985, pp. 31-53.

Martin, Joanne and Caren Siehl. Organizational Culture and Counterculture: an Uneasy Symbiosis. *Organizational Dynamics* 12:2, 1983.

Maslow, A. H. A Theory of Motivation. *Psychological Review* 50, 1943, pp. 370-396.

McKeown, Greg. If I Read one more Platitude-Filled Mission Statement, I'll Scream. *Harvard Business Review Blog*, 4 October 2012.

Meehan, Paul, Orit Gadiesh and Shintaro Hori. *Culture as Competitive Advantage*. London: Bain & Company Publications, 01 January 2006.

Menkes, Justin. *Better Under Pressure: How Great Leaders Bring Out the Best in Themselves and Others*. Harvard: Harvard Business Press, 2011.

Miller, Chris. *Ryanair and Easyjet: The History of the Peanut Airlines*. BBC News, 20 June 2013.

Murphy, Mark. *Hiring for Attitude: Research and Tools to Skyrocket Your Success Rate*. LeadershipIQ.com, 2012.

Nieminen, Levi, Lindsey Kotrba, Felix Thai, Ia Ko and Dan Denison. *The Impact of Work Unit Culture on Telework Performance*. Unpublished Manuscript, 2013.

Nitin Nohria, William Joyce, and Bruce Roberson. *What Really Works?* Harvard: Harvard Business Review, July 2003.

Nord, J.H., Nord, G.D., Cormack, S. and Cater-Steel, A. IT Culture: Its Impact on Communication and Work Relationships in Business. *International Journal of Intercultural Information Management,* 2006.

Parr, Shawn. Culture Eats Strategy for Lunch. *Fast Company*, 24 January 2012.

Risberg, Annette. *Mergers and Acquisitions: a Critical Reader*. London: Routledge Press, 2006.

Rock, David. SCARF: A Brain-Based Model for Collaborating with and Influencing Others. *Neuroleadership Journal* 1, 2008.

Schein, E. M. *Organizational Culture and Leadership*. Third Edition. San Francisco: Jossey-Bass, 2004.

Schein, E. M. *The Corporate Culture Survival Guide: Sense and Nonsense about Culture Change*. San Francisco: Jossey-Bass, 1999.

Schwartz, Howard and Stanley M Davis. Matching Corporate Culture to Business Strategy. *Organizational Dynamics* 10:1, 1981.

Senn, Larry and John R. Childress. *The Secret of a Winning Culture: Building High Performance Teams*. Los Angeles: The Leadership Press, 1999.

Sherman, Andrew. *Mergers and Acquisitions from A to Z*. Third Edition. New York: Amacom, 2010.

Shook, John. How to Change a Culture: Lessons from NUMMI. *MIT Sloan Management Review* Winter 2010.

Sinoway, Eric. *When to Fire a Top Performer Who Hurts Your Company Culture*. Harvard: Harvard Business Review, 15 October 2012.

Smith, Martin E. Success Rates for Different Types of Organizational Change. *Performance Improvement*, 41:1, January 2002, pp.26-35.

Soderquist, Don. *The Walmart Way: The Inside Story of the Success of the World's Largest Company*. Edinburgh: Thomas Nelson Publishers, 2005.

Stieglitz, Richard G. and Stuart H. Sorkin. *Expensive Mistakes When Buying and Selling Companies*. Acuity Publishing, 2009.

Stoddard, Nat with Claire Wyckoff. *The Right Leader: Selecting Executives Who Fit*. London: John Wiley & Sons, 2009.

Taylor, Carolyn. *Walking the Talk: Building a Culture for Success*. New York: Warner Business Books, 2005.

Towers Perrin. *Closing the Engagement Gap: a Road Map for Driving Superior Business Performance*. New York: Towers Perrin Global Workforce Study, 2007-8.

Tualli, Tom. *The Complete M&A Handbook: The Ultimate Guide to Buying, Selling, Merging, or Valuing a Business for Maximum Return*. Prima Lifestyles, 2002.

Turturici, Deborah. Neuroscience Sheds New Light on Change Management Strategies. *Bpminstitute.org*, 12 April 2013.

U.S. Government. Deep Water: the Gulf Oil Disaster and the Future of Offshore Drilling. *The Report of the National Commission on the BP Deepwater Horizon Oil Spill and Offshore Drilling.* 11 January 2011.

Van Wassenhove, Luk, Neeraj Kumaar and Ramina Samii. The Tale of Halewood – Jaguar: The Story of a Ramp-Up. *Management Today.* 01 May 2002.

Wallach, Ellen J. Individuals and Organizations: The Cultural Match. *Training & Development Journal* 37:2, 1983.

Waller, David. *Wheels on Fire: The Amazing Inside Story of the DaimlerChrysler Merger.* London: Hodder & Stoughton, 2001.

Whitelegg, Drew. 'Flying for Peanuts: the Rise of Low-Cost Carriers in the Airline Industry.' *Journal of Transportation History* 26: 2, September 2005.

Wiley, Jack and Brenda Kowske. *Respect: Delivering Results by Giving Employees What They Really Want.* London: John Wiley & Sons, 2011.

Williams, Richard, Wallace Higgins and Harvey Greenberg. 'The Impact of Leader Behavior on Employee Health: Lessons for Leadership Development.' *Northeast Human Resources Association*, 11 February 2011.

WorldatWork. *Telework 2011: A WorldatWork Special Report.* 2011.

PRINCIPIA ASSOCIATES

FASTBREAK: The CEO's Guide to Strategy Execution

A unique synthesis of how-to, philosophy, principles of effective leadership, and case-study examples to help the CEO and business leader improve their organization's ability to deliver on their strategy and business promises.

FASTBREAK is filled with breakthrough thinking that is practical and applicable in any industry and any organization, private or public.

This is clearly a book for the CEO and business leader. As Childress states "strategy is a contact sport", and from my experience successful strategy execution requires consistent dedication to detail, communication and a willingness to modify as conditions warrant. You will find it all in this highly useful book.
- Robert Dangremond, Alix Partners

This book is the best synthesis on strategy execution I have read. It gives the CEO a sure-fire process to effectively engage the executive team in executing the strategic intent including principles, templates, examples, and most importantly, tips to avoid costly mistakes.
- Frank Tempesta, former President and CEO, Textron Systems Corp

While a turnaround is one of the most challenging and stressful of business situations, it is also one of the most rewarding to see good people take control of their business again and create a sustainable future. The principles described in **FASTBREAK: The CEO's Guide to Strategy Execution** *are solid and sound, as is the advice, processes and templates. A complete synthesis for the CEO.*
- Joe Bione, President, The Whitehall Group

Lightning Source UK Ltd.
Milton Keynes UK
UKOW06f1547290814

237772UK00013B/97/P